The Intercultur

The Intercultural Mind is a nascent exploration of the interrelationship between cultural neuroscience and intercultural competence. It provides an accessible and intelligent introduction to the potential blend of these two areas. Joseph Shaules' rich international experience and scholarly exploration allows both seasoned and novice professionals an entry point into this topic, which will surely be influential in the future of the field.

—Janet Marie Bennett, Executive Director, Intercultural Communication Institute

"*The Intercultural Mind* is an invitation to travel mentally and physically. Joseph Shaules is a knowing guide and a shrewd teacher who makes some difficult concepts come alive and dance."

—Michael Kelly, Professor of French, University of Southampton

"With *The Intercultural Mind*, Joseph Shaules goes beyond the excellence of his previous books. A much-needed exploration drawing on neuroscience, cultural psychology, and exciting reports from the field."

—Stefan Meister, Managing Director, intercultures

"A fascinating and important book about understanding cross-culturalism. Lively, well-written, incisive and fun to read. I learned a lot."

—Robert Whiting, Pulitzer Prize nominee and best-selling author of *Tokyo Underworld* and *You Gotta Have Wa*

"Joseph Shaules, well known in academic circles for his work on 'deep culture', has written an original and highly readable book which will engage anyone wondering about how they will experience life in another country and culture. He uses research and cases studies to explain such matters as culture shock, stereotyping and in-group/out-group behavior, but the research, and the researchers, are presented in a personalized way which will appeal to the wider public. His particular emphasis on neuroscience and cognitive psychology will however also interest the more specialized reader."

—Mike Byram, Professor Emeritus University of Durham

the intercultural mind

Connecting Culture, Cognition
and
Global Living

JOSEPH SHAULES

Illustrations by Matthieu Kollig

INTERCULTURAL PRESS
an imprint of Nicholas Brealey Publishing

BOSTON • LONDON

First published by Intercultural Press in 2015.

53 State Street, 9th Floor
Boston, MA 02116, USA
Tel: + 617-523-3801
Fax: + 617-523-3708

Carmelite House
50 Victoria Embankment
London EC4Y 0DZ
Tel: 020-7122-6000

www.nicholasbrealey.com

Printed in the United States of America

20 19 18   4 5 6 7 8 9 10

ISBN: 978-1-94117-600-9
E-ISBN: 978-1-94117-601-6

Library of Congress Cataloging-in-Publication Data
The intercultural mind : connecting culture, cognition, and global living / Joseph Shaules.
pages cm
ISBN 978-1-941176-00-9 (paperback) -- ISBN 978-1-941176-01-6 (ebook) 1. Cultural relations.
2. Intercultural communication. 3. Cross-cultural studies. 4. Culture conflict.
5. Ethnopsychology. 6. Visitors, Foreign--Psychology. I. Title.
HM1271.S465 2014
303.48'2--dc23
2014010027

table of contents

introduction

I love Tuesday afternoons. That's the day I teach forty international students—from more than fifteen countries—about cultural difference and adapting to life abroad. I say *teach*, but that's not quite accurate. There's already so much global living experience in the room that I am more of a facilitator than a lecturer. Many are study-abroad students living abroad in Japan. Others have international backgrounds—perhaps they moved around the world with their family or have parents from different countries. Some have not traveled much, but aspire to international careers. They share stories about their experiences—cultural surprises, the excitement of foreign places and people, cross-cultural misunderstandings, and the ups and downs of adjustment stress. At the end of each class, I have more energy than when I began.

My students are fortunate. Even a generation or two ago, such international experiences were reserved mostly for the elite. A trip abroad was often considered an adventurous journey to far-away places, and the people living in distant lands were seen as exotic or mysterious. Today, of course, intercultural living is getting more common. As communities become more diverse and interconnected, cross-cultural experiences are becoming the new normal—even for many people who don't spend much time traveling. We increasingly come into contact with cultural diversity both in our neighborhoods *and* abroad.

Intercultural living is not, however, always easy. I also work helping expatriate executives, multicultural teams, and companies trying to internationalize. I see first hand that increasing intercultural contact doesn't automatically produce mutual understanding. Bringing diversity into the room creates discord as often as it creates synergy. I regularly hear complaints about the unreasonable people from country X, Y, or Z, and see that smooth international collaboration is the exception rather than the rule. My Tuesday students often struggle too. They experience culture shock, foreign language difficulties, and trouble making local friends. Some of them hang out mostly with their compatriots and spend more time interacting with electronic devices than with the people in the country they are staying in.

Unfortunately, globalization can contribute to a form of naïve internationalism. I regularly meet highly informed sojourners caught off guard because they take the metaphor of the "global village" a bit too much to heart. They have been educated to believe that "people all over the world are basically the same." They have read that technology is making the world flat. They have a philosophical commitment to cultural diversity. They feel that they are global citizens. These things, however, sometimes lead them to underestimate how hard it can be to adapt to life in a foreign country, work in a diverse environment, or gain a deep understanding of foreign ways of thinking. Despite increased connectivity and technological advances, cultural misunderstanding, differences in language and culture, ethnic conflict, intolerance, and even genocide are not disappearing anytime soon.

For many global citizens, the word *culture* has become a way to talk about cultural heritage, customs, or traditions. What they may miss, however, is that culture can also be found in the subtle and taken-for-granted patterns that shape our thinking and acting. The more deeply you involve yourself in foreign cultural communities, the more likely you will be confronted by this deeper cultural difference. This is particularly true where I live in Tokyo—a high-tech, post-modern city with every conceivable convenience. Visitors and foreign residents here find it easy and efficient to use the spotless subways, but still a big challenge to learn Japanese and become something of an insider here. In modern Japan, as in many places around the world, much cultural difference has gone underground.

There are two ways to learn about this deeper side of culture. One is to dive fully into life abroad, immersing yourself in, and adjusting to, everyday living in a foreign environment. There are, of course, some risks. One is that adjustment stresses can catch you off guard. In the pages that follow, for example, we'll meet sojourners who were surprised and dismayed by the cultural difference they found. But there's an opposite risk as well. Modern convenience is allowing more and more people to *avoid* deeper intercultural encounters. It's possible to spend extended periods away from home without truly immersing oneself in the local community. We may skim the surface of globalized living without noticing the profound differences to be found by exploring at greater depth.

Fortunately, there's another way to learn about deep cultural difference—one that can help people in both these situations. Recent advances in cognitive neuroscience have started to shed light on questions of culture and mind that are relevant to sojourners. In particular, there has been great progress in understanding the unconscious mind. Long a bastion of psychoanalysis, it is now understood to involve highly complex cognitive processes that shape our experience of the world and influence our behavior in hidden ways. We have understood for some time, of course, that parts of our mind are inaccessible to conscious reflection. What we are now learning, however, is that our ignorance is more profound than we had realized. Of particular interest to me is research from the emerging fields of *cultural neuroscience* and *cultural psychology* that examines the hidden influences of culture on how we think, our sense of identity, and our way of making sense of the world. While still in its early stages, insights from such research can be of practical value to sojourners.

This book brings a cognitive perspective to questions of intercultural understanding. Cognitive and cultural neuroscience is providing clues to longstanding puzzles such as: What is cultural shock? How does culture affect our thought processes? Why are we blind to our own cultural conditioning? What is bias? Can cultural difference be measured empirically? What does it mean to have an international mindset? We do not have final answers to these queries, but a cognitive perspective is bringing a new set of empirical tools to bear on them.

Don't be put off by big words, such as *cognitive neuroscience*. This is not a technical book that tries to explain, for example, the structure of the brain. Instead, the focus is on the *intercultural experience*. The study of cognition is, after all, largely an investigation of mental experience. We will learn about mental processes involved in common intercultural experiences, such as the "Oz Moment" sensation of noticing cultural difference abroad, the stresses of culture shock, and our tendency towards bias and ethnocentrism. We'll see, in a variety of ways, how our thinking is subtly but powerfully affected by culture. The ultimate goal is to help sojourners understand—in a straightforward way—what is going on inside their own minds during foreign experiences. I believe this can help develop a more *intercultural mind*—an awareness of one's own cultural conditioning, and a greater ability to understand the cultural worlds of others.

One final word about my Tuesday students. At the beginning of each chapter, you'll notice brief quotes that they wrote in response to the question: "What advice would you give to someone planning an international experience?" I found their answers original (*Don't judge the gravity. Each planet has its own way of regulating the ecosystem!*), heartfelt (*It takes a long time to become a bridge person.*), and reflective of hard-won insight (*Culture learning is blind!*). They worked hard to learn from their intercultural experiences, and in sharing their stories with me have helped me explore deep cultural learning. In the process, they have taught me more than they can imagine. Their insights are hard won and deserve a prominent place on the page.

1.

culture and cognition

Culture learning is blind.
—Takashi

In recent years, neuroscientists have made great strides in understanding the cognitive processes that give rise to our everyday mental experience of the world. Drawing on this new science of the mind, this book explores the connection between culture and cognition. It argues that we are often unaware of the cultural configuration of our own mind.

The New Science of Mind

The most famous person in the history of brain research is also one of its least fortunate. Perhaps you've heard of Phineas Gage, a twenty-five-year-old blasting foreman. While working at a railroad construction site on September 14, 1848, Gage inserted a long iron rod into a borehole and tamped it down on a blasting charge, only to have it explode unexpectedly, hurtling the rod upward. It penetrated below his cheek, passed completely through his skull, and flew through the air, landing some eighty feet away "smeared with blood and brain."[1] Remarkably, however, Gage remained conscious and even described the accident to an attending physician—who didn't believe what he heard. Gage survived the ordeal and went on to live another twelve years.

Gage's miraculous survival made news at the time. The nature of his eventual recovery, however, is what has kept his story alive even today. While the damage to Gage's brain didn't affect his physical functioning, it had a clear effect on his personality. He reportedly became impulsive and scattered—no longer the even-tempered and responsible man he once had been. We know now that the rod likely damaged the left hemisphere of his brain, including the orbitofrontal cortex, which is involved in cognitive processing and decision-making. For scientists, Gage's story provided the first clear evidence that specific parts of the brain are responsible for discrete mental functions. This hinted at something that we now have come to accept as quite ordinary. The rich inner life we lead—our dreams, emotions, creative urges, brilliant insights, and romantic sparks—is a product not of muses or spirits, but of biological processes in our skull.

How does the brain work? How does mental experience emerge from brain functioning? These are among the most difficult questions that science can ask—so difficult that until recently they remained largely in the realm of philosophical speculation. Well into the twentieth century, the study of mental processes was considered by many to be beyond the reach of science. Some psychologists, such as Sigmund Freud, focused on introspection. Others, like John B. Watson and B. F. Skinner, insisted that only by focusing on quantifiable aspects of behavior could we scientifically study mental processes.[2] For a long time, we learned about cognitive functioning largely thanks to people—like Phineas Gage—with damage to specific parts of the brain. This only provided, however, a rough map of the brain areas associated with particular mental functions,[3] and a more detailed understanding of how the brain works was a distant dream.

In recent years, however, progress has accelerated, and there has been a revolution in our understanding of cognitive functioning. We've begun to understand the biochemical processes of the brain and how its neural networks function. New neuroimaging technology has allowed scientists to monitor brain activity while subjects carry out different tasks. A better understanding of information processing has allowed us to develop new models of cognition.[4] And we are finally starting to get a "big-picture" view of the brain's complex connective pathways.[5] As a result of all this progress, we're getting a bit closer to understanding the big questions of brain and mind.[6]

This has brought the realm of brain science closer to our daily lives. Perhaps most obviously, neuroscience is contributing to the treatment of medical conditions—depression, schizophrenia, dementia—that used to be seen as purely psychological or supernatural maladies.[7] We've also been flooded with new information related to a wide range of topics related to the unconscious mind[8] in areas such as learning, education, the experience of wellbeing,[9, 10, 11] decision making,[12] unconscious bias, and unconscious intuition.[13] We have gained further insights into psychological change, religious experience, morality, and rationality,[14, 15, 16, 17] and even such difficult subjects as linguistic meaning, empathy, and consciousness.[18, 19, 20]

Several strands run through much of this new research into brain and mind. One is a value placed on ideas grounded in empirically testable models—we get less philosophizing and speculation and more research and facts. Another is an appreciation of the complexity of our own mental systems. We keep finding that things that seem natural and easy—recognizing faces, reading emotions, using

Figure 1-1: Phineas Gage

language—involve highly complex cognitive processes. An increased understanding of unconscious cognition is also teaching us that our common sense can fool us—we're often unaware of the reasons for our behavior, how we make decisions, and what motivates us. A better understanding of human cognition has revealed, ironically, that we often don't truly know our own minds.

Culture and Cognition

In 2003, Richard Nisbett published a book—*The Geography of Thought*—that was an important marker of progress in our effort to understand the brain and mind.[21] Nisbett is a groundbreaking psychologist who studies cognition—the information processes of the brain. In 1977 he published a highly influential article (together with Timothy Wilson) that argued convincingly that we are often unaware of our own cognitive processes. Since then, in addition to studying cognitive processes in general, he and other researchers also started looking at the relationship between culture and cognition. Much cognitive neuroscience seeks to understand universal processes common to all humans, with a starting assumption that brain function is fundamentally the same all over the world. Nisbett, as well as other pioneering cultural psychologists such as Shinobu Kitayama, have wondered just how true that was.[22]

Nisbett has been looking at cultural variation in cognitive processing, trying to identify the ways that cultural patterns shape our experience of the world. His work was part of an increased interest in culture and cognition, as evidenced by the emerging fields of *cultural psychology* and *cultural neuroscience*. These disciplines seek to understand how culture shapes neurobiological processes and how brain function and genetics may give rise to cultural practices. They assume that there is a dynamic interdependence between body, mind, and culture.[23, 24, 25] Whereas in the past nature and nurture have been seen in opposition to each other, we now see that biological processes and environmental factors are intertwined with each other in complex ways.

The Geography of Thought carried a provocative subtitle: *How Asians and Westerners Think Differently . . . and Why*. Nisbett describes, for example, how his American students, when shown an underwater scene, tended to focus on salient objects such as the fish, whereas his Japanese students focused more on the background environment. Shown a picture of a cow, a chicken, and grass, East Asians were more likely to draw a connection between the cow and the grass based on a contextual relationship—cows eat grass. Westerners were relatively more likely to associate the cow with the chicken, because they belong to the same category of objects—"animal."

Such results provide clues to the broader influence of culture on thought processes, identity, and values. Or, as Nisbett puts it: "The Westerner sees a wall where the Asian sees concrete."[26] These tendencies are reflected in cultural practices, intellectual traditions, and social systems. For example, traditional Chinese medicine is holistic, focusing on restoring balance to the whole body, whereas Western medicine emphasizes discrete symptoms and illnesses. East Asians tend to be more collectivistic, seeing society more as an organic whole, whereas Westerners often assume that a community is the sum total of its individual parts. These differences are reflected in forms of identity: Westerners see themselves as individuals independent of others, while Asians develop a more interdependent sense of personal identity—your "selfness" is manifest in the relations you have with others.

There is a curious corollary to this sort of research. As cultural differences in cognition, perception, and identity have become better understood, it becomes more obvious that while culture shapes our thinking in measurable ways, we usually fail to notice this influence. Cultural patterns are, in effect, such an integral part of our thinking that they are invisible to us. To be clear, I'm not saying that culture determines what we think. Rather, cultural patterns help configure our cognitive processes and in so doing shape our perceptions. Some people find this surprising, vaguely assuming that cultural knowledge is a kind of informational content poured into our minds as we grow up—that it's stuff we know, whereas cognitive processes and perception are universal. As we'll see, it's not that simple. The new science of mind is revealing that cognitive processes are highly plastic—that they change and develop over time, and are highly responsive to their environment. The idea that culture plays a role in our cognitive processes, and that we may be largely ignorant of its influence, is looking less and less surprising.

The Confounding Mystery of Global Living

It is fitting that Nisbett's work was published at the dawn of a new century of globalized living—just in time for the work that I do. As an intercultural educator, my job involves helping people understand cultural diversity. I work with executives doing business internationally, conduct intercultural trainings for expatriates, help multicultural teams collaborate successfully, and teach international students studying abroad. My clients and students are educated, often highly traveled, and tech savvy—the cream of the crop in our twenty-first century global village. Yet despite their sophistication, and despite all the conveniences of our flat-earth interconnected world, they are often caught off guard by issues of intercultural adjustment and cultural difference.

I frequently see sojourners struggle with culture shock and cross-cultural misunderstanding. They may find foreign values and customs exotic and interesting at first, for example, but frustrating over time. They regularly find foreign behavior inefficient or inexplicable. Sometimes, however, they face the opposite problem, remaining blissfully ignorant of how others perceive them, or misreading the intentions of their foreign counterparts. Such difficulties are not universal, of course. Most people enjoy their international experiences, and life away from home is more convenient than ever. Still, the longer people stay and the more interaction they have, the higher the risk of significant barriers to smooth relations and positive experiences.

The new science of mind helps us better understand these challenges. One critical insight is that unconscious patterns of perceiving and valuing can be very important on the one hand, and largely invisible on the other. We tend to think of powerful influences as being obvious, but that's not always the case. Often the deeper trends in any complex system or process—whether cognitive, social, or historical—are diffuse, so it's easy to miss the forest for the trees. I see this reflected in the most confounding mystery of intercultural education—our blindness to the culture-cognition connection within our own minds. By this I mean that almost without exception, we find our own cultural view of the world natural. Our cultural viewpoint is "built-in," so to speak, to our perceptions and judgments.

It can be surprisingly difficult to understand the cultural impact on one's own way of thinking or experiencing the world. Many people don't discover this until they interact extensively with people whose perspective is different from their own. In a similar way, communication in our native language is natural and taken for granted until we must work with non-native speakers or use a foreign language. It's not that we're biased in the sense of being prejudiced or insensitive; it's just that we are so habituated to our own cultural and linguistic patterns that it is difficult to step outside ourselves far enough to perceive them. Contact with difference sheds light on parts of the self that we had been unaware of.

The difficulty of perceiving the influence of culture on self can be illustrated with a thought experiment: Imagine, in some bizarre twist of fate, that you had been taken away as a baby and raised elsewhere. What if instead of being raised in a secular society, you had been raised in a strongly Muslim community in Pakistan? What if instead of marking the passage to adulthood with a high school graduation, you had your teeth filed by a Hindu priest in Bali? What if instead of growing up where modesty is paramount, you had been raised in Germany where mixed saunas are considered unsurprising? What if instead of sleeping separately from your parents and being encouraged to develop independence, you were raised in Kenya and were almost never alone? What if instead of growing up in the crowded streets of Katmandu, you were raised in Finland where the streets are nearly empty and everyone seems locked away in individual houses and apartments?

It's difficult to imagine such an alternative cultural self—the kind of person we'd be. Many of our core values, assumptions about life and death, priorities, habits, and tastes would be different. Some things would be the same, of course, but a lot would not. Yet conjuring an image of this other possible self is nearly impossible. The places we know, the language we speak, the perspectives common to our community—all of these are such an integral part of who we are that they can't be separated out and examined apart from the entirety of our being. We are, in more ways than we often notice, a product of our cultural background.

Being blind to our own cultural conditioning has important consequences. The human capacity for prejudice towards those considered "different" is the most obvious. A more everyday example that I see, however, is the common tendency to jump to ethnocentric conclusions. American students studying in Japan, for example, sometimes describe Japanese students as "shy" because they speak up in class less than those in the United States. When saying this, my students feel they are simply "reporting the facts" about "how people are" in Japan. Yet they are actually projecting their own cultural interpretations onto behavior that is not an indication of shyness at all.

For their part, Japanese students sometimes find American students to be "selfish," hogging class time with unprompted questions or comments. Yet Japanese aren't exhibiting shyness any more than Americans are being selfish. "Shyness" and "selfishness" are words associated with personality traits; they're not neutral descriptors of cultural patterns. They assume a comparative norm—one is shy or selfish relative to shared expectations of what is normal. If Japanese are shy, then what does that make Americans? If Americans are selfish, then what does that make Japanese? In both cases, students interpret the behavior they see using unnoticed cultural standards—perceiving the cultural other as deviant from an unconscious cultural norm.

This is not a criticism. It can be very hard to accurately interpret behavior in a foreign environment. Even the simplest of actions reflects many unconscious cultural assumptions and choices. In a classroom, for example, if you have a question should you raise your hand? Or is it more typical to approach the teacher after class? What are the proper roles of teachers and students? Is it fundamentally a relationship between equals, one of whom simply happens to be an expert on a particular subject? Or is it more parental and hierarchical? What are attitudes towards showing respect? Is it best to do so in obvious ways, with titles and formality? How much deference is expected from students? Is it acceptable, or perhaps even desirable, to disagree openly with a teacher's point of view? Which is the best way for people to learn: through a dialectic process, or through memorization and absorption? What is the perception of the individual versus the group? Is the classroom primarily a community, or more simply a collection of individuals?

"They're so shy..."

"They're so pushy..."

Figure 1-2

I'm not, of course, saying that all American or Japanese or Swedish students follow identical cultural rules. We are not like robots following some form of cultural programming. My point is that the accurate interpretation of simple behaviors—such as speaking up in class—rests on interpretive knowledge that is largely cultural. This background knowledge, however, is such a natural part of our thinking that we may not be aware of it. Because of that, my students easily jump to conclusions about shyness and pushiness. Each side finds the other not quite "normal" because it can be hard to view the classroom from the other's perspective.

Culture and the Unconscious Mind

Within the field of intercultural communication, the idea that culture's influence is invisible is common. Educators frequently invoke the metaphor of the iceberg, which illustrates the idea that much of culture is beneath the surface of awareness. Another common simile is that culture is like water to a fish—invisible to us because it is the medium that we move in. While these figures of speech can be helpful, I've found they don't go very far. First of all, they give the impression that culture is like an object or substance. Thinking of culture as an iceberg may give the impression that it is a static trait embedded inside our minds—the same trap my students fall into when they say, "Japanese are shy."

In addition, these figures of speech cannot answer certain fundamental questions, such as: What sorts of cultural differences can we find hidden beneath the surface of our mind? Is there an overall structure or universal grammar to these hidden cultural patterns? And if culture is like water to a fish, then how can we become more aware of the water around us? Such metaphors don't contain testable hypotheses. They point us towards a question, but they don't provide any answers.

This is where the new science of mind is useful. We are still in the early stages of cognitive and cultural neuroscience research, yet foundational insights are emerging that recast our understanding of the relationship between culture and mind. For example, it's increasingly clear that we remain largely ignorant of the influence of culture on us because *many cognitive processes involved in daily living are inaccessible to conscious reflection.* Conscious thought—the active paying of attention, the stream of thoughts in our head, the mental images we manipulate in our minds, our imagined hypothetical outcomes—represent only one part of human thinking. There is another set of mental processes that are vital but more hidden, indeed often noticed hardly at all.[27] It is primarily this more unconscious part of our minds that is shaped by cultural patterns. By the time a thought pops into our heads, it has already been processed by the unconscious mind.

This hidden cognition will be a major focus of this book. What used to be simply called *the unconscious* is now referred to by a range of different terms, depending on the specialists and what they study. These include: the *cognitive unconscious*, the *adaptive unconscious*, the *new unconscious*, *fast thinking*, the *intuitive mind*, or simply *system 1*. I'll talk more about terminology in a bit. For the moment, I'll just point out that unlike the Freudian unconscious, which was conceptualized as consisting of powerful emotions and hard-to-control urges, we now understand the unconscious mind to be a collection of interrelated, high-level cognitive processes.

This unconscious mind is highly sophisticated. It generates judgments, inclinations, and feelings, and thus subtly guides our behavior in certain directions.[28] This is why you may arrive at the refrigerator door before having the conscious thought that you are hungry. It produces skilled responses and intuitions. That's why a basketball player can instantly "read" the state of play as she dribbles at top speed down the court.[29] It creates coherent interpretations, which we experience as things "making sense." It infers and invents intentions and causes. That's why it feels natural to see a rolling object eventually stop moving, and why we intuitively know that other people look at the world from a particular viewpoint and are driven by particular motivations.[30] It draws attention to novelty, which is why we notice countless small everyday differences when we arrive in a foreign country.[31]

Unconscious cognition is much more complex than Freud could have imagined. Yet it feels simple because its workings are cloaked in everyday normalcy. Take, for example, the seemingly simple act of seeing. A common conception of vision is that our eyes are like cameras reporting our surroundings to us. In fact, vision is a constructed experience—a mental simulation that correlates to our external environment.[32] Yet we remain unaware of this process until its eccentricities are pointed out. For example, you don't notice your blind spot (everyone has one), or that peripheral vision is so out of focus (you see no detail off to the side), or the jumping around of your eye as it gathers information (unconscious processing directs the eye to details you are interested in). Seeing, as well as many other cognitive functions we rely on every day, feel natural *not because they are simple, but because our highly complex cognitive systems work so smoothly.*

This is the first lesson that we can glean from the new science of mind—the fact that our perceptions seem so natural and obvious doesn't mean that they are simple or necessarily accurate. As we'll see, the generation of our feelings, judgments, and intuitions are largely automatic and instantaneous. The speed of our "gut reactions," however, comes at a price. The intuitive mind is also home to hidden biases and a tendency to jump to conclusions. It generates motivations we are unaware of, unconsciously influences our behavior, favors the familiar, neglects ambiguity, is biased towards a confirmation of previously learned patterns, and tends to frame decisions narrowly.[33]

These processes are not limited to some abstract form of cogitation, but are embodied—they involve feelings and physiological processes as well. Cognitive processes, far from being like the computations performed by a computer, are a whole-body experience, engaging our heart, our mind, our fears and aspirations, our survival instincts, and our social drives.[34] And, as a corollary to this, if we rely heavily but unknowingly on cognitive functions that take place out of awareness, it should come as no surprise that at least some of them are influenced by cultural factors as well.

Social Cognition

Many of the cognitive processes that we are typically unaware of are critically important in social cognition—the interpretations, intuitions, and judgments that help us manage human relations.[35] Naturally, the unconscious judgments and reactions that are appropriate in our home environment may be ineffective or inappropriate in unfamiliar cultural settings. My American students, many of whom quickly learn *not* to raise their hands in class in Japan, often feel frustrated by their inability to express themselves as they normally would. They discover that the social instincts they developed back home—how to participate in class, how to read behavior, how to make friends—may not work so well abroad.

Our unconscious cognition relies heavily on what social psychologists call *schema* (networks of meaning that we use to interpret our experiences) and *scripts* (behavioral expectations relevant to a particular context). We'll come back to this, too, but for the moment I'll simply say that this extensive body of social knowledge is very important for everyday social functioning, and naturally it's shaped by culture. Its role is similar to language, which is also a critical tool of human interaction. We all follow certain linguistic conventions, but we use them in unique ways to form social bonds, collaborate with others, and express our individual feelings and thoughts. Tied with these linguistic conventions are social expectations and shared cultural knowledge. Taken together, they all form a web of shared standards that we can rely on and don't need to think about—until relations break down.

As we learn more about our cognitive processes, it becomes less surprising to think that our social and cultural background has such a big impact on our experience of the world. For many people, however, the functioning of the brain, and thus the mind, is regarded as a sort of "standard equipment" that cannot be affected by one's cultural background. I, for one, was raised to believe that people everywhere are basically the same. To imply that one group of people was different was equated with prejudice and racism. The ideals of egalitarianism may lead us to the idea that cultural difference is a superficial part of our humanity—a kind of flavored icing on the uniform cake of human nature. If taken too far, however, this assumption can lead to questionable conclusions. Since we all share a similar human nature, the thinking goes, the cultural differences we will encounter abroad shouldn't cause us too much trouble. For better or for worse, however, that's often not how it works.

Brain, Mind, Culture

So far, I've been talking almost as though specialists understand the brain, how the mind works, how culture affects cognition, and so on. That's really not true. We are still at the earliest stages of knowledge, and words like *mind* and *culture* still generate plenty of heated debate. With that in mind, I'd like to define some basic terms so you can see where I am coming from. Let's start with a working definition of *culture*, including its relationship to mind (also known as "psyche"), courtesy of Shinobu Kitayama, a pioneer researcher in the field of cultural psychology:

> [Culture] is not a "thing" out there; rather it is a loosely organized set of interpersonal and institutional processes driven by people who participate in those processes. By the same token, the psyche is also not a discrete entity packed in the brain. Rather, it is a structure of psychological processes that are shaped by and thus closely attuned to the culture that surrounds them. Accordingly, culture cannot be understood without a deep understanding of the minds of people who make it up and, likewise, the mind cannot be understood without reference to the sociocultural environment to which it is adapted and attuned.[36]

This definition is very broad. It doesn't attempt to define what precise elements make up a conceptual understanding of the term *culture*. It simply points to the patterns of behavior and thinking that exist in the world and that shape psychological processes. It points to culture as a *general phenomenon*, one that needs to be taken into account when trying to understand the mind and, indeed, human nature. Research into culture and cognition does not use a rigid definition of culture as its starting point; it instead tries to identify the environmental factors that could be productively referred to as culture. This sort of research can be understood as an attempt to *discover* the relationship between cultural patterns out in the world and the cognitive functioning we find in the brain. This definition is a starting point for research; it is not the endpoint of a conceptual argument. This may contrast with the many other possible definitions we can find for the word *culture*, each of which has its own value and purpose.

With this broad, functional definition in hand, I want to briefly discuss a few issues that complicate our understanding of culture and cognition. First of all, we normally study the brain (the physical organ used in cognition), the mind (our mental experience of the world), and culture (in the broad sense of patterns of shared behavior and meaning in a community) at very different levels of analysis—each of which is highly complex in its own right. When we mix up these levels of analysis, it's easy to create confusion. If, for example, we ask the question "Where in the brain is culture?" we are mixing up two different scales of analysis. The study of the physical properties of the brain requires different methodologies than the study of a meta-property like culture. There are connections between the two, of course, but they aren't easily talked about in simple terms.

To get a sense of what I mean, let's start by looking at the brain. It is, of course, a physical organ, like a spleen or a pancreas, made up of living cells that can be studied with the tools of biology. Using a microscope, we can look at neural cells and glial cells. Examining a neuron, we see its branching dendrites and long snake-like axons, which transmit electric charges through neurotransmitters, across a synaptic gap, to the receptor cells in other neurons. Our brain consists of something like 20 billion such neurons, each of which may have a thousand synapses, pushing the number of connections within our head into the trillions.[37] The structural connections of our brain, referred to overall as the *connectome*, are so intricate that scientists have only just now begun to map them.[38] One of the major difficulties of such mapping is that brain systems function at so many different levels—from the micro scale of biological processes to the macro scale of the brain's higher-order processes.

The gap between the micro study of neural processes and the macro scale of culture has, until recently, seemed unbridgeable. Great progress has been made, however, through the study of *cognition*: the elaboration, storing, reduction, recalling, and use of sensory information.[39] The study of cognitive processes puts us conceptually into the realm of mental experience—phenomena that can't be studied directly with a microscope. Cognitive processes result in mental functions such as attention, awareness, memory, reasoning, learning, language, problem solving, and consciousness. Cognition is built upon the physical properties of neural networks, yet it results in mental experiences that have no place in the physical world. Adding numbers in your head, remembering the name of your dog—such activities are real to us in terms of our everyday lives, but they do not correspond to any single physical place in our brain. Cognitive neuroscience has helped us connect these high-level processes of experience to the neural structures that they are built upon.

The mental worlds we live in are not, of course, experienced in isolation—we are joined together in shared networks of meaning. If I say, "The unicorn buried the microwave next to the tree in the back yard," I create a series of images in your mind using the phonological, morphological, syntactical, and semantic patterns of English. You know what a unicorn is, even though unicorns don't exist. And this sentence makes sense, even though it's hard to picture how a unicorn could bury a microwave. The shared concepts of "unicorn," "microwave," and "back yard" provokes a mental experience that will be similar among English speakers. The shared knowledge of language provides a shared system of meaning we rely on to communicate. And of course we rely on shared cultural information as well. If I say, "The child approached and kissed her grandfather's knee" you may find it puzzling, but not if you are from Ethiopia where it's a traditional way of showing respect.

In terms of cognition, culture exists as networks of shared meaning. It can be found, in some form, in the patterns of knowing and interpreting within your mind. Those internal patterns, however, are not static, nor do they exist in isolation. They develop and emerge through interaction between you and other people. They are absorbed through interaction within a cultural community. The boundaries of these communities are not fixed or static, of course. A family will have its own conventions and communicative patterns just as a nation-state will. Cultural communities exist on many overlapping levels, and each is made up of unique individuals that use and interpret cultural patterns in distinct ways. Just as each of us uses the patterns of our native language to express our individual self, the shared patterns of culture enable meaningful interaction among distinct individuals.

If you find this description rather abstract, don't worry. Most of this book will focus on the intercultural experiences of real people. I'll try not to get lost in theory or technical detail. But brace yourself for some complexity. Any inquiry into culture, cognition, and international living necessarily touches upon difficult subjects that even specialists are just beginning to grapple with. We won't find easy answers, but I think you'll find that even a cursory exploration will provide insights into the pitfalls and rewards of our intercultural experiences.

The Structure of This Book

This book traces—roughly speaking—the trajectory common to the traveler's experience of a foreign land. Chapter two sets the scene for intercultural experiences in the twenty-first century, and asks whether globalization is moving us beyond cultural differences. Chapter three gives an account of arriving in a foreign environment. It examines our cognitive response to this challenge, revealing that the small differences we notice abroad are in fact a sign that our unconscious mind is hard at work detecting, interpreting, and judging anomalies in our surroundings.

Chapter four takes a tour of the everyday functioning of our cultural mind, arguing that we are often less aware of our mental functioning than we believe. We'll meet Ned Hall, an intercultural pioneer who understood that our mind is deeply affected by cultural patterns that we aren't fully aware of. In chapter five, we discover that many sojourners don't anticipate the cognitive impact of foreign experiences. They share stories of unexpectedly difficult adjustments and culture shock. Their reactions make sense when we see them for what they are—cognitive overload.

In chapter six, we will see how cultural configurations are an integral part of the way our minds work. We'll look at the brain's plasticity and see that culture is not just an idea, custom, or set of symbols; culture is embodied. We'll look at research into parenting that shows how we pass on cultural patterns without being aware of it. In chapter seven, we will look at bias, exploring ways in which our reactions and interpretations are influenced by cultural conditioning and subject to mental shortcuts.

In chapter eight, we will examine *expert intuitions,* our unconscious ability to learn and interpret patterns. We'll see that cultural knowledge is a form of expert intuition—an ability to identify and read subtle cultural patterns. In chapter nine, we'll learn how researchers are using new research techniques, including brain imaging, to understand the complexities of cultural difference.

Chapter ten will examine the language-culture-cognition connection. We'll see that new research into *embodied simulation* is giving us new ways to think about how our minds process cultural meaning. In chapter eleven, we'll take a closer look at the "intercultural mind"—the increased cognitive flexibility that foreign experiences can help us attain. We'll see that people with extensive experiences in different cultural worlds may learn to switch between different cultural frames, thus becoming effective *bridge people.*

This book doesn't wade into debates about big questions, such as "How does the brain produce consciousness?" or "What is culture?" It is not intended as an academic overview of cultural neuroscience or cultural psychology. There is, of course, already a vast body of literature that touches on issues of culture and mind from a wide range of disciplines, including cultural anthropology, sociology, psychology, and philosophy. A fair overview of such an enormous body of work is far beyond the scope of this book, intended, as it is, for busy internationalists—travelers, expatriates, immigrants, study-abroad students, and so on. Here I limit myself to emerging ideas from the study of cognition and culture that I find useful in my intercultural work. The main goal is to spark interest in the culture-cognition connection, with an eye to better appreciating the deep learning that can result from intercultural experiences.

The Intercultural Mind

The organizing concept at the center of this book is the *intercultural mind*. This term brings together two main ideas: (1) *The human mind is cultural by nature.* By this, I mean that just as our native language becomes a natural part of how we communicate, the cultural configuration of our mind plays an essential role in of our cognitive functioning. (2) *Foreign experiences make possible a process of deep cultural learning,* one that can make us aware of the cultural configuration of our unconscious mind, and make us more effective interculturally. This learning process can be experienced in negative ways—such as culture shock or cross-cultural misunderstanding—but it also can stimulate personal growth and provoke deep-seated changes in our perception, worldview, and identity. Many of these reactions and changes, however, take place at the hidden level of unconscious cognition. By learning about how our minds work, we're therefore better equipped to make the best of our intercultural experiences.

In subsequent chapters, we will alternate between personal stories of intercultural experiences and a few key ideas about culture and cognition. Before taking a detailed look at cognition, however, we'll ask a few more basic questions. Does globalization dilute the intercultural experience? Is modern technology taking us beyond cultural difference? What are the intercultural challenges of the twenty-first century?

KEY CONCEPTS

Mind: *The constellation of mental phenomena that makes up our everyday experience of the world—thoughts and images, wakeful attention, consciousness and self-awareness, memory, imagination, abstract problem solving, and so on.*

Culture: *Culture is not a "thing" out there; rather it is a loosely organized set of interpersonal and institutional processes driven by people who participate in those processes.*[40]

The mind-culture connection: *Culture cannot be understood without a deep understanding of the minds of people who make it up and, likewise, the mind cannot be understood without reference to the sociocultural environment to which it is adapted and attuned.*[41]

Discussion Quote: *Cognitive processes, far from being like the computations performed by a computer, are a whole-body experience— engaging our heart, our mind, our fears and aspirations, our survival instincts, and our desire for connection with our fellow humans.*

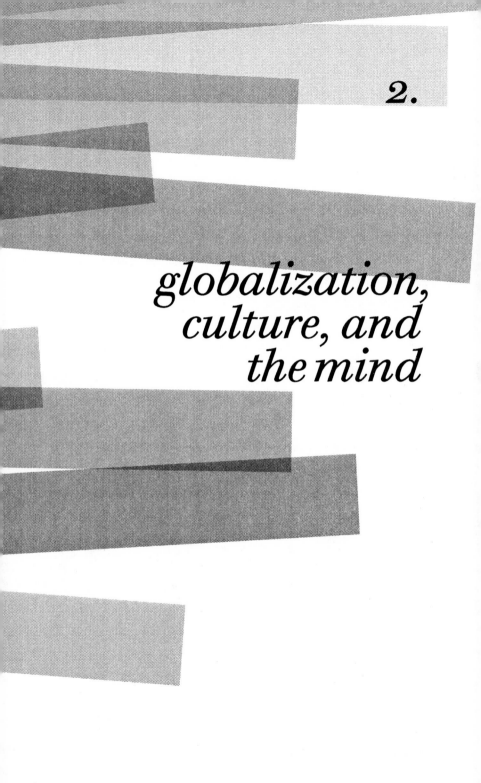

2.

*globalization,
culture, and
the mind*

You'll never know how big the world is
unless you experience it on your own.

—Sum Yi

We may live in a global village, but it's still not easy to adjust to life abroad, understand
cultural difference, or develop an international mindset. The conveniences of
globalization help us explore the world, but they also can prevent us from experiencing
deeper encounters with human diversity. We face choices not only about where we travel,
but how deeply we look into our intercultural experiences.

Lost in Bali

I was lost among the back roads of Banjuwedang in northwest Bali. Fortunately, the narrow dirt track I was navigating led me to a modest compound where I could ask for directions. Cobs of corn were drying on a blue plastic tarp in the yard, and several people were lounging on a covered platform. Children, seemingly immune from the burning sun, were chasing each other around in flip-flops. A young man stepped forward to greet me. With soft-spoken courtesy he pointed towards a sandy path that passed by a tethered goat, continuing along a field and towards the ocean. I thanked him, asked his name—it was Dan—and was introduced to his family. I met his cooing newborn daughter, his wife, and other relatives, along with a neighbor. He invited me to join them. So before getting back on my scooter, I shared a spot in the shade of their open platform.

I sipped coffee, played with the baby, and chatted within the narrow limits of Dan's English and my Indonesian. Time slowed down as I slipped into the rhythm of Balinese life. I was born and raised in laid-back Southern California, but I live and work a world away in Tokyo, a frenetic megalopolis of glass and concrete, scramble crossings, and bullet trains that depart at precise twenty-minute intervals. Life in and around Banjuwedang, suffused with local tradition, is another world still. "Going to work" often involves fishing, farming terraced rice fields, or hiking into the hills with a long knife to cut fodder for cows. Temples and mosques are central to community life, and offerings are placed daily on the family altars of Hindu homes.

The opportunity to step a bit more deeply into that world with Dan, if even for a few minutes, was magical. Dan's father had immigrated to Bali from Java as an agricultural worker, but was now, like Dan, a snorkeling guide at a nearby marine sanctuary. Dan's father patted his round stomach and made jokes about puffer fish. Several children had gathered to stare for a time, but soon went back to playing. The pace of conversation was unrushed. After some more chatting, though, it was time to leave. I thanked Dan, expressed pleasure at our encounter, and said I hoped that we would meet again. I was conscious that my flight would soon take me back to a very different set of routines—and that this compound, with its drying corn and foot-loose children, would soon feel far away.

That's when Dan asked, "Are you on Facebook?"

Figure 2-1: Dan (second from the right) with his family

Culture and Globalization

If you're interested in travel, culture, or life in faraway places, globalization can feel like a double-edged sword. On the one hand, foreign places and cultural diversity are more accessible than ever. I researched Bali online and clicked my way to hotel and flight reservations, and I now stay in touch with Dan on social media. I live in Tokyo but regularly talk to my family in California—the global village now fits into a device I keep in the front pocket of my Japan-purchased, American-branded, Chinese-manufactured jeans.

The flip side of such convenience and interconnectivity, of course, is that it can seem increasingly difficult for travelers to find places that are truly "exotic." To find Banjuwedang, for example, I traveled from the southern slopes of Bali, with its teeming beachside tourist beehive of Kuta, through the less commercial but still traveler-packed Ubud, up through rice fields and past Lake Beratan through the lesser-known but still popular Munduk, and over to the northwest coast. Eventually, I found the town of Pemuteran, which became my base of operations while exploring the local area. While still maintaining many Balinese traditions, this region too is changing because of international tourism, connective technology, and economic development. Dan's texting is as fast as tech-savvy teenagers everywhere, and despite the relative isolation of his hometown, he is connected to the outside world in ways unimaginable even a few years ago.

For many travelers, this raises questions: Is there any place that's unexplored? Do we have to rush out and find *unspoiled* places in order to have a profound travel experience? This raises a more fundamental question as well: What are we looking for from our foreign adventures? It can feel like globalization is diluting the intercultural experience—that it's becoming *too* easy to see the world. We find Facebook in Fiji, McDonald's in Moldova, Toyotas in Timbuktu, and ethnic foods in our neighborhood. Even a generation ago, foreign travel was seen as an exotic adventure. Increasingly, no matter where we go, we are greeted with things we already know. Dan's Facebook page and his job with international tourists are emblematic of much larger trends. The owner of the hotel I stayed at in the village near Dan's place is a German—one who has spent many years living in Indonesia. At the airport in Denpasar, a McDonald's competes with a Burger King and a Starbucks for both international *and* Indonesian customers.

I've come to believe, however, that appearances of standardization and watered-down local culture can be deceiving. Throughout this book, I argue against the idea that communication technology, economic development, and virtual communities are making intercultural experiences less powerful or meaningful. Despite the conveniences of industrialization, information technology, global branding, borderless commerce, international sports, and global pop culture, traveling and living abroad are still powerful, potentially transformative experiences. Cultural difference is alive and well. Culture shock is still a challenge.

Profound cross-cultural experiences await travelers who make the choice, and have the patience, to look beneath the surface of globalization.

In today's highly interconnected world, however, *where* you have intercultural experiences is becoming less important than *how* you have them. You can jet to Kenya yet stay pampered in a luxury safari camp, or live in Hong Kong without speaking any Cantonese. You can go on a study-abroad program yet Skype with your loved ones back home every evening—what the international educator Richard Slimbach calls "cocooning."[1] In the past, travel forced you to confront diversity, whereas staying home protected you from it. That has changed. Now, the choice is more often yours. If you are interested in foreign experiences, you can have them, whether you travel to faraway places or not. If you seek familiarity, you can cut yourself off from those who are different from you—even when you are abroad. It's not the distance traveled that matters; it's the *depth* of our experiences that count. Globalization, Dan reminded me, is what we make of it.

Cultural Learning

Travel brings us face-to-face with fundamental questions of human diversity. To make sense of foreign experiences, we must juggle competing notions about human nature and cultural difference. On the one hand, we believe that cultural and ethnic differences between peoples are important, interesting, and worth trying to understand—we try to learn from different lifestyles, customs, and ways of seeing the world. At the same time, we believe that all people are fundamentally the same—that we share a common human nature that connects us in fundamental ways. Yet these ideas seem to contradict each other—we are the same, yet different; cultural difference is important, yet shouldn't be over emphasized; we want to honor diversity, and yet feel part of a unified humanity.

The way we think about these issues can affect our foreign experiences. Visiting Dan, for example, confronted me with these contradictory ideas. If I look for commonality between us, I will find it. His pride in his daughter, or the laughter of the children as they play, can be understood by anyone, regardless of culture or background. At the same time, I cannot discount how different his world is from mine. I grew up in the so-cool Southern California surfing city of San Diego, had a secular education, and was raised in a country that values, among other things, self-determination and individualism. I was thrilled, for example, to become independent from my family as a teenager. Dan, on the other hand, grew up in a village where community life is centered on family and the local mosque. He is a minority Muslim in predominantly Hindu Bali and lives enfolded in a multigenerational household.

While foreign travel may remind us of our common humanity, the longer we spend away from home, or the more we attempt to adapt to life abroad, the more that difference comes to the fore. For me to move to Banjuwedang and integrate myself into local life would be a challenge. Likewise, it wouldn't be easy for Dan to go live in the neighborhood where I grew up, and adapt himself to the social world that seems so normal to me . While we may feel humans are fundamentally the same, in practice it's not easy to take on a new lifestyle, learn a new language and way of communicating, accept different social obligations, appreciate different moral orientations, or become a smoothly functioning part of a new cultural community.

People react differently to this contradiction. After walking through the streets of faraway places, interacting with foreigners, and eating different food, some travelers resolutely come to the conclusion that cultural difference is of little importance because people are the same everywhere. One expatriate in Japan states this position rather forcefully:

> The thing about travel is that it's unnecessary. You don't need to go somewhere to have a "direct experience." That's the kind of nonsense that we tell ourselves to justify the expense, hassle, and time spent getting somewhere. It's the same day everyday in Bosnia as it is in Detroit. The people aren't any more interesting. There are no incredible insights. Seeing a place you've never been is not necessarily any more valuable than the shit you're surrounded with all day everyday. It's not guaranteed to make you a more interesting or even a more "well-traveled" person.[2]

It's true, of course, that simply walking in the streets of Cairo or Kiev won't *automatically* make for a meaningful foreign experience. And it's also true that we can have powerful cultural learning experiences in our hometown. To that extent, at least, this sojourner has a point.

But it's hard to miss a note of cynicism in this dismissal of cultural difference. This expatriate seems to have turned what *could have been* a "direct experience" abroad into a set of safe and bland generalities. This sort of thinking is sometimes buttressed by the argument that, after all, people everywhere are "basically" the same. If we share a common humanity, then the cultural differences encountered abroad are only secondary.

Yet once taken to such an extreme, the Tokyo expat's position becomes less convincing. Growing up as a Bosniak Muslim in Sarajevo *is* different from growing up in Detroit as an African American. How could it not be? If we adopt a strong universalist stance—that people everywhere are the same—we may be pushed to agree that "there are no incredible insights" to be had from foreign experiences, and that people in foreign places "aren't any more interesting" than those back home. This conveniently excuses us from any need to take cultural difference seriously—since we believe we already understand people everywhere. The international traveler who adopts this stance is like a man who says to his female date: "All women are the same, so I don't need to bother getting to know you."

The convenience of travel can also make us blasé about the differences we find around the world. I was reminded of this recently when reading the diary of Edward Morse, a naturalist who first came to Japan in 1877. Morse was so fascinated by the day-to-day differences he found that he kept a detailed diary, complete with hundreds of meticulous drawings, describing daily life and everyday objects. His assumption was precisely the opposite of our modern-day Tokyo expat—Morse believed that the little differences he found were indicative of something profound. Instead of focusing on commonality and searching for universality, he developed a sharp eye for cultural contrast and pondered on its significance:

> [I]n many operations we do just the reverse of the Japanese. . . . The Japanese plane and saw toward them instead of away from them as we do; they begin a book on what we should call the last page, and at the upper right-hand corner and read down; the last page of our books would be the first page of theirs; their boats have the mast near the stern and the sailor sculls from the side; in the sequence of courses at dinner candy and cake are offered first; they drink hot water instead of cold and back their horses into the stall.[3]

Morse's detailed observations are accompanied by broader musings about Japan, the changes brought about by industrialization, and the larger lessons that could be gleaned about humanity. Unlike the Tokyo expat, his starting assumption was that the differences he observed were like pieces of a puzzle that gave clues to the thinking of Japanese people. Rather than looking for universal qualities, he sought out the novel, the inexplicable and the mysterious, and only then attempted to form a new understanding of the cultural worlds he witnessed.

The differing stances of our Tokyo expat and Edward Morse act as a reminder that our assumptions about human nature and cultural diversity are important. They affect our reactions to our experiences—whether we look for bigger meaning in small details, or perhaps downplay significant differences that are obvious to everyone. People differ in what they find meaningful in foreign places. For example: Is it significant that Japanese books traditionally are read from right to left, rather than left to right? That they use kanji characters rather than an alphabet? Some travelers are tempted to dismiss such details, while others look at them as clues to understanding something profound. Focusing on difference provokes questions: What does this mean? Why do people act that way? What's expected of me? Is this person being rude? How should I interpret that?

These questions are what drives cultural learning, though finding answers is often not easy. For one thing, not all novelty is equally meaningful. In England people drive on the left side, whereas in France they use the right—yet there's no deep symbolic significance to this. Deciphering what is significant and what isn't can be difficult. The fact that Japanese and Chinese people use ideographic writing systems is perhaps simply an accident of history. On the other hand, neurolinguists have found evidence that reading in Chinese activates different parts of the brain than reading in English, perhaps because of the visuospatial nature of the characters.[4] Perhaps, then, using different writing systems has cognitive effects beyond reading tasks. There is evidence, for example, of differences between how Asians and Westerns perceive and attend to visual objects and contexts. It has even been found that when Asians look at faces, they tend to focus more on the nose and less on the eyes and mouth compared to Westerners, though the reasons for this are not clear.[5]

How are we to make sense of all this? It's not easy. We are still at the beginning stages of such research. Such work is, however, a reminder to pay attention to the differences we find abroad, and learn as much as possible about how our minds work, and in particular the role of culture in cognition. To lay some groundwork for this, and before looking more specifically at cognition, it's important to look at the many ways that we use the word *culture* in everyday life, and contrast that with how researchers are using this term.

In Search of Culture

I recently received an e-mail from a student that said: "Now that I have a little free time before going to college, I'm really happy to be able to travel to Japan and get to know the country, its culture, and its people." Her message made me curious about what precisely she means by "getting to know" Japan's "culture, and its people." Are culture and people separate? What's the culture she is referring to here? Temples and kimonos? Crowded subways in Tokyo? Her message seems, on the surface at least, clear enough. Yet as soon as we look more closely, the meaning becomes quite fuzzy. Often, our use of the word *culture* is vague. When I ask, "What did you learn from your foreign experiences?" I hear: "I learned about the culture." Or "I was able to see the culture first hand." Yet if I dig a little deeper and ask, "What do you mean by culture?" people get stuck.

The vagueness of this usage is not, I don't think, a product of sloppy thinking. It results from the fact that culture, as a phenomena, is experienced in a highly intuitive way—it's not typically something we analyze with our conscious, problem-solving mind. We *get a feeling* for culture, or *experience* culture, or *come into contact* with culture—all intuitive experiences. The powerful elements of intercultural experiences aren't related to conscious knowing and precise conceptualization. We don't visit the Great Wall of China in order to learn facts about its construction. We want to *feel* this structure and *get a sense* for its importance in China. Intercultural experience affects us more at the level of feeling and intuition, rather than reasoning and conscious reflection. Our understanding of culture, and of our intercultural experiences for that matter, is largely intuitive.

There's a lot to be gained, however, from reflecting on what we mean when we use the word *culture*. In the last chapter, we were given a broad technical definition—as an environmental factor that influences cognitive process—but we should also look more closely at how this word is used in everyday life, as a way of clarifying in our own minds how we are using it. This can help us examine our intercultural experiences more closely and more critically.

In everyday communication, the word *culture* has an impressive range of usages, and it can refer to related, yet very different, sets of ideas. As I go through some examples, consider the common threads that run through disparate usages. We might refer, for example, to Elizabethan literature as representing *English culture*, refer to the *company culture* at our workplace, decry a *culture of violence* that leads to increased crime, make a distinction between *high culture* and *low culture*, or may refer to someone with a high level of education as being *cultured*. We also talk about yogurt being *cultured*.

In American politics, you sometimes hear about the *culture wars* or that financial service companies have a *culture of greed*. I heard a traveler proclaim that he experienced *Tunisian culture* in North Africa, and in multiethnic California I hear people say they are *proud of their culture*. People living in societies with repressive regimes may experience a *culture of fear*. Some say that "Americans have very little culture," except perhaps for *pop culture*. A newspaper headline for a recent article about traditional music in China reported that "Once the Villages are Gone, The Culture is Gone."[6] The word *culture* is pulled into so many directions that the whole concept starts to seem flabby and shapeless indeed.

Specialists often aren't much more precise. The encyclopedia of cultural anthropology doesn't even define culture. Instead, you will find a history of its changing conceptualizations over time.[7] Wikipedia's crowd-sourced definition is a historical account that stretches back to Cicero.[8] Broadly speaking, however, the use of the word *culture* as related to intercultural experiences has its roots in the nineteenth century. In 1871, Edward Tylor, a foundational thinker in the field of cultural anthropology, created an enduring definition of the word: "Culture, or civilization, taken in its broad, ethnographic sense, is that complex whole which includes knowledge, belief, art, morals, law, custom, and any other capabilities and habits acquired by man as a member of society."[9] This definition contains many of the elements common to the diverse usages we looked at, namely that culture is shared by groups of people, and it's learned and passed on. The roots of the word *culture*, I'll point out, are the same as that of "cultivate."

We are now quite used to the idea of culture as a shaper of our humanity. In the nineteenth century, however, even progressive thinkers commonly believed that physical characteristics were an important determinant of behavior. The great emancipator himself, Abraham Lincoln, said, "There is a physical difference between the white and black races which I believe will forever forbid the two races living together on terms of social and political equality."[10] Eugenics, the idea that we could improve society by improving its genetic makeup, was popular well into the twentieth century, supported by luminaries such as Winston Churchill, Theodore Roosevelt, and the Atlantic-hopping celebrity pilot Charles Lindbergh.[11] With a backdrop of this type of thinking, arguing that "culture" was an important determinant of behavior, rather than biology, was a progressive step. It was less deterministic, more egalitarian, and emphasized the capacity of humans to learn and develop.

During the twentieth century, many people starting shifting towards the idea that human behavior is shaped largely by nonbiological factors in the environment. The first people to systematically explore the idea of culture believed deeply and passionately in the equality of all humans everywhere. Linguists like Sapir and Whorf argued that language, and by extension culture, affected our perceptions.[12] Pioneering anthropologist Margaret Mead went to Polynesia in 1925 and came back with sensational stories about taboo-free sexuality.[13] She sought to show that many things that people considered "human nature" were in fact artifacts of socialization. Culture seemed to be an all-powerful shaper of human behavior independent of biology. Linguist Stephen Pinker calls this way of thinking the "tabula rasa" understanding of human nature—the belief that humans are blank slates ready to be written on by our cultural background.[14]

These days, however, cognitive neuroscience is leading us towards a more integrated perspective—one that looks for human nature in the complex interplay between the environment, genes, and the brain.[15] In this view, culture is one of many environmental factors that affects the development and functioning of the brain. Evidence for such environmental influence on cognition has been found by researchers in a number of areas. One example is that meditation can bring about differences in brain function (a greater volume of particular brain frequencies). Another is that taxi drivers with an extensive knowledge of a city have been shown to develop larger hippocampi—a part of the brain important in spatial navigation. It has been shown that gymnasts develop different elements of their sensory motor systems compared to practitioners of the Afro-Brazilian art of capoeira. Although standing on their hands is common in both art forms, the trainings emphasize different techniques, resulting in differences in how practitioners maintain their balance.[16]

While we might think of culture as merely symbolic, or something to be discovered in remote places, researchers trying to understand brain function are developing a view of culture grounded in open systems theory. This refers to the idea that humans are in constant interaction with their physical and social environment. In the words of neurocognitive researcher Bruce E. Wexler, M.D., professor emeritus of psychiatry and senior research scientist at Yale School of Medicine and director of the Neurocognitive Research Laboratory at the Connecticut Mental Health Center:

> There is a neurological imperative that an individual's internal neuropsychological structures match key features of his or her external

environment, a principle of internal-external consonance. This principle is of great importance, since people are linked to their environments by obligatory, continuous multimodal sensory stimulation. It is not possible to turn off the sensory receptors. The developing nervous system requires sensory stimulation in order for brain cells to live and develop.[17]

From the neurocognitive perspective, culture is a form of sensory stimulation. Our environment provides us not only with food and shelter, but with the social interaction that our brain needs to function normally. Our cultural environment shapes our mind, and we in turn shape the communities that we belong to in an ongoing feedback loop. Seen in this way, culture is something that is both "out there" in the environment and "inside" the human organism—embodied in the structures of our biology, our brain, and the cognitive processes that produce mind.[18] This broader understanding of human nature incorporates our ongoing interaction with our environment while highlighting the fundamental role that cultural patterns play in our mind.

Deep Culture

There are a few things to keep in mind when using the word *culture* to talk about our intercultural experiences. Some precision is needed to avoid a few common confusions. First of all, we sometimes talk about culture as though it's a *thing*. ("I saw the culture," or "I'm proud of my culture.") This is called the reification fallacy—treating an abstraction as though it were an object. In terms of cognition, however, we cannot see culture directly, since it is a meta-property found in patterns of social interaction and shared meaning. Of course cultural communities create cultural artifacts, like Aboriginal didgeridoos, or Alsatian flammeküeche or coming of age ceremonies.. But such artifacts are, more precisely, residues of human interaction—not cultural patterns themselves.

The tendency to reify culture might lead us to use the word *culture* in the singular—e.g., "The culture in Greece is fascinating." But cultural patterns are not countable "things." Similarly, we might say, "She did that because of her culture," as though culture were a singular trait possessed by an individual that also determines that person's behavior. These uses of the word *culture* are typically well intentioned and easily understood. But once we cross cultural boundaries, these common ways of thinking and talking about culture may not be adequate. When interacting across cultures, it's easy to overlook differences in *deep culture*. This is the term that I use to talk about patterns of habit and meaning that are internalized in the unconscious mind, and that we rely on when we communicate and interact with others. Deep culture is easy to overlook because it operates in the background, providing us the tools to communicate (through shared linguistic knowledge), guiding us in our interactions with others and providing us with interpretive frameworks for looking at things. It includes the linguistic knowledge that allows us to effortlessly use our native language, and the social knowledge to successfully interpret the intentions and messages of others in our community. This background knowledge produces an intuitive sense of what's normal in a given situation and acts as a glue of shared habits and standards.

We often don't notice how much we rely on implicit cultural knowledge until it fails us in a foreign environment. I recently gave a cross-cultural training course to Frederick, a German executive who had relocated to Japan. He was an intelligent man—sharp with numbers as well as an experienced and competent manager. He wanted advice on how to gain the trust of the Japanese staff. "At meetings, they don't speak up," he complained. "They seem passive and don't ask questions. I don't know what they are thinking. What can I do to get them to open up?"

Frederick's inability to "read" the behavior of Japanese staff is rooted in differences in deep culture. Frederick's pre-departure training had given him rules to follow about Japanese business etiquette—how to pour drinks for others, grasp business cards with both hands, and so on. But these concrete behaviors are grounded in cultural values and habits that take a long time to understand. Behind the simplest of actions is a world of meaning and interpretation. Frederick's first impression had been that it would be easy to work in Japan, but over time, he kept bumping up against more subtle cultural differences.

If we are unaware of deep culture, we may overestimate the unifying force of globalization. Scott Lash, a professor of cultural studies, has called this unifying trend *extensive culture*, by which he means the homogenizing, systematizing forces of increased economic exchange, shared media, and intercultural contact.[19] People around the world share more with each other than ever—pop culture, brand names, common technology, foods, and so on. Customers in more than fifty countries can go to Starbucks and share in a coffee-drinking experience similar from Seattle to Singapore. Extensive culture makes life abroad more convenient and makes cross-cultural interaction easier. Hundreds of millions of people around the world share some knowledge of European soccer, Chinese food, pop music, Hollywood movies, the latest gadgets and video games, and on and on. We've got more common points of reference than ever.

Accustomed to thinking of the world as a global village, sojourners such as Frederick are sometimes startled to discover just how different things really *are* in other places—once you scratch the surface. They discover what Lash refers to as *intensive culture*, the local perspective of a given community—things that are untranslatable to outsiders. All human communities—even virtual ones—develop shared social expectations and points of commonality that become second nature. Intensive culture, or what I refer to as deep culture, is internalized such that it becomes a natural part of how we relate to others—it is configured into our minds at the level of intuition and unconscious expectations.

The supply chains of extensive culture allow Frederick to spread Nutella on the bauernbrot he buys at specialty food shops in Tokyo. He can find a lot that is familiar if he seeks it out. Yet he runs into deep culture differences in his silent meetings. His staff really *does* have a different way of communicating and getting things done. Like many sojourners today, Frederick found that the convenience of globalization is often not enough to achieve deep levels of understanding abroad. Extensive culture can mask the need for deep culture knowledge, but it can't make it go away.

Culture in a Globalized World

Globalization provides entry points into many different communities, but it's up to sojourners to look more deeply into our experiences and step more fully into other cultural communities. Despite technological cushioning, cultural differences—large and small—still abound. This means that twenty-first-century travelers have an important choice to make. Those who choose *not* to seek out meaningful differences, to downplay novelty and cultural variation, can do so. I believe, however, that this comes at a price. As one of my students, Francois, explains:

> I have seen friends living the same semester as me in Tokyo, but who could have been anywhere else. They did not have an international experience. Not only do I think that it is a shame because they missed something great, but I also think it is really sad because they are leaving with bad feelings against Japan and the Japanese people. So

I guess I learnt that an international experience is a great challenge, and that as [with] any challenge it can be failed.

Francois' point is that if we make the choice—perhaps unconsciously—to avoid engaging with cultural difference, we pay a price. Francois warns us that his friends ended up leaving with "bad feelings against…the Japanese." Why? Because downplaying cultural difference puts us in an untenable position. It requires us to judge things we don't fully understand, relying only on our own common sense. This is a mistake because our cultural background flavors our everyday thinking, judgments, and interpretations in important ways. It's harder to "understand culture" than we might think. In the next chapter, we'll learn more about why this is, starting with a look at the cognitive processes that are engaged as soon as we step into a foreign cultural environment.

KEY CONCEPTS

Extensive culture: *The homogenizing, systematizing forces of increased economic exchange, shared media, and intercultural contact.*

Intensive culture: *The local perspective of a given community—things that are untranslatable to outsiders.*

Deep culture: *Embodied networks of shared meaning and behavior that enable communication and collaboration within a community.*

Discussion Quote: *It's not the distance traveled that matters; it's the depth of our experiences that count.*

3.

the oz moment and the intuitive mind

The more you experience culture,
the more you will be confounded.

—Jumpei

The small differences we notice abroad—Oz moments—are a sign that our unconscious mind is hard at work detecting, interpreting, and judging anomalies in our surroundings. These experiences can have powerful effects on our "intuitive mind," which is one reason travel can be so stimulating, stressful, and transformative.

Aki in LA

Aki has clear memories from her first trip abroad—starting with the toilets in the LA airport. Bleary-eyed after a long flight from Tokyo, she walked into the restroom and stopped short. A fluorescent glare illuminated a long row of stalls stretching to the back wall, as well as a glimpse of something unexpected—the feet of a woman inside. In Japan, toilet stall partitions typically start at the ground and reach nearly to the ceiling, so entering one isolates you completely. But these American stalls reached barely above head level and only extended down to the knees. Weighing her embarrassment against her immediate needs, and after making a quick calculation of potential wait time, she resigned herself and stepped inside, wondering about this strange new country with such public toilets. Welcome to America!

Oz Moment Memories

A foreign experience can be like a scene from the 1939 film *The Wizard of Oz*. At the beginning of the movie we meet Dorothy, a sweet, plucky girl from Kansas. A tornado rips her house off its foundations, lifts it into the sky, and whirls it through the storm until it crashes down far away in the magical Kingdom of Oz. Curious, yet with trepidation, she opens her door and steps out to explore this new realm. She is greeted by a fantastic landscape of shimmering green leaves, mushroom-shaped houses, and a tiny village square in Munchkinland. She slowly looks around, dazzled by the other-worldliness of her surroundings. The scenes of Dorothy on her farm in Kansas are filmed in sepia, dreary and everyday, but Oz is saturated with the vivid color of a dream world. Clutching her dog, she stares wide-eyed and declares, "Toto, I've the feeling we're not in Kansas anymore."

Aki's Oz moment

Figure 3-1

I call this the *Oz moment*—a feeling of disorientation or surprise when encountering novel surroundings or hard-to-interpret phenomena. Aki's reaction to the bathroom in LAX was similar to Dorothy's—an I'm-not-in-Japan-anymore feeling of heightened awareness and vigilance. She felt self-conscious in this foreign environment, like an actor on an unfamiliar stage. She noticed tiny details that contrasted with life back home: the sounds of English and the gun strapped to the leg of the customs agent. Exiting from baggage claim, she saw a bus "kneeling"—lowering itself down—to allow a person in a wheelchair to enter, something she'd never seen in Japan. She remembers the wide LA boulevards and the fact that traffic drove on the right while the steering wheel was on the left. Like many who have experienced Oz moments, she has a heightened recall of tiny impressions like these.

It's curious, really, that entering a foreign environment can bring such tiny details to our attention and provoke such lasting images. Such memories often lack any particular symbolic importance—they don't have some obvious meaning—and may involve minor points we never bother to discuss with others. Aki's restroom story, for example, lay buried in her mind, unreported to anyone, until I asked her what she noticed when she first went abroad. Yet if they are such minor details, why should they stick with us? After all, we typically remember very few of our daily activities—routine experiences are stored for a fraction of a second then lost. In evolutionary terms, long-term memory is only worthwhile for high-value data, such as the location of a fruit-laden tree. Our brain is mostly designed to forget; yet these tiny memories seem to stick with us for years.

Why do we remember Oz moments? One way to look at them is as a conscious echo of an intuitive, largely hidden cultural learning process—a sign of an unconscious mind hard at work. They are a cognitive response to the anomalous patterns surrounding us in a foreign environment. If we want to understand intercultural experiences, a first step is to examine the cognitive processes that produce such sticky memories. This will help us see one way in which our background shapes the experiences we have away from home.

Discovering Difference

From the cognitive perspective, foreign experiences are a wake-up call to the information processing systems of the brain. It's no wonder that many of us dream and plan all year for an annual vacation, or talk about being "hooked" on travel. If routine is a tranquilizer, then novelty is a stimulant. As one of my students describes it:

> Living in another country gave me another view of things. It requires much more mental energy, but it also is very rewarding. Wherever you go, whatever you do—be it having a drink with a friend, paying your rent, or going to school—has a special taste to it. Of course, it is because it is different, more complicated . . . but I think it also comes genuinely from the fact that you are doing it somewhere else.

The attraction of difference motivates many of us to head abroad—we want to chew new foods, traipse through unknown streets, and look into the faces of people who speak and act differently than we do. The excitement, stress, and transformative power of our experiences abroad all revolve around our response to difference. It's difference that makes things feel exotic; it's difference that causes culture shock; it's difference that creates cross-cultural misunderstanding; it's difference that challenges us to see the world in new ways. In a broad sense, dealing with difference is the essential driving factor of cultural learning.

We often use the words "discover," "find," or "see" when talking about the differences we encounter abroad—as though coming across an object in our path. Aki might say she "discovered" that American toilets have short stall doors. Yet this is misleading because the things we "discover" abroad are often things that the locals don't notice. For their part, Americans who use the LAX restrooms are largely unaware of the gap between the floor and the door—it is part of the background and doesn't enter their conscious awareness. This reminds us that *the discoveries we make abroad are a result of our previous experience, including unconscious expectations we have about the world.* In Aki's case, her Oz moment was caused by a sort of "toilet mismatch"—the public restroom in LAX was not "normal" relative to her previous experiences.

This is an important lesson that Oz moments teach us. The things we will notice depend as much on our expectations as on the particular details found in our new environment. Our unconscious mind is quite skilled at steering our attention to novelty. The cognitive processes responsible for this are not well understood, but they are related to an automatic process of pattern recognition and categorization.[1] One theory about how this works is that it involves *template matching*, a comparison of what we see to patterns held in long-term memory. It may also involve *feature analysis*, in which stimuli are analyzed in terms of simple features, or *prototypes*, idealized mental forms that we use to interpret what we see.[2]

Regardless of the particular mechanisms involved, sticky travel memories are a result of an unconscious process of filtering and selection.[3] Our unconscious mind makes judgments about what is noteworthy, flagging certain things for attention while ignoring others. These judgments are made based on unconscious expectations and help guide our behavior.[4] Yet this process involves more than simply noticing. We also activate interpretive frameworks in order to *make sense* of our experiences. This may trigger thoughts in our conscious mind ("Wow, the bathroom doors are short!"), or provoke physiological responses—such as making Aki blush in embarrassment. We may end up with a set of interpretive questions to consider: Are these doors typical? What kind of people find it normal to be so exposed in the toilet? Are Americans shameless? What larger significance, if any, do these toilet stall doors *have*?

It's impressive to think that Aki's unconscious expectations about public restrooms, when violated, can trigger such an elaborate series of responses. While she probably had never thought consciously about what a "normal" public toilet is, her previous conditioning shaped her response to this situation. This is the most important lesson of Oz moments—namely, that *perception and attention are not neutral. They are largely the result of mental habits that we don't normally notice.* This, of course, is what makes foreign experiences interesting. Travel raises questions about what is "normal" and what things mean, and it provides us with an opportunity to notice the hidden patterns that shape our thinking.

Oz Moments and the Intuitive Mind

Oz moments are more than curious mental phenomena. They can help us to distinguish between two different sets of mental processes: those that are more conscious and others that operate largely beneath the surface of our minds. As I mentioned briefly in chapter one, research in cognitive neuroscience is shedding new light on the importance of *unconscious cognition*. This refers to mental processes that affect our behavior yet remain out of reach for our reflective mind.[5] When we hear the words "thinking" or "cognition," we often imagine the *content* of our mind—thoughts, images, or problems we might actively be thinking about. Unconscious cognition, however, refers primarily to *processes* rather than this kind of mental content.

By way of illustration, let's look at some examples. When you recognize the face of someone you haven't seen for a while, some part of your mind must identify the patterns of that individual's face from the store of implicit knowledge gained from your previous experience. Likewise, as you read these words, some portion of your mind must translate the shapes of these letters and words into meaning. If I spell a wrod incorrectly, an unconscious pattern detection system may bring it to your attention. Unconscious cognition runs in the background, taking care of these and many other cognitive functions. For sojourners, an understanding of unconscious cognition is important because *our reactions to novelty and cultural difference when we are abroad are signs of an unconscious learning process.* Understanding what goes on beneath the surface of our mind helps us get the most out of our intercultural experiences.

In chapter one, I referred to some of the competing terminology that specialists use when talking about unconscious cognition. We'll talk a bit more about that in the next chapter. For the moment, know that I frequently (though not exclusively) use the term *intuitive mind* to refer to these more hidden processes. I will frequently be using the term *attentive mind* to refer to more conscious cognition. This is nothing more than shorthand. Talking about two minds is only a way of referring to a whole range of intermeshed mental processes, some of which are more automatic and hidden from conscious reflection. It is a contrivance intended to draw attention to the fact that many elements that go into creating our mental experiences are hidden from us.

We can find elements of both conscious and unconscious cognition in Oz moment experiences. What I am calling *attentive mind* involves cognition that we typically associate with noticing thoughts, reflecting on a situation, or consciously trying to analyze or solve a problem. We experience attentive mind in many different ways: as the string of ideas that float through our mind at any given moment, the attention we focus on an object or a problem, the images in our mind as we consciously plan out our day, the analytic process of adding numbers in our head, and so on. When Aki first confronted the short toilet stall doors, for example, she did a quick mental calculation to decide whether to wait until later to satisfy her biological needs. While she was actively directing her attention to the stall doors and suppressing her embarrassment, she was using her attentive mind. The attentive mind is intentional and often purposeful. We are aware of its processes and have the impression that we control them.

The other set of cognitive processes that go into Oz moment experiences is what is sometimes referred to as *intuitive mind* (as I said, more on other terminology in the next chapter). I use this term because it captures something of how we experience these processes—as feelings, sensations, urges, and intuitive rightness and wrongness. For the moment, the important point to remember about the intuitive mind is that we rely on it more than we realize. The intuitive mind acts as a sort of gatekeeper that highlights or ignores features in our environment. It also produces reactions to, and initial judgments about, our experiences.

With this distinction between conscious and unconscious processes in mind, let's look again at Aki's experience of the Oz moment. The scanning function of the intuitive mind is what is responsible for bringing the short doors into conscious attention. Her conscious mind received a kind of anomaly report, since the restroom didn't match previous patterns. At this point Aki stopped short—

whereas conditioned reactions and intuitive responses are instantaneous, Aki's attentive mind required more time to take stock of her situation, consider the possibility of waiting until later, then take the decision to suppress embarrassment and enter the stall. These two systems have, of course, evolved to work smoothly together. In a miracle of evolutionary psychology, we are able to manage highly complex behaviors using unconscious processes, freeing up active cognition for novel situations and step-by-step problem solving.

As you can imagine, while our intuitive mind is remarkably efficient in a familiar environment, it often gets tripped up when trying to function abroad. Oz moments are a tiny sign of an unconscious process of adjustment and adaptation. Spending time away from home, living abroad, speaking a foreign language, and trying to understand a new cultural perspective—all of these activities challenge the hidden patterns in our intuitive mind. We are often only dimly aware of that process, however, because much of it takes place deep in the underground of our psyche. When we notice Oz moment experiences, we are given noticeable clues to hidden cognitive processes, like the traffic cones around a manhole cover cautioning us about underground works in progress below.

Figure 3-2 attempts to visualize some of the hidden elements of the Oz moment experience, and cultural learning in general. It starts on the upper left as we enter a foreign environment, creating a *mismatch* between the familiar patterns our intuitive mind is used to, and the novel patterns perceived through our senses. An ongoing scanning process draws attention to *anomalies*—detection of difference—which activates our interpretive schema and alerts the attentive mind. Our reflective and analytic capacities thus engaged, we *make sense* of what we are experiencing, and face *choices* about how to respond. We may *suppress* certain responses and make a conscious *decision* to take particular action. We also react at the intuitive level, with negative or positive feelings and *associations.* We may intuit *new patterns* and become more inclined to *avoid* or *seek out* similar situations in the future. Our attentive mind may *not notice* many of these intuitive reactions, or it may *reflect on* or seek to *solve problems* we have consciously identified.

I refer to the sum total of these responses as the *cognitive impact* of the experience. Those impacts may be short term or long term, and might include learning *new behavior*, gaining a *new perspective*, or perhaps on the contrary, having *prejudices* or *negative associations* reinforced. The term *cognitive impact* is simply a technical way to talk about the things that we learn from intercultural experiences, many of them at the level of unconscious cognition. Oz moments change us, sometimes in ways that we are not fully aware of.

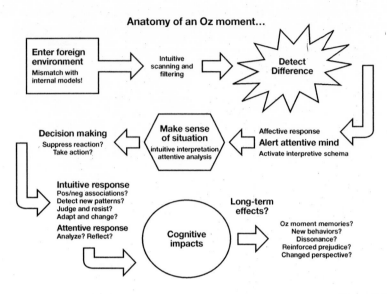

Anatomy of an Oz moment...

Enter foreign environment
Mismatch with internal models!

Intuitive scanning and filtering

Detect Difference

Decision making
Suppress reaction?
Take action?

Make sense of situation
intuitive interpretation, attentive analysis

Affective response
Alert attentive mind
Activate interpretive schema

Intuitive response
Pos/neg associations?
Detect new patterns?
Judge and resist?
Adapt and change?

Attentive response
Analyze? Reflect?

Cognitive impacts

Long-term effects?
Oz moment memories?
New behaviors?
Dissonance?
Reinforced prejudice?
Changed perspective?

Figure 3-2

Looking at the cognitive architecture that produces Oz moments sheds light on an ongoing cycle of cultural learning that is largely hidden from conscious reflection. Encountering difference often constitutes an *adaptive demand* that our neurocognitive systems respond to—we either need to *modify* (i.e., adapt) our behavior and perceptions to take new patterns into account, or perhaps *resist* the difference we find and seek to preserve existing habits. Dealing with these adaptive demands leaves a cognitive residue, creating memories of the experience while alerting us to things we might want to avoid, be attracted to, or puzzle over in the future. This experience will inform our reactions should we come across such phenomena again.

Oz Moments Are Meaningful

As a general rule, our mind seeks coherence—it tries to integrate new information into existing mental structures.[6] In everyday life, we experience this in terms of things "making sense" or not. We dislike loose ends and contradiction, and feel the need to come to conclusions about our experiences. Because of this, when experiencing cultural difference, we tend to make judgments. When tasting exotic foods—let's imagine, for example, trying escargot in France—we typically make conclusive statements: "Oh, it's really good!" or "How can anyone eat this?" Once we've experienced something once, we tend to feel that we *know it* in some definitive way.

Our intuitive mind not only draws attention to physical difference; it plays a role in making sense of behavior and human interaction. This can lead to feeling puzzled, or bothered, by what people say and do:

> A Tunisian man was struck by the skimpy clothes worn by American women in the summer. He thought to himself, "Don't women respect themselves in this country?"

> A traveler in Korea was surprised to see someone selling a vegetable cutter on the subway, proclaiming, "She even stuck a slice of cucumber to her face, and no one reacted at all!"

> A Chinese woman felt abashed witnessing two Americans kissing on a park bench, and said, "I would be embarrassed."

Events like these can set off storms of mental activity as we struggle to interpret our experiences. Mari, for example, recounts, "When one of my Thai friends took me to the local department store, I was secretly so surprised that a cashier kissed my bag at the checkout counter." She had no idea how to interpret this behavior. What did it mean? Did she need to respond? Did it symbolize something she needed to know about?

This struggle to make meaning when we are abroad is a key element of learning about life in another place. A Japanese student at a U.S. university recounted in great detail his fascination with an American next to him in class. On one occasion, she pulled an apple from her bag, rubbed it on her jeans, crunched a bite, set it on her desk, then went back to taking notes. This sequence of events was remarkable from the Japanese perspective for a whole slew of reasons: (1) She had an apple in her bag. An uncut, whole apple? (2) She intended to eat in class. Isn't that rude? (3) She rubbed it on her jeans. Isn't that dirty? (4) She took a big, loud bite. Doesn't that disturb others? (5) She set it on her desk. That's not a clean place to put it! (6) She went back to taking notes. So this is normal here?! One minor act set off a storm of attempted interpretation generated by intuitive and attentive cognition.

This brings us to perhaps the most important point about the Oz moment: *Much of the cultural learning, adjustment, and adaptation that we experience in foreign environments is a two-mind process. It involves facts, explicit knowing, and conscious realizations, as well as adjustments at the hidden level of intuitive mind and body.* By *cultural learning,* I mean the process of acquiring a familiarity and understanding of new physical and social environments. It includes concrete things such as the layout of streets, as well as more abstract patterns, such as communication styles and cultural values.

This learning process involves taking in new information, acquiring new behaviors and habits, absorbing new interpretive schema, and developing new interpretive frameworks to make sense of our experiences. It also includes acquiring new habits—both physical habits and mental habits. Cultural learning involves some form of *adaptation* or *adjustment*—the changes we undergo in response to contact with a new environment. We may try hard to fit in, or instead may resist modifying our behavior or attitudes. In both cases, we are responding in some way to the *adaptive demands* of being in a new environment.

An important premise of this book is that the cultural learning process can have a big impact on the more hidden parts of our mind. We may not even be consciously aware that we are engaged in a learning process. It's possible for us to become stressed without knowing why, to jump to wrong conclusions and never notice, or to feel alienated or offended without being able to pinpoint the sources of our frustration. The hidden side of cultural learning is important. The better we understand the cognitive processes involved, the better we can manage our experiences.

Cognitive Impact

Common sense tells us that foreign experiences can have a long-term impact on our mind. While a trip abroad or a foreign assignment can stress us out, it can also be a highly meaningful life event that leads to personal growth and an expanded perspective. Yet how do cross-cultural experiences change or affect us? It's clear that foreign experiences can teach us something—but what? For her part, Aki describes arriving at the Los Angeles airport as an a-ha moment, saying, "It was my first time abroad, and I had a realization that the people I saw were living their whole life in this other world." What impressed her was that things that seemed so novel to her were so *normal* there. "Until I visited LA," she explains, "foreign countries were like the moon, just this distant thing. Suddenly they became real." She compares the change that she felt to losing one's virginity, saying, "You can't go back to the way you were before." This is a remarkable assertion. Aki reports that spending a few weeks abroad provoked a shift in her perceptions that was permanent—*you can't go back to the way you were before*. At some level, this is unsurprising, since it is rather cliché to say that travel expands our horizons. From the perspective of unconscious cognition, however, it's a radical thesis—encountering cultural difference can provoke noticeable long-term changes in perception and a seemingly permanent shift in perspective.

This is, strangely enough, easy to believe yet difficult to fully understand. I regularly hear stories of seemingly simple Oz moments that provoke deeply felt sensations of change—like the ground shifting beneath one's feet. Take, for example, the reaction of Kentaro to his arrival in Canada for a brief homestay:

> All people around me speak English! The scale of the place, house, everything in Canada was huge! We eat steaks all meals! . . . My host family keeps 695 cows! They don't have a key on the door of the house! All family members have their own cars! They don't have trains! They don't have mail drop at the door! And so on and so on. I had [all] kinds of shocks because the way of their lives is quite different from ours in Japan. And I could not understand all about that, and I would not try to understand all about that because I thought unconsciously the way of life in Japan is normal and the way of life in Canada is weird.

At first blush, Kentaro's reactions seem rather superficial and perhaps even quaint. There's something curious, however, about the elements of his experience that he finds meaningful. He says, for example, "All people around me speak English!" Yet this is something that he knew would be true before arriving—it's the whole reason he went on a homestay in the first place, to learn English. His intellectual knowledge of Canada as a country where English is spoken did not, however, prepare him for the cognitive shock of being in this English-speaking world. He feels the need to point out details—the cows, the cars, and the mail drop—that are mundane and have little deep significance in and of themselves. Yet he mentions them to communicate the *alienness* of his surroundings. In this we get a hint at the perceptual shift that is taking place within his mind.

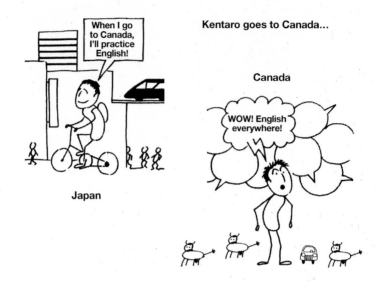

Figure 3-3

While Kentaro is able to tell stories about the things he found remarkable in Canada, the cognitive processes that brought those details to his attention, and the subtle perceptual changes he experiences, take place largely at the level of hidden cognition and the intuitive mind. His intellectual knowledge of Canada does not increase by much, but something does seem to be shifting. We can call that shift an *expanded perspective* or *cultural awareness* or a more *international outlook* or whatever we like. Labeling it in this way, however, doesn't fully explain it.

As I've said, I refer to psychological reactions, changes in perception, and mental adjustments as *cognitive impact*. This is a catchall term to describe the effects of intercultural experiences on our body and mind. The difficulty of clearly understanding or describing just how we change because of intercultural experiences reminds us that: (1) *Many reactions to foreign experiences engage hidden cognitive processes,* (2) *we often cannot anticipate our reaction to cross-cultural experiences,* and (3) *we ourselves may be only partially aware of their effects on us.* Yes, we know where we've been and what we've done. We can tell stories and work them into the larger narrative of our lives. But we may not be fully cognizant of the full impact of our own experiences.

In my work, I hear a wide range of stories about the lessons of international living. At one end of the spectrum are those who seem unimpressed by what they see—the "been there; done that" attitude exemplified by the Tokyo expat I mentioned earlier. I also hear stories of transformation:

When I was nineteen years old, I decided to go to India by myself, to explore a new culture and know more about myself. When I came back to France . . . my eyes were different. Everything around me looked different. My friends, my family, my routine changed. I didn't feel good with my best friends. They were children for me, less mature. They did not recognize me. "You have changed, Michel." Yes, I had changed. After India, I was someone else. I was someone who put things into perspective. I was someone who does not always find a problem in a problem. Before India, I was very confident. I thought I was the best, I was selfish, and I despised people. After, I doubted about myself, I accepted everyone, and furthermore, I wanted to know about people that I met. I was very interested in their life stories.

It's hard to say why these experiences trigger such a wide range of reactions. It's also hard to say how a brief journey could so powerfully alter perceptions that have been developed over a lifetime. Does it represent a reframing of our experience? Is it a form of metacognition? Does it entail an expansion of the psychological territory of our personal identity? I don't know. In any case, it's not likely to be a single cognitive change that can be simply defined and easily measured.

Obviously not everyone feels such dramatic changes after intercultural experiences. One traveler, for example, says, "Now that I'm back, the big question seems to be, 'How are you different today than you were when you left for your globetrot?' In short . . . not as different as I had hoped."[7] This person left home seeking change, but never found it. This led him to reflect and reach the following conclusion: "This search for direct experiences is where I don't think I succeeded quite like I wanted to. Mostly because I was resistant to embracing them . . . my primary method of 'dealing' came in the form of 'ignoring.'"

Another reason we may not feel different after a foreign experience is that we simply don't notice changes because they are intuitive. Some only pay conscious attention to the cognitive impact of cultural learning after they go back home, once they realize that their perceptual systems have been in some way reconfigured.

I believe I first realized a substantial change in me when I went back home to Sweden during the winter break for a month [after having been in Japan for four months] and caught myself bowing to clerks, professors, and office workers, getting slightly annoyed by the lack of proper, straight queues to buses and trains, feeling too uncomfortable to eat whilst walking on the street, and feeling slightly surprised by the seemingly empty roads and squares. Whilst being in Sweden still felt the same as it always had, as the patterns stored and recognized by my unconscious mind simply were brought forth again from my mind's repertoire, I could still feel the presence of those gained in Japan, and it felt slightly odd.

Sarah

It may be that the deepest changes are those that are the most difficult to verbalize. Aki, like Michel, says that her first trip abroad fundamentally altered the course of her life. Yet until I asked her, she had never attempted to articulate it. She knew she had changed, but couldn't quite describe how.

Oz Moments and the Intercultural Mind

I advise my students and other sojourners to pay attention to their Oz moment experiences and to the mental and emotional responses that they provoke. The same adaptive stresses that transformed Michel's perceptions can also overload the cognitive systems. Far from always being a positive, affirming experience, Oz moments can provoke stress, highly critical thoughts, and negative feelings. This too is a natural part of deep culture learning. As Antoine, a Frenchman spending a semester in Tokyo, says:

> In the first days I was here—after the arrival excitement was gone—I was angry. I would leave convenience stores swearing in French because the shop clerk said *irasshaimasse* (welcome) once too often. I was grumbling and sweating with my heart pounding in my chest. "I hate them; I hate their manners, their politeness, their driving on the left, and their hot cans that burn my fingers!" At other moments, though, I said the exact opposite of all these things.
>
> I would have said, at that time, that the Japanese made me angry because they did not make eye contact in the subway, and kept scream-

ing "*Irasshaimasse*" when I came into a shop, or because cashiers would talk to me every time I bought something. I was definitely searching for the reason, though. I was searching for the reasons that could explain why I was having such a visceral reaction to such small differences.

Antoine's story is a reminder of the cumulative impact of ongoing Oz moments. Little things can chip away at our mental equilibrium. The longer we stay, and the more human interaction we have, the greater the chances for powerful reactions. Oz moments can act as signposts on the road to an intercultural mind. When abroad, we must fiddle with the settings on our intuitive autopilot, challenging mental habits and dredging up reactions from parts of ourselves that we normally can't access. As I see it, *developing an intercultural mind revolves around an awareness of the cultural learning process, rather than aiming for some idealized reaction to our experiences.*

Introspection, making a critical analysis of our own experiences, is one tool we can use to those ends. But there's something else I have found useful—the larger story of the study of culture and the mind. In the next chapter, we'll learn about Edward Hall, an intercultural pioneer who was among the first to speculate in detail on the connection between culture and the unconscious mind. We'll see what researchers in cognition are saying about the structure of the unconscious mind. This can put our travel adventures into the broader context of the human desire for cultural self-understanding. Oz moments may be tiny and fleeting, but they fit into a much larger picture of learning.

KEY CONCEPTS

Oz moment: *A feeling of disorientation or surprise when encountering novel surroundings or hard-to-interpret phenomena.*

Cognitive impact: *The psychological reactions, changes in perception, and adjustments in sense of self that are associated with intercultural learning.*

Discussion Quote: *Much of the cultural learning, adjustment, and adaptation that we experience in foreign environments is a two-mind process, involving facts, explicit knowing, and conscious realizations, as well as adjustments at the hidden level of intuitive mind.*

4.

the intuitive mind

*Only through the deeper understanding of culture can
one really understand one's true self.*

—Peeratat

*Intercultural experiences open a window into the deeper workings of the mind.
This was first articulated in detail by Edward Hall in 1959. We'll take a brief tour
of the discoveries about unconscious cognition that have been made
since then. Millions of people today have the opportunity follow in Hall's
footsteps, using foreign experiences as a springboard for deeper
cultural- and self-understanding.*

Ned in Arizona

B umping along the dusty, dry-packed dirt roads in a remote corner of Arizona in 1933, Ned Hall knew he was a lucky man. In the midst of the Great Depression, he had a steady job working for the Bureau of Indian Affairs. At his side, swaying with the swings and shudders of their pick-up, sat Sam Yazzie, a young Navajo assigned to help Ned supervise the construction of dams on Native American lands. Pulling into the job site raised a cloud of dust, but instead of quickly jumping out of the cab, Ned turned off the engine and let things settle. After a suitable pause, Ned and Sam slowly climbed down and greeted the men gathering around—not like "the bosses," but as though they were guests.

The foreman came over, smiled, and greeted them with *Yatahei* while offering his hand. Ned had learned to grasp the hand gently without making direct eye contact. The Navajo handshake was a chance to ease into another person's presence, not a declaration of self-confidence and individuality. After this, the workers gathered and sat in a circle. Tobacco was passed around, and each man hand-rolled a cigarette. After taking the time to smoke together, Ned reviewed the time book, got to know the men, and learned who had worked on what days.[1]

Ned's willingness to adapt to the way of the Navajo he worked with was unusual at the time. He didn't accept the then-common stereotypes of Native

Americans as simpletons or savages. But he discovered that respect for the Navajo, in and of itself, was not enough. He found himself getting tripped up by his Anglo thinking and communication style. Even basic rituals, like greetings and shaking hands, had to be relearned. Often, his explanations while working ended up creating more confusion than they resolved.

Over time, Ned concluded that while Western thinking often emphasizes abstraction, the Navajo approached things with concrete pragmatism. Time was different, too. Instead of being experienced as a straight line with a finite number of points between now and the future—the "time is money" approach to managing activities—Navajo time was more situational. You give important things more time, with less concern for the specific number of minutes or hours. Absorbing these lessons was a slow process. Ned couldn't simply say to his Navajo colleagues, "Tell me about how you use time." He learned by trial and error, clarifying his thoughts by discussing the details of his interactions with Sam. In these things, Sam was more than just Ned's assistant—he was his guide to the Navajo world.

In 1959 Ned Hall published *The Silent Language*, which became the foundational work of the new field of *intercultural communication*. He was fascinated by people's ignorance of their own cultural patterns. He realized that the communication gap between the Anglos and Native Americans he worked with was not simply a result of prejudice. Even well-intentioned Anglos often bungled their attempts at being helpful, and the Native Americans truly had trouble understanding the particular obsessions of the Anglos they were forced to work with. The problem, as Ned saw it, was that our cultural background programs our thinking and behavior in unconscious ways. Thus, when communicating across cultures, we jump to wrong conclusions, get offended, feel frustrated with "inefficiencies," or get the impression that people lack common sense, intelligence, or whatever.

Hall viewed the unconscious as something that worked systematically, that was affected by culture, and that guided our habitual patterns of acting and thinking.[2] He hoped to understand the influence of culture on perceiving and acting, and he spoke of "the way in which deep cultural undercurrents structure life in subtle but highly consistent ways that are not consciously formulated. Like the invisible jet streams in the skies that determine the course of a storm, these hidden currents shape our lives: yet their influence is only beginning to be identified."[3]

Hall pointed out that cultural difference often catches us unaware: "Things begin, most frequently, not only with friendship and goodwill on both sides, but there is an intellectual understanding that each side has a different set of beliefs, customs, mores, values or what-have-you. The trouble begins when people have to start working together."[4] Hall felt that intellectual learning alone was insufficient to come to an understanding of this deeper element of culture, arguing that "The investigation of out-of-awareness culture can be accomplished only by actual observation of real events in normal settings and contexts. It is not amenable to philosophizing—at least not yet!"[5]

While Ned's intercultural experiences may sound exotic nearly a century later, they are no more unusual than what awaits a German expatriate posted in China, or a Mexican student studying in the UK. In fact, many more people are in cross-cultural situations than when Ned was writing—and they are still bumping into the hidden cultural differences that he pointed out. But there is also a more widespread awareness of the need for intercultural understanding. It could be that the globalized twenty-first century is making possible some of the "philosophizing" that Hall felt people weren't ready for in the past.

The Unconscious

For Ned Hall, as for most people in the twentieth century, ideas about the unconscious mind were largely shaped by Sigmund Freud. Born in 1856 in the Czech Republic, Freud was a spare, highly cerebral man who changed the way people thought about their inner lives. He was, by training, a neurologist. Like many people at the time, he assumed that mental illness was caused by imbalance in the nervous system. Freud believed that there were hidden parts of the mind that could be investigated and understood, and that this could lead to new techniques for treating mental illness. Little was known about brain function, however, so he was forced to create his model of the unconscious with limited tools—observation of memory errors, hypnosis, dream analysis, introspection, and conversations with patients.

Freud saw the unconscious mind as a realm of powerful urges, painful memories, violent emotions, and repressed memories—a jungle of primitive forces held in check by the civilizing structure of our conscience and rational mind. Freud's radical thesis was that our conscious control was not as complete as we might think. A slip of the tongue might actually reveal a hidden resentment or desire; a childhood trauma might unconsciously affect our behavior many years later. Freud's ideas put a major crack in the assumption that humans largely understood their own mental states and could accurately explain the reasons for their own actions.

This fundamental insight still stands, but an increased understanding of unconscious cognition has allowed us to go beyond Freud's conceptualization. The overall metaphor of Freud's theory of the unconscious is that hidden forces are held in check by a conscious controlling mind. This idea—that our conscious mind regulates our behavior and acts as a sort of master controller—is very commonsensical because it matches our experiences of everyday life. After all, we make conscious decisions about such issues as whether to have pancakes rather than waffles, or whether to buy a house or rent an apartment. This creates the impression that our conscious mind has a high degree of control and functions like the pilot of our mental ship. What we're finding, however, is that this control may not be as complete as we might think.

In the last chapter, we discussed the difference between the conscious thinking of the *attentive mind* and the unconscious cognition of the *intuitive mind*. Broadly speaking, this approach to understanding cognition is called the *dual processing* model.[6] It contrasts with commonsense assumptions—which the psychologist Jonathan Evans calls our *folk psychology*—that many people have about how the mind words. In our everyday view of things, it's easy to think of mind as a kind of master controller, as is depicted on the left side of figure 4-1. This assumes our behavior is controlled by a *conscious executive mind*. *Explicit representations* refer to the thoughts and images that we manipulate in our minds, be they memories or words or concepts. Beneath these representations are unconscious support systems, such as creative processes or inspirations that we may draw on to accomplish the tasks we set out for ourselves. This diagram is intuitive—it matches how it feels to think and speak and act. Evidence is building, however, that this is not how our mind actually works.

The New Unconscious

Although we typically experience our mind as the master of our behavior, this is in many ways an illusion. It's more accurate to say that there are a multitude of mental functions that operate independently of conscious cognition. Conscious and unconscious elements work separately, but they are networked together, each affecting our behavior in different ways. The unconscious mind doesn't filter *through* the conscious mind; it often operates independently of the conscious mind, often without us ever noticing.

Jonathan Evans diagrams this new view of mind as on the right side of figure 4-1, which shows that the intuitive mind often influences our behavior without us being aware of it. The intuitive mind draws on implicit knowledge, evaluates situations, makes judgments, produces urges and intuitions, and influences our behavior in many ways. The arrows going from intuitive mind to implicit knowledge are a reminder that our intuitive mind also learns. The larger point for people crossing cultures is that many of the most powerful effects of intercultural experiences take place at the level of unconscious cognition.

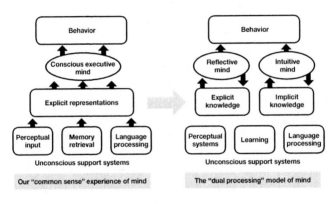

A changing view of mind...
Adapted from Evans, 2010

Figure 4-1

Specialists use different terms to describe unconscious cognition and have different understandings of how it works. Despite competing conceptual models, it is clear that unconscious cognition is not carried out by a single place in the brain, nor is it a single brain function—rather, it's a whole conglomerate of different mental processes that affect our judgments, feelings, and behavior without our conscious awareness.[7] Some specialists refer broadly to these hidden processes as the *new unconscious*, to distinguish it from the more traditional Freudian unconscious.[8] Cognitive psychologist Timothy Wilson uses the term *adaptive unconscious*, which emphasizes the role of evolution in shaping our mind to help us survive in the world.[9] He describes it in this way:

The mind operates most efficiently by relegating a good deal of high-level, sophisticated thinking to the unconscious, just as a modern jumbo jetliner is able to fly on automatic pilot with little or no input from the human 'conscious' pilot. . . . [P]eople can no more observe how they are unconsciously categorizing their environments, setting goals, and generating intuitions than they can observe how their kidneys work.[10]

This metaphor is particularly useful if we recognize that our unconscious autopilot has autonomous systems—which the conscious pilot is unaware of—that also influence the direction of travel. The autopilot may choose or change the course (through motivations, desires, urges, or cravings) in ways that the conscious pilot has little control over. This is why we sometimes find ourselves putting French fries into our mouth even after telling ourselves to stop, or get jealous when we tell ourselves we shouldn't.

Daniel Kahneman is a Nobel Prize–winning psychologist who researches biases, judgment, and decision-making.[11] He has been highly influential in the development of behavioral economics, which emphasizes that humans don't always act naturally in their own self-interest, and that intuitions can lead us astray. His conceptualizations, it should be noted, have informed this book in many ways. Kahneman divides cognitive processes into two systems: *system 1*, or *fast thinking* (the intuitive, associative, automatic form of cognition), and *system 2*, or *slow thinking* (paying attention, step-by-step analysis, and conscious reflection).

As described by Kahneman, fast thinking is typically effortless, while slow thinking has clearly limited resources. Evolution favored fast, intuitive appraisals that allowed our ancestors to escape when they heard the grass rustle. But this speed and automaticity means that our intuitive mind is the home of lots of sloppy thinking. It has a tendency to jump to conclusions and a bias towards familiarity. We have short tempers when hungry, an appetite for sweets and fat, a desire to gossip and judge others, a powerful identification with ingroups, a sense of territoriality, and many other tendencies that may not serve us so well today.

System 1 and system 2 cognition contrast with each other in a number of ways. They are usually complementary, but can be at odds with each other as well. The lists in Table 4-1 will give you a sense of some of the differences between the two.[12]

SYSTEM 1 (intuitive mind)	SYSTEM 2 (reflective/attentive mind)
Unconscious reasoning	Conscious reasoning
Implicit	Explicit
Automatic	Controlled
Low effort	High effort
Large capacity	Small capacity
Rapid	Slow
Default process	Inhibitory
Associative	Rule based
Contextualized	Abstract
Domain specific	Domain general
Evolutionarily old	Evolutionarily recent
Nonverbal	Linked to language
Includes recognition, perception, orientation	Includes rule following, comparisons, weighing of options
Modular cognition	Fluid intelligence
Independent of working memory	Limited by working memory capacity
Pragmatic	Logical

Table 4-1

Matthew Lieberman, another researcher of unconscious mental processes, uses a different set of terms to talk about these contrasting types of cognition: the X-system (after the "x" in "reflexive") and the C-system (for the "c" in "reflective"). His work emphasizes the fact that these two systems are not as separate as, say, the digestive system and the visual system. Rather, they are integrated in a complementary and interrelated whole.[13] These different forms of cognition serve the larger unified purpose of helping the human organism manage its relationship with the outside world.

Jonathan Evans—with yet more competing terminology—refers to unconscious cognition as the *intuitive mind* and conscious cognition as the *reflective mind*. This choice of words represents the fact that we consciously *reflect* on problems and objects of our attention. As Evans says:

> The reflective mind *feels like* the all-controlling executive mind to its owner, but this is largely illusory. In reality, it competes for control of behavior with the intuitive mind, often unsuccessfully. Moreover, the two minds have access to different kinds of knowledge: explicit memory for the reflective mind and implicit memory for the intuitive mind. . . . The reflective mind only *thinks* it is in control. In fact, one of the major functions of the reflective mind is confabulation. In other words, we (conscious beings) make up stories to maintain the illusion that we are the chief executive who is really in control.[14]

I'll add here that referring to cognition in binary terms (conscious–unconscious / system 1–system 2 / reflective–intuitive) creates the impression that there is a clear-cut dividing line between different mental functions. But it's not that simple. A great deal of conscious cognition is produced using unconscious processes. Meanwhile, unconscious processes are experienced at least indirectly in conscious form. Evans describes this distinction:

> If we meet an old friend, memories of our previous meeting or beliefs about her personality that come to mind may inform our decisions about what to say or do. But the mechanisms that identified and retrieved these memories cannot themselves be conscious. . . . If the reflective mind cannot be entirely conscious, then the intuitive mind cannot be entirely unconscious either. The latter has access to both emotions and what I call "cognitive feelings," which result in conscious experiences. When we choose intuitively we often have a feeling of confidence or rightness in the choice, even though we have no access to the underlying process.[15]

For sojourners, all of these distinctions and competing terminologies can be confusing. As an educator, I am most interested in helping my students become more aware of the hidden elements of intercultural experiences. There's still a mix of different terms, as can be expected with such a new area of research. And no set of labels will capture the complexity of the multiple processes involved. At the same time, we need *some* terminology to talk about the unconscious elements of cognition and mind, so that we can pay more attention to them and understand how they may affect our lives.

Throughout this book, I tend to follow Evans' terminology by referring to unconscious cognition as the *intuitive mind*, and I use the term *attentive mind* to refer to more conscious cognition. My choice is not intended to favor one researcher's conceptualization over another, but to find terminology that's easy to grasp and that matches our experience of these cognitive phenomena. These terms also remind us that what we *pay attention to* when traveling abroad is important, but so is our *intuitive* sense for things.

Navigating Everyday Life

Let's take a closer look at ways in which unconscious cognition—intuitive mind—helps us manage our lives. Most fundamentally, this includes body management, the automatic biological processes like breathing and regulation of body temperature. These are things that we can't easily control through conscious effort. In addition, there is plenty of unconscious calculation required for navigating the physical world—for seeing, walking, grasping, or manipulating objects with our hands. Some of these abilities, like seeing and walking, are developmentally programmed into us and don't have to be learned intentionally. Other skills, like learning to crack open an egg or play the piano, require intentional practice to learn, but are performed automatically once mastered. These activities end up feeling totally natural to us, freeing up conscious cognition to take on novel challenges. The intuitive mind's job is to create *automaticity*. Once you've internalized the pattern of shoe tying, you can plan your date even while lacing up your sneakers.

To give a sense of why it's important for sojourners to understand unconscious cognition, below are a few characteristics of unconscious cognition and how it relates to intercultural experiences. The terminology and the statements in italics come from Kahneman.[16]

System 1 (Intuitive Mind)

Generates impressions, feelings, and inclinations; when endorsed by System 2 these become beliefs, attitudes, and intentions
When abroad, our reactions and impressions of our new environment are produced through unconscious processes. We must be careful when choosing which of these reactions to endorse, or we may jump to wrong conclusions.

Operates automatically and quickly, with little or no effort, and no sense of voluntary control
We rely on it more than we might expect and can be surprised when our System 1 has difficulty functioning in a new environment (e.g., because of culture stress or culture shock).

Can be programmed by System 2 to mobilize attention when a particular pattern is detected (search)
In foreign encounters, we may see only what we want or expect to see. Education or training can sensitize us to particular elements of our experiences. We may catch ourselves, for example, thinking in terms of stereotypes.

Executes skilled responses and generates skilled intuitions, after adequate training
Learning to function in a new environment involves an unconscious learning process as we acquire a new set of intuitions and responses. This includes skills like mastery of a foreign language, which requires practice and developing of a sense for how the language is used.

Creates a coherent pattern of activated ideas in associative memory
Cultural learning requires acquiring new patterns, including ways of interpreting situations, so we can make sense of new experiences.

Links a sense of cognitive ease to illusions of truth, pleasant feelings, and reduced vigilance
We have a tendency to be biased against the unfamiliar and foreign. Novelty is tiring.

Distinguishes the surprising from the normal
What we find normal is often experienced as right. We have little conscious control over our initial "gut reactions" to the novelty we experience.

Infers and invents causes and intentions
We may be poor at inferring intentions and interpreting behavior in foreign settings. We may jump to unjustified conclusions but not realize it.

Neglects ambiguity and suppresses doubt
If we have preconceived notions or strong first impressions, we can easily find things that confirm our biases.

Represents sets by norms and prototypes, does not integrate
We may rely on stereotypical thinking when interpreting foreign behavior. We sometimes read too much into a single event or experience. Even after a short time we get the feeling that we basically understand things

Sometimes substitutes an easier question for a difficult one (heuristics)
We may jump to wrong conclusions or misinterpret behavior without noticing it.

Sojourners are uniquely positioned to become aware of these hidden processes because going abroad involves a constant barrage of tasks that the brain cannot easily handle on autopilot. The intuitive mind relies on a predictable environment, so even the simple act of walking the streets of a foreign city can be mentally exhausting. As one traveler put it to me, "You don't have eyes enough to see everything around you." The *automaticity* of much of our hidden cognition—a great strength of our cognitive architecture—creates problems for us when spending time abroad. Many tasks that we previously performed with little conscious effort suddenly require our full attention.

Deep Culture and the Social Autopilot

As I've said, interacting with others requires a lot of cultural knowledge. Think of this *deep culture* as the cultural programming of our mental autopilot—the settings that let us *forget* that we are using language, meeting the expectations of others, reading situations correctly, and so on. As Timothy Wilson says, "There is considerable evidence that the adaptive unconscious has a stable characteristic way of responding to the environment."[17] He points out that "People develop constructs to make sense out of and predict their environments. As a result of their background and learning history, people develop regular, idiosyncratic ways of construing the world."[18] Naturally, when people share a similar background and learning history—when they share cultural patterns—their ways of construing the world will overlap to a greater degree.

Deep culture knowledge is the backdrop against which we judge things. Americans are unsurprised when offered a choice of soup or salad; they have learned to nod, not bow, when entering their boss's office; they automatically stand at arm's length when talking to someone; and so on. When those expectations aren't followed—if we are given a choice of soup or drink, for example—we notice. This sort of background cultural knowledge can be added to Jonathan Evans' diagram of the mind as in figure 4-2. The shaded rectangle of deep culture configuration represents knowledge about our own cultural community, both explicit facts that we can explain and implicit expectations and patterns that we can't.

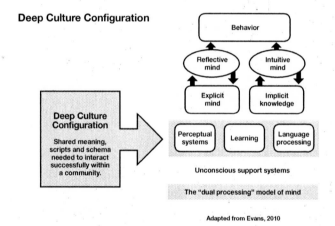

Deep Culture Configuration

Behavior

Reflective mind   Intuitive mind

Explicit mind   Implicit knowledge

Deep Culture Configuration

Shared meaning, scripts and schema needed to interact successfully within a community.

Perceptual systems   Learning   Language processing

Unconscious support systems

The "dual processing" model of mind

Adapted from Evans, 2010

Figure 4-2

Deep culture patterns involve conditioned responses—we react automatically to particular stimuli. Americans, for example, reach out automatically to shake hands in certain situations, while an Indian's hands may just as automatically form the namaste gesture. These patterns require highly contextualized judgments. In France, people kiss on the cheek when greeting certain people and shake hands to greet others—depending on the broader social context. Someone might refrain from kissing a girlfriend when greeting her in front of the girlfriend's grandmother, for example. We make these choices intuitively on the fly, with minimal input from conscious analytic processes.

Social psychologists refer to this as *social knowledge*—the shared knowledge and learned patterns that we rely on to guide us through everyday social interactions.[19] We can tell unconscious cognition is involved because we know intuitively whether behavior is right or wrong, typical or unusual, but often can't say *how we know*. An American or Brit has a feeling for when it's permissible to use first names and when titles are more appropriate, but would be hard-pressed to explain this in detail. Social knowledge provides a steady hand of intuitive guidance that we rely upon all the time, yet which we may seldom actively think about, notice, or question.

The Clash of Normals

There's another way to find evidence for the deep culture conditioning of the intuitive mind—through intercultural experiences. As Hall, Aki, and millions of others have found, foreign experiences confront us with previously undiscovered cultural patterns within our own mind. I often hear stories about reactions to what I call a *new normal*. Hall discovered this, for example, in relation to cultural expectations about time. When others violate unconscious cultural expectations about time, we may at first find them irresponsible, or like slaves to the clock, yet later realize that there is a different time logic in play.[20] Finding that our sense of normal is rooted in our cultural configuration can be destabilizing. Antoine, a French student in Tokyo, describes it this way:

I soon realized that what was giving me such a hard time were not the Japanese waitresses or shop clerks, but that what really bothered me was that all this was *normal here*. . . . I really see deep culture at this breaking point, where two *normals* collide. Everything you usually did not ever think of—you start not only thinking of it, but also reflecting on it, criticizing it, maybe rejecting it.

The clash of normals that Antoine is talking about occurs not only because we have different habits of mind, but because we experience those habits as such a natural part of ourselves. The cultural content of our intuitive mind is not like the oil in the engine of your car—something that can be replaced with a functional equivalent. It is not simply a set of abstractions that we can examine objectively in our analytic mind—it is an intimate part of who we are.

Other sojourners tell me similar stories—of small experiences that drive home just how different people from other cultural communities can be. Ray, for example, says:

> I left North America for the first time when I was twenty-one. I can remember quite clearly the first time I felt intercultural shock. I was in Zanzibar, entering the house of my Zanzibari friend. His very pregnant sister-in-law, dressed in traditional Zanzibari hijab and kanga, with arabesque foot and hand tattoos, got off the couch which she was sleeping on and lay on the floor so that I could sit down. I had to very strongly refuse, and for the first time a very heavy lump of deep culture shock sank down my esophagus. People in this country were different; not in the way Chinese and American food are different. People here were psychologically completely different, and it scared me.

Ray's reaction highlights just how powerful the experience of a new normal can be. Ray recognized that had he been raised in Zanzibar, he most likely would have perceived the sister-in-law's behavior to be unremarkable. Ray found the idea of a pregnant woman giving up the sofa for him to be profoundly discomforting. He recognized, however, that his reactions were based at least in part on his own cultural conditioning. It was "scary" for Ray to discover that Tanzanians are "psychologically completely different" because it forced him to acknowledge that the world that he found normal was, to no small degree, a matter of cultural conditioning.

Towards an Intercultural Mind

We don't need cognitive neuroscience to have powerful cultural learning experiences. But learning about culture and cognition is like looking through a user's manual for a camera with highly advanced features. We typically snap pictures on auto mode, paying little attention to how the camera works. But when shooting conditions are incompatible with our camera's preprogrammed parameters, our photos might get washed out or underexposed. In these situations, we can choose to muddle along with the limitations of our automatic settings, or we can dig out the manual and learn more about the hardware we are using and its factory-configured settings. Armed with this knowledge, we can make the necessary adjustments and take full advantage of the technology at our disposal. Shooting in tricky surroundings becomes an opportunity to learn more about photography. In the same way, learning about our cognitive processes helps us expand our intercultural repertoire. It helps us become more effective abroad and expands our understanding of shared humanity and cultural difference. We should not worry too much about cultural differences, but neither should we underestimate the difficulties we might face, or just how profound cross-cultural experiences can be. The cultural learning challenges faced by Ned Hall in the 1930s have not gone away; in fact, they're more common than ever since there is more intercultural contact now than then. This creates conflict and frustration, but provides a learning opportunity as well. In the next chapter, we'll try to apply some of this new knowledge of the mind by looking at the process of adjusting to a new cultural environment.

KEY CONCEPTS

Intuitive mind: *consists of primarily unconscious cognitive functions. It acts as a sort of autopilot and affects our behavior in ways we are often unaware of. (Different specialists refer to unconscious cognition using different terms, including the new unconscious, the cognitive unconscious, the adaptive unconscious, the x-system, system 1, and fast thinking.)*

Attentive mind: *the more conscious, intentional set of cognitive functions that we engage when actively paying attention and doing analytic problem solving. (It also called the reflective mind, or simply the conscious mind.)*

Discussion Quote: *We don't notice deep culture knowledge because it is the backdrop against which we judge things.*

5.

managing our minds abroad

Don't feel stressed. Take it easy.

—Lina

We often cannot anticipate the cognitive impact of foreign experiences. Sojourners share stories of unexpectedly difficult adjustment and culture shock. Our reactions make sense when we see these challenges for what they are—cognitive overload.

Cathy from LA

Cathy touched down in Tokyo as something of a poster child for a multicultural, postmodern society. As a vivacious Asian American student from Los Angeles, her decision to take part in a study-abroad program in Japan seemed like a natural life choice and a boost for a future international career. She was a double major in Global Studies and Japanese and felt "ready to take on whatever cultural adjustment issues [she] might encounter." Raised in a diverse neighborhood by parents originally from Taipei, Cathy embraced her cultural heritage and had traveled to Taiwan and spent time connecting to her relatives there. This sort of heritage wasn't unusual in her high school, where she had many friends of different racial and ethnic backgrounds. She grew up in California at a time when the minority population of the state passed the 50 percent mark.

Even before leaving, she expected her trip to be a journey of growth and discovery. She had historic and cultural knowledge of Japan—including the Japanese language—and had visited as a tourist before. The transition from one diverse metropolis—Los Angeles—to another—Tokyo—did not seem like such a big jump. If anyone had reason to expect a smooth transition to life abroad, she did. Yet despite her preparation and positive attitude, Cathy was blindsided by the difficulties of adapting to life in Tokyo:

> Little did I know how wrong my assumptions were, and how many cultural adjustment issues I was going to face. All of my expectations

were challenged, and the image of Japan in my mind was completely uprooted, causing me to experience an extreme case of culture shock. I became depressed, negative, and withdrawn—the complete opposite of the person I really am. Even now, I am still in the middle of getting over my culture shock, and the old me is slowly trying to break free.

I regularly meet students like Cathy: smart, emotionally healthy people who struggle with the challenges of life abroad. Some find that there's a big gap between being a tourist abroad and being a longer-term resident. Others find that their expectations were off—perhaps because they idealized their destination, or felt more lonely or stressed than expected. Occasionally I meet people who find life abroad much *better* than they expected. Rarely, however, are foreign experiences just as we imagine they will be.

Cathy was much better prepared than most. She had done a lot of thinking and studying about internationalism before her stay. She had studied Japanese (many Americans are painfully monolingual), had visited Tokyo before, had a philosophical commitment to cultural diversity, was proud of her own cultural heritage, and aspired to a career in international business. She was also an outgoing and friendly person. Moreover, she was thoughtful and willing to reflect on her experiences in an honest way. How can we make sense of her strongly negative reaction? If Cathy struggled, then who wouldn't?

Transformation Abroad

Entering a new environment stimulates us at many levels of self. This helps explains the addictive attraction of travel, with its potential for mind-expanding, even transformational experiences. Many people accept the idea that foreign experiences can change us and help us grow. As one intercultural communication scholar says, travel has the potential to teach "radical lessons about the possibility of living a different everyday life."[1] Foreign experience gives us a new point of comparison to evaluate our own choices in life, and breaking our routines provides a fresh perspective on how we spend our time.

The idea of life-changing travel is seen in popular bestselling books like *Eat, Pray, Love*,[2] which portrays living abroad as an adventure in personal growth, and in the work of popular travel authors like Pico Ayer, who describes himself as a "global soul."[3] Travel is often portrayed as a sort of meaningful life quest, something that "has outcomes that rekindle the spirit, rejuvenate the body, and even ignite a shift in consciousness."[4] One article in a counseling journal states that a week in Aruba is "worth three years of therapy."[5] The idea that foreign experiences expand our horizons has become so popularized that some college admissions counselors advise applicants *not* to write about insights gained from travel in application essays, since that theme is so common and often cliché.[6] One guide to studying abroad has the ambitious title *Becoming World Wise.*[7]

Few would deny that foreign experiences at least have the *potential* to expand our horizons, change us, or help us develop in any number of ways. From the cognitive perspective, however, there's a catch to all of this talk of transformation and growth. When we travel, we not only get away from our usual environment—giving us a chance to reflect on our lives in a new way—we also must adapt to new, unexpected surroundings. These two elements of travel exist in uneasy opposition to each other.

Leaving home and seeking a comfortable retreat—a vacation resort for example—is very different from putting ourselves in a situation that requires learning, improvisation, and adaptation. Naturally, doing the latter is often what provokes unexpected reactions. Our attentive mind may map out a travel itinerary, sign up for a homestay program, choose an intensive language course, or decide to take a foreign posting, but *it's the intuitive mind—the autopilot of everyday life—that bears the brunt of intercultural adjustment.* We can opt for a more insulated experience, such as a pre-planned tour or luxury cruise, but protecting ourselves from adaptive challenges changes the nature of the travel experience. Put simply, *the more adaptive demands we face, the more powerful—yet also the more unpredictable—our intercultural experiences will be.*

Adjustment challenges can catch anyone off guard. Cathy may not have understood the difference between a philosophical commitment to diversity (a largely conscious intellectual stance) and the ability to successfully adjust to foreign environments (an unconscious process of learning and change). Having the former doesn't guarantee success with the latter. Cathy was raised in California, where cultural diversity is often couched in the language of ethnic pride and tolerance for other lifestyles. Confronted with the day-to-day stresses of cross-cultural adjustment, she found life abroad more foreign than expected. I meet some sojourners who expect life abroad to be like a vacation, except longer. They may discover, however, that stress builds as the initial novelty of their surroundings wears off. Some do manage to successfully treat their time away like a long holiday—hanging out with their compatriots and making little effort to learn about their new surroundings. Sensitive, emotionally engaged sojourners like Cathy, on the other hand, report powerful emotional ups and downs, but may also have more deeply satisfying experiences.

At the core of these challenges are the profound learning demands made to both our attentive and intuitive mind. For starters, our conscious mind has little control over how we react to the challenges we face. We may imagine what it will be like to be abroad, yet find our guesses way off. Ray, an American studying in Japan, says:

> My attitude towards intercultural experience was like what John Lennon sang: "nothing's going to change my world"; I thought I was impervious to being changed by international experiences. I have now come to know that this is completely false. International experiences have been a major impact on the formation of my identity.

Like many who have highly satisfying international experiences, Ray's adjustment process involved a lot of unexpected change. Yet like many travelers, he was unrealistic about what it would be like, or how he would respond.

Even those with significant experience abroad sometimes miscalculate potential stresses. Consider Maria, a Romanian who was planning a study abroad stay in Tokyo. She recalled previous struggles when studying at a high school in the UK, and decided to be better prepared for her Japan adventure:

> Before coming over I spent many hours on the Internet trying to find accommodation first, then looking on Google maps and learning all the streets around my new flat. At the same time I searched many travel websites and personal blogs about Japan, so I felt like I was an "expert" in everything Japan had to offer (apart from the language, of course). But how wrong I was! Having previously had the opportunity of relocating to another country, I thought that all the stress of my first experience was because I was not prepared and did not know a lot about the Welsh culture. I was confident that my research about Japan should have dealt with this gap. But nothing had prepared me for having to try and function "normally" in a language that I had no confidence in communicating and a culture that is so complex and different from what I knew that a few websites could not describe it properly.

Two things stand out about Maria's account. First, despite her previous experience, *she herself did not understand the underlying causes of the adjustment stress she had experienced in the past*. Because of this, she was caught off guard by the adaptive challenges in Japan. On her second try, she came to understand that it's the more subtle cultural differences found in everyday life that make long-term adjustment difficult—the parts of our experience processed by the intuitive mind.

The Intuitive Overload of Culture Shock

The term most commonly associated with difficulties adjusting to a foreign environment is *culture shock*, which made its first-known public appearance in Brazil on August 3, 1954. The Women's Club of Rio de Janeiro had invited Kalervo Oberg, a Canadian-born anthropologist and educator, to talk about the challenges of adapting to life abroad. He spoke to a well-heeled group of relatively privileged expatriates—whose status did not, however, protect them from adaptive stress reactions.

Oberg talked about "fear of physical contact with attendants or servants" and people who "take refuge in the colony of your countrymen and its cocktail circuit." He referred to culture shock as an "occupational disease." He talked about its "symptoms," which he said included an absentminded, far-away stare, feelings of helplessness, fits of anger, and a refusal to learn the language of the host country. He described stages of culture shock and gave advice for dealing with it. His talk was then published in the journal *Practical Anthropology*, where it became a widely quoted classic.[8]

In some ways, the talk—which Oberg gave more than a half century ago—is dated. We are, after all, living in a hyper-connected global village with greater awareness of cultural diversity. Today's sojourners are usually less isolated than his audience that day. But the essence of his description, of the mental strains caused by cultural adjustment, fits our current understanding of cognition and the intuitive mind. The causes of culture shock that he identifies all relate to the largely *unconscious process of learning and adjustment*:

> Culture shock is precipitated by the anxiety that results from losing all our familiar signs and symbols of social intercourse. These signs or cues include the thousand and one ways in which we orient ourselves to the situations of daily life: when to shake hands and what to say

when we meet people, when and how to give tips, how to make purchases, when to accept and when to refuse invitations, when to take statements seriously and when not. Now these cues, which may be words, gestures, facial expressions, customs, or norms, are acquired by all of us in the course of growing up and are as much a part of our culture as the language we speak or the beliefs we accept. All of us depend for our peace of mind and our efficiency on hundreds of these cues, most of which we do not carry on the level of conscious awareness.[9]

The mental functions Oberg describes, such as the processing of "familiar signs and symbols of social intercourse," are handled largely by the intuitive mind. He refers to implicit cultural knowledge as the "thousand and one ways we orient ourselves in the situations of daily life." He identifies elements in our environment—gestures, facial expressions, customs, and norms—that are the natural domain of unconscious cognition. Above all, Oberg's description refers to the stresses of getting used to new patterns of *everyday behavior*. He doesn't talk about new foods, different architecture, weather, or any other concrete, easy-to-identify differences we might find abroad. It's the little, yet pervasive, differences that end up overloading our intuitive mind.

Culture Surprise and Culture Stress

A cognitive perspective cannot provide an easy antidote to culture shock, but it can help us understand what's happening beneath the surface of our minds. In chapter three, I talked about Oz moments, the noticing of novel elements in a new environment. Intercultural specialists sometimes call these experiences *culture bumps* or *culture surprises*.[10] They can be viewed as an initial response—the first stage of cognitive adjustment to a foreign environment. These early Oz moments are often perceived as exciting, interesting, or exotic. Remember, for example, Kentaro's surprise that everyone around him in Canada spoke English. Because his stay was short, he likely returned home to Japan with the impression that life in Canada would always consist of an exciting series of novel experiences. If he had stayed longer, however, he might have found that the culture surprise experience contains frayed threads that may start to unravel. The difference that stimulates us at the beginning of a stay can start to wear us down.

Culture stress is what we feel when our cognitive processes start to get overwhelmed by culture surprises.[11] The novelty in our environment, so exciting at first, exhausts the attentive mind's ability to pay attention and solve problems. Perhaps it also overloads the intuitive mind's capacity to process new patterns. In any case, it's easy to underestimate the toll that everyday adjustment can take on us. Jane, for example, undertook what she assumed was an easy task, finding whole-grain bread in Tokyo:

> I spent a couple hours going to every local grocery store, not finding anything but these weird pseudo-wheat breads. By the end of it I was exhausted and frustrated. I went home. A friend called asking if I wanted to go out drinking, and I realized how ridiculous I would sound if I told the truth and said, "I can't; I spent all day looking at bread." So I said I was tired and went to sleep.

This experience was part of a larger trend for her. She found herself unexpectedly stressed, despite having traveled abroad previously:

> I noticed that things seemed to be going downhill. Everyday tasks that I used to find interesting and exciting had become stressful obstacles. Why wasn't I as sociable and optimistic about everything as I was in my first semester of international college? I had been shown the diagram of the "W curve" over and over, before every plane flight away from home, and every time I thought they got it all wrong. Thing was, though, that I had never been in a foreign country long enough to go "down the W."

The "W curve" Jane refers to is sometimes used by intercultural educators to talk about the process of adjustment stress, with a dip, a recovery, and then another dip when adjusting to life back home. Jane believed that she was immune from culture shock simply because she had never been in a foreign environment long enough for it to hit her.

Ego Depletion

Although we primarily think of cultural adjustment stress as a mental phenomenon, there are physiological reasons for our reactions. Unlike the intuitive mind, which largely functions effortlessly, our ability to consciously focus our attention and actively solve problems is limited. Social psychologists refer to the mental exhaustion of these capacities as *ego depletion* and have shown that we become more irritable and judgmental when we are tired or mentally strained.[12]

Think of the attentive mind as having batteries with a limited amount of energy available for intentional mental activity. We experience ego depletion whenever we must exert self-control, suppress emotion, make difficult decisions, or focus our attention on solving problems.[13] An awareness of ego depletion can help sojourners be more sensitive to their own moods and have more realistic expectations about how much novelty they can handle. When overloaded, we may simply need to reduce stimulation to recover our sense of balance and be ready to explore the streets again.

As culture stress increases, foreign experiences may cease being fun. Kaoru, on a home-stay in the United States, describes her transition from culture surprise to culture stress in this way:

> In the first two or three days, I was being happier rather than getting stressed, and I was excited at finding something new for me in the new culture. But from the fourth day or so, I gradually came to feel stressed, mostly because I couldn't speak English fluently and communicate as I would like. Although I wanted to talk with my host family, I often shut up in my room so that I no longer had to use my poor English with them.

> What's more, there were other problems than just the language. For example, the Japanese culture of elaborately made lunch boxes, taking a bath every night, and safe nights doesn't exist there. That is, what I thought was the natural order of things in Japan didn't apply there. I tried to learn how to take care of myself not to bring troubles to my host families. For example, how to take a bus or go shopping in a supermarket by myself. I even rehearsed for table talk in English.

One characteristic of culture stress is that activities that are normally handled by the intuitive mind require active mental attention. Small talk is normally something we do without thinking, yet Kaoru has to consciously practice it. And other things that are largely habitual for locals, such as taking a bus or shopping in a supermarket, require an active process of conscious problem solving.

While culture stress and ego depletion are associated with particular tasks that require increased levels of conscious attention—"How does this stupid ATM work?"—*culture shock*, as conceptualized by Oberg and others, is a more vague and potentially quite alienating sensation.[14] An accumulation of tiny adaptive stresses can lead to a deep sense of malaise, experienced in different ways—feelings of tiredness, irritability, emotional instability, homesickness, depression, and so on.

The difference between *culture surprise* (stimulating and interesting differences we first notice), *culture stress* (ego depletion from so much conscious problem solving), and *culture shock* can be compared to the reactions of our muscles when we exercise. Culture surprise is like the joy of stimulating our muscles when we start our workout. It feels good, and we feel enthusiastic about the idea of coming regularly to the gym. As the exercise continues, we reach culture stress—and the panting and heavy limbs that come from the strain of a longer workout—we start to perform poorly and lose motivation to continue. Finally, culture shock is an exhaustion of the muscles—they are sore even if we are not exercising at the moment.

I have not yet found any research into the physiological changes that take place during periods of severe culture shock. I do know, however, that mental exhaustion can make people highly sensitive to things that might otherwise seem inconsequential. It can feel like one is surrounded on all sides, as this student expressed while talking about her first year abroad:

> First year: Culture shock, tears every night. Here is the list of my thoughts back then:
>
> Why are people here dressed so normal? OK, my fashion doesn't fit here at all!
>
> How can students speak and understand English so well?
>
> They must think I am a lame, boring person because I am so silent.
>
> It seems like there is a certain invisible common sense here, but I don't get it.
>
> I am so scared.
>
> My English teacher is gay, and students seem to accept that, and he is very popular. This is so different from Japan.
>
> Why are they so loud during class?

Why do they throw food at each other?

How could bus drivers and teachers be late for the time or class without apologizing?

Why does this Chemistry teacher make and drink coffee during his lesson?

Why do people bite their nails! It's disgusting!

While this sojourner was able to identify things that bothered her, others find that they feel down for no identifiable reason.

Peace Corps volunteers, who often spend a period of months or years in radically different cultural surroundings, often face big challenges. Chris, for example, is an easygoing Californian who once moved to a rural village in Thailand. He received language training, housing, a teaching job, pocket money, and Thai civil servant status. At first he drank in the novelty—using a squat toilet, walking dirt roads, and seeing farmers bent over in the rice paddies. People were unfailingly polite and smiling. The things Chris thought would cause problems—spicy food and humid weather—didn't really bother him. But he hadn't counted on how incompetent he would feel.

Even after many months, communication in Thai required an enormous mental effort but yielded only superficial communication. To the villagers, Chris was an alien presence whose comings and goings attracted constant attention. At times, he felt such an overpowering urge to escape that he would strap on his helmet, kick-start his motorbike, and head out of the village along trails that snaked into the rainforest. Taking a deep breath, he would scream obscenities at the top of his lungs. As he explains it:

> The pressure to adapt was intense. I stood out like the proverbial sore thumb, so everyone knew what I was doing and everyone discussed my doings. I could not discuss my problems, stress, etc. with anyone. I felt a tremendous sense of relief when I was riding my tiny motorcycle through the rainforests on the small, winding roads where few people went.

Fortunately, Chris' story has a happy ending. As his Thai improved, he started to deepen his bonds to the community. Unfortunately, just when he was feeling deeply connected to his new home, it was time to leave. He now describes the Peace

Corps as the "toughest job you'll ever love"—a boot camp of interculturalism. When Kalervo Oberg spoke of culture shock, he used the language of sickness—referring to it as an *occupational disease*. That's partly because when he was writing, living and working abroad was less common, and culture shock was typically only faced by people in particular professions—such as missionaries abroad. I mostly see culture shock not as a psychological ailment but as *a side effect of unconscious learning*. Having said that, these stresses are real, and psychologists recognize symptoms of culture shock as an *adjustment disorder*.[15]

I tell sojourners that if you feel no adjustment stress, then that's good, but don't assume that you're immune—it may be waiting around the corner. On the other hand, if you find yourself suffering unexpectedly from depression, extreme emotions, sadness, homesickness, irritability, or similar symptoms when you are abroad, go easy on yourself. Usually, the intuitive mind simply needs the opportunity to digest its experiences, and the attentive mind needs a break from its nonstop problem solving. Don't push yourself. Take a break; even visit home if you need to. Travelers who do so often get their batteries recharged and are soon ready to resume their adventure. Don't hesitate to reach out if you are finding adjustment difficult. You are not the first person, nor will you be the last, to feel the way you do.

Hidden Cultural Patterns

Globalization sometimes masks the challenges of cross-cultural adjustment. For sojourners today, the physical adjustments necessary for life abroad are often minimal—you can find shopping malls in Kuala Lumpur and pizza in Nairobi. If an institution sponsors your stay, its staff may take great care to provide for all your physical needs. A longer stay, however, can present you with a deeper, subtler set of challenges—often related to things that may seem trivial at first. Cathy, who we met at the beginning of this chapter, for example, says that small cultural differences bothered her more and more as time went on. She had unexpected trouble getting restaurant staff to customize her food orders as they would in the United States. As she explains:

> I was extremely frustrated when I went to [restaurants] and the person taking my order refused to make any changes to it. I was surprised when my vegetarian friend could not get the waitress to take

out the meat in her pasta order. At a sandwich shop, I wanted to add avocado to my chicken sandwich, and was again denied . . . It's like Japanese people are robots and just say they are sorry, but do nothing more. Apologies come out of their mouths, but no further action happens beyond that. How useless and backwards is that?

In and of itself, the inability to get a food order customized is a small thing. Yet Cathy started to understand that these seemingly isolated incidents were indicative of deeper layers of cultural difference. There was something *systematic* going on that Cathy had trouble understanding—as though she was walking through an invisible maze and bumping into unexpected cultural walls. We have a natural desire to understand the significance of the patterns in our new environment, and when we can't make sense of things, it can bother us.[16]

The problem with these more subtle cultural patterns, of course, is that they can clash with our values and social expectations. Americans and Europeans are used to being given choices. Order food in an American restaurant, and you'll be given a long series of choices to make—*Soup or salad? What kind of dressing? Would you like it on the side? Rice or potatoes? French fries or baked? Any food allergies? An extra plate so you can share?* This emphasis on choices is not simply good service; it's a *particular form of good service* that rests on hidden cultural patterns. One hidden assumption of individualistic thinking is that personal choice is critical to expressing one's true self.[17]

The cultural values underlying attitudes towards choice have been explored by psychologist Sheena Iyengar. As an Indian American, she brings a unique perspective to the discussion of the cultural values of choice. She argues that people from individualistic societies feel making choices is a central way of defining and expressing themselves. It is also associated with personal freedom and self-actualization. You are, the thinking goes, the choices that you make. Westerners may assume that such attitudes are universal to all humans and have trouble making sense of things, such as arranged marriages, that hint at different attitudes towards choice.

American attitudes towards choice have an impact beyond everyday things like ordering food in restaurants. They are part of an individualistic construction of identity, one that sees human beings as discreet and fundamentally separate from others. Those who grow up in more collectivist communities, on the other hand, develop an identity constructed in a more interdependent way. Humans are self-actualized by coming together with others, rather than by setting oneself apart. This makes for a greater emphasis on *collective wellbeing and choice*—choices should benefit everyone.

As a way of exploring these issues, Iyengar asked different groups of people to write down areas of their life for which choice was important, versus areas for which they were happy to have choices left up to others.[18] Americans created detailed lists of choices they wanted to make—little was given for other people to do. Japanese people, on the other hand, were happy leaving many choices up to others. Such differences in attitudes towards identity and choice are reflected in other areas as well: parenting and family life, how people socialize, and even restaurant service. In the more collectivistic society of Japan, good service often involves *eliminating* choice by anticipating customer needs. The best possible service involves providing you something that is *better* than what you could have imagined on your own. An expensive meal in a Japanese restaurant often involves no decision-making at all. So while modifying a food order is not unheard of, Japanese restaurants are less oriented towards that kind of service.

These hidden value differences help explain why Cathy had such a negative reaction when restaurants in Japan failed to give her choices. Yet she had trouble making sense of the underlying cultural difference because it was so foundational. Cathy worried that she was overreacting, saying, "I know that these feelings of frustration and anger and negativity towards the Japanese way of never changing orders or making exceptions comes from cultural differences." Yet this intellectual knowledge didn't resolve her inner conflict. As she explains:

> What I think are silly rules are actually principles that stem from the fundamentals of Japanese society. But knowing these issues are because of cultural differences . . . does not make it any easier to accept them. I still have to go through a painful change of getting used to doing things completely differently. . . . Of course Japan isn't going to bend over and change for me, but for me to change who I am to live here is hard.

Cathy was, in effect, at odds with herself. Her intuitive mind was habituated to valuing choice, and she had a negative "gut" reaction to losing it. Her attentive mind, on the other hand, had trouble figuring out why "normal" choices were being denied to her. In this way, little things that touch on deep cultural elements of the self started to rankle over time. Despite Cathy's multicultural heritage, education, positive attitude, and natural curiosity, it was her unconscious American values—

largely taken for granted—that created some of her biggest adjustment challenges. Unfortunately, it's hard to prepare for experiences like this. We usually don't recognize our own deep cultural values until our expectations have been violated. And we can't simply ask the locals to explain events like this. Many of the cultural scripts that we follow are unconscious. What advice could North Americans, for example, give to Mayuko, a Japanese exchange student?

> It took me one school year, two weeks of summer camp, and some nice American friends to understand what is a hug and what I should do when somebody opens his or her arms to greet me.

Not only is it hard to know the unspoken rules of when and how hugging is appropriate, customs about hugging relate to deeply felt values about gender roles, physical contact, and expressiveness—very deep elements of self. Getting a feel for what's expected and becoming comfortable with a new way to relate to others can be a challenge. And here's a story from Joanna:

> I was born in China, and raised in Japan and Canada, so with my cultural background I always thought I would be a bit more immune to the "cultural shock" that everyone else experienced. When I moved from Japan to Canada . . . there was still one thing that I could not get used to—when people asked me, "How are you doin'?" Knowing that Canadians used this phrase interchangeably with "Hi," I still found myself accidently trying to scramble for the right word to describe how I was feeling, only to find that the person who asked me was already gone by the time I was prepared to answer their question.

I think you get my point. The cultural patterns we rely on in daily life are felt deeply and often cannot easily be analyzed by the attentive mind. For short-term sojourners, these challenges may never come up. But for those who interact more, or who attempt to adapt to the local way of doing things, there is often no quick end to adjustment challenges.

An Open Systems View of Adjustment

While we often can't predict our reactions to a new environment, we *can* learn to see our reactions as part of a larger process of cultural learning. Just as learning about culture shock can help us take steps to deal with it, learning about the *process of cultural learning* can help us feel more in control of our reactions and feelings. It provides us with a conceptual framework to make sense of our experience. With that in mind, let's look at cultural adjustment not simply from the cognitive perspective, but from the broader point of view of all biological systems.

Like even the simplest single-celled organism, humans are sensitive to, and in constant interaction with, our physical and social environment. This interactive outlook is sometimes known as the *open systems* view of living systems.[19] The open systems view, though describing a basic principle found in physics and biology, can also be used to describe the intercultural adjustment process.[20] Like all living things, we naturally strive to stay in balance with our environment—mediating between our inner states and the external world. As the neurobiologist Antonio Damasio puts it (in admittedly dry terms):

> Through thick and thin, even when large variations occur in the environment that surrounds an organism, there is a dispositional arrangement available in the organism's structure that modifies the inner workings of the organism. The dispositional arrangement ensures that the environmental variations do not cause a correspondingly large and excessive variation of activity within. When dangerous variations have already occurred, they can still be corrected by some appropriate actions. . . . The specifications for survival that I am describing here include: a boundary; an internal structure; a dispositional arrangement for the regulation of internal states so that those states are relatively stable. . . . It is intriguing to think that the constancy of the internal milieu is essential to maintain life *and* that it might be a blueprint and anchor for what will eventually become a self in the mind.[21]

Damasio points out that regulation between inner and outer states is a fundamental element of all living things. We seek out comfortable temperature ranges, favor nourishing environments, flee from threats, and so on. Yet Damasio also proposes that our psychological processes—our experience of self and mind—may follow the same principles. From this perspective, the psychological process of cultural adjustment is simply an extension of this basic biological process, and it can therefore be understood as a form of psychological and cultural boundary management.[22]

Seen in this light, Cathy's frustration with Japanese restaurant service is more than a difference in customs—it's a threat response produced by her intuitive mind. As she tries to make sense of cultural difference, she is attempting to keep her inner mental life in balance with the patterns she finds around her.

Resistance, Acceptance, and Adaptation

Cathy's powerful response to cultural difference is frustrating to her in part because *she has trouble making sense of her own reactions.* In other words, her analytic, attentive mind has trouble categorizing the feelings and sensations produced by her intuitive mind. Rationally speaking, the restaurant's refusal to customize her order *shouldn't* be a big deal, yet she finds that it bothers her a lot. Some sojourners may become defensive or self-critical, suppress their feelings, or feel isolated because they "can't cope" in the way they think they should.

I try to provide sojourners with a simple, non-judgmental approach to categorizing and making sense of their cultural learning process, one that is consistent with an open-systems view of adjustment. This theoretical starting point is used by others as well, notably by intercultural communication specialist Young Yun Kim.[23] In line with this, the model I use is built on some very simple assumptions: (1) it's natural that we have internal reactions to changes in our external environment; (2) it's natural that difference is sometimes experienced as a psychological threat of some sort; and (3) our adjustment responses are highly intuitive and thus may not be easily manageable through conscious effort or analysis.

Furthermore, I assume that our conscious mind is better able to analyze and understand more explicit elements of difference, like new foods and subway systems. On the other hand, more abstract patterns of cultural difference, such as behavioral patterns, values, and ways of thinking, are felt intuitively. Adjusting to these hidden patterns of difference requires a *deep cultural learning process* that our conscious mind is only indirectly aware of. The longer we spend in a new environment, and the more we interact with people there, the more likely we are to encounter these less obvious learning challenges.

With these assumptions in mind, I give learners a set of labels that describe the possible reactions to the experience of cultural difference: *resistance, acceptance*, and *adaptation*. *Resistance* can be seen as the equivalent of a psychological threat response, in which we resist integrating new patterns into our way of being. We experience resistance as a negative judgment or denigration of the difference we encounter. If we find ourselves thinking, "They eat with their hands? That's uncivilized!" we recognize that we are experiencing an intuitive resistance to the experience, accompanied by a corresponding negative judgment. Concluding that something is "uncivilized" is, of course, a form of denigration that includes a negative value judgment.

Acceptance, on the other hand, involves recognition that the patterns of cultural difference simply represent another way of doing things. We experience acceptance when we acknowledge that a particular local practice is fine for others, but still not something we choose to do, as when we find ourselves saying, "It's normal here to eat with your hands, but I still prefer to use a spoon." Finally, *adaptation* involves changing ourselves to better fit into our new environment. It implies that we learn new things, adopt new behaviors, see things in a new light, and so on. I have written about this overall approach previously and refer to it as the *deep culture model* of cultural learning.[24]

Let's take a look at these possible reactions in a bit more detail. Resistance is characterized by critical judgment—a hesitation to accept a phenomenon as a reasonable and normal way of doing things. Recall that Cathy, for example, compares Japanese people to robots and exclaims, "How useless and backwards is that?" These words are not a product of racism or prejudice; rather, they are a product of her cognitive self-protection reflex. They contain a negative value judgment. In terms of open systems theory, resistance is a *defensive reaction that seeks to maintain the primacy of one's internal configuration in the face of an environment perceived as threatening.* It is an attempt to maintain the cultural status quo within one's own mind.

As I see it, not all negative reactions constitute resistance. I describe *dislike* as a negative feeling that is not accompanied by a negative value judgment. Perhaps I find the idea of blood sausage found in Germany rather gross, but recognize that there's nothing inherently disgusting or wrong about eating it. Simply finding something distasteful or uncomfortable doesn't automatically mean we judge it as "not normal." Resistance involves drawing the conclusion that there's something *wrong* with the difference we've encountered, whereas *dislike* involves recognition that one's distaste is a matter of personal preference or habits, and that there's nothing intrinsically bad about the difference itself.

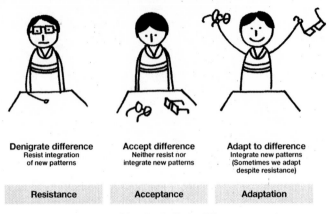

Intercultural Adjustment
Cognitive reactions to patterns of difference

Denigrate difference	Accept difference	Adapt to difference
Resist integration of new patterns	Neither resist nor integrate new patterns	Integrate new patterns (Sometimes we adapt despite resistance)
Resistance	**Acceptance**	**Adaptation**

Deep Culture Model — Shaules, 2007

Figure 5-1

From the perspective of open systems theory, *adaptation* is an internalizing process by which patterns from the new environment are integrated into the self. It creates more concordance between our inner self and the environment we find ourselves in. Sometimes we may embrace such change and easily feel at home in a new environment. On other occasions, we may change because we have little choice, resisting and judging negatively even as we are forced to *adapt*. This is psychologically unhealthy but not uncommon. I sometimes find cynical expats who stay abroad for the money or status it brings, even while looking down on the host community. By staying, they are forced to adapt to local life, even though they resist doing so. This cognitive dissonance can lead to conflicted feelings, as they force themselves to get along in an environment they feel critical about and don't fundamentally accept.

Acceptance is a sort of neutral middle ground between the defensive posture of resistance and the receptive response of adaptation. We choose not to change ourselves, yet don't make negative judgments either. Acceptance can be a transitional stage as we move from resistance towards adaptation. It's not uncommon to have an initial reaction of *resistance*—feeling critical and judgmental about differences we find—and then shift to *acceptance* as we become accustomed to, and start to better understand, those differences. That can make it easier for us to adapt—to change ourselves in line with those differences. Naturally, people have complex and overlapping reactions to difference. Cathy, like most people, probably adapted to some things in Tokyo quite easily even as she resisted others that she found hard to accept. This model assumes that we react to different elements of our experience in different ways, and that our experiences can and do change over time.

Surface and Deep

As we've seen, subtle cultural patterns may escape the focused attention of our attentive mind. We do easily notice, however, the most explicit elements of cultural difference, such as food, clothing, architecture, ceremonies, and so on. Sometimes referred to as *visible culture*, or *explicit culture* (though I tend to use the term *surface culture*), these things are, more strictly speaking, *products* of culture—the objects a community uses and the symbols it shares. Surface culture may be related to the traditional (ceremonies, dance, temples) or the everyday (food, clothing, subway systems). Because surface culture is represented in explicit form, it can be captured by a camera or written about in a Wikipedia entry. Surface culture is perceived more directly by the focused attention of conscious analytic thought. When you look through guidebook entries about the sights you are seeing, you are using your attentive mind to focus your learning on explicit culture.

In contrast to this, more subtle *deep culture* patterns are experienced indirectly through the pattern recognition capacity of our intuitive mind. This includes things like communication styles, values, standards of politeness, or, in Cathy's case, expectations about choice. Deep culture patterns are not observed directly. Rather, they are experienced over time as patterns of behavior and interaction. When I first arrived in Japan, for example, I knew what a bow was, but I really couldn't "read" Japanese bowing because I wasn't familiar with the more subtle patterns of bowing etiquette. The intuitive mind needs time to identify these patterns such that we have a "feel" for them. The longer we spend abroad and the more we interact with locals on their terms, the more our intuitive mind has to decipher and manage these subtler patterns of difference. Short-term visitors may not notice such subtleties at all.

I believe that we experience *resistance*, *acceptance*, and *adaptation* at different depths—as responses to both explicit and hidden patterns of difference. In effect, both the attentive and intuitive mind are engaged in learning about and adjusting to different elements of cultural difference. Learning how to buy tickets for the

Metro in Paris is a more concrete (thus, *surface*) cultural adjustment challenge, for example, than getting a feel for French communication styles (*deep*). We can visualize this as in figure 5-2. The top of the diagram represents our adjustments to differences in surface culture, while the bottom represents reactions to deeper cultural difference. Surface culture is easier to talk about and analyze with our attentive mind, while deep culture is experienced intuitively.

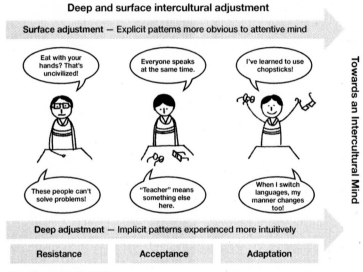

Figure 5-2

I've included a few sample statements to illustrate *resistance*, *acceptance*, and *adaptation* at both the surface and deep level. For example, if someone describes Indonesians eating with their hands as "uncivilized," we can guess that this denigration represents a *resistance* to rather obvious (explicit) difference (top left). I once heard a Brit make the following comment after living in Spain: "Everyone speaks at the same time." This is an observation about surface behavior without any sort of criticism attached—*surface acceptance*. Many sojourners will point out something that they learned, for example, using chopsticks or eating new food. This *surface adaptation* reflects the integration of these concrete skills into their behavioral repertoire.

With longer, more involved interactions, we encounter patterns we might not have noticed before. On one occasion, a German engineer complained about the problem solving of his Japanese colleagues. (It was a more bottom-up, data gathering–oriented approach than he was used to.) His conclusion, however, was simply that "These people can't solve problems." His intuitive mind rejected and denigrated the pattern he found—a form of *deep resistance.*

This perspective can be contrasted with that of an American teacher in Korea who found that he could accept the deference given to teachers in Korea, even though he didn't feel comfortable taking on those values himself. He didn't want to be treated with great deference, but recognized this practice to be a valid alternative way of thinking and valuing. We can find *deep acceptance* in his statement that "'Teacher means something very different here than what it means back home."

When we spend long periods in foreign environments, and integrate many new patterns into our intuitive mind, we may go through a process of *deep adaptation.* As our intuitive mind integrates new patterns, we become increasingly comfortable speaking a new language, relating to others in a new way, and looking at things from the cultural perspective of our hosts. Deep adaptation often requires an adjustment in our sense of identity. We may start to wonder where we belong, or feel that family and friends back home don't understand us anymore. This is sometimes talked about in terms of *marginality,* a feeling of not quite belonging. People who have long experience in foreign environments may develop a sense of identity centered on this marginality. One might feel like a kind of bridge person who has entry into different cultural worlds, but who also remains in some sense detached from them.[25]

The deep culture model I present is intended to help learners reflect on, and thus get a better handle on, their process of intercultural adjustment and change. It attempts to describe how people *do* react to adaptive challenges, not how they *should* react. I believe that as we get over our resistance and eventually reach acceptance and adaptation, we develop an increasingly sophisticated understanding of cultural difference, allowing for a greater degree of *intercultural sensitivity.*[26] By this, I mean that we are better able to perceive the foreign environment from the local point of view. We accept that our judgments and interpretations need to be informed by this insiders' view, and we broadly accept the validity of contrasting ways of looking at the world. This doesn't imply that we agree with or adapt to everything we find, but we do understand the importance of the local perspective when interpreting our experiences. It should be pointed out, however, that not everyone progresses in equal measure. Some may spend years resisting and denigrating the differences they encounter, while others may accept and embrace these same differences.

Cultural Adjustment and the Intercultural Mind

Throughout this chapter, I have emphasized the need to recognize that cultural adjustment takes place at the level of both the attentive and intuitive mind. In my work, I try to sensitize sojourners to the more intuitive elements of their intercultural experiences. I've found that many embrace the opportunity to gain insights into their own minds. At the very least, they recognize that spending time in a foreign environment may provoke reactions they may not expect. Reflecting on these reactions can be reassuring for those who, like Cathy, struggle without knowing quite why. This sort of reflection can help us reduce stress, and ultimately contributes to the development of a more intercultural mind.

KEY CONCEPTS

Resistance: *A psychological threat response in which we resist the integration of new patterns. It is experienced as a negative judgment or denigration of difference.*

Acceptance: *A recognition that patterns of cultural difference simply represent another way of doing things, though we choose not to adopt those patterns.*

Adaptation: *Allowing for change in ourselves so as to better fit into a new environment. It implies that we learn new things, adopt new behaviors, see things in a new light, and so on.*

Surface culture: *The explicit elements of cultural difference that we notice and experience in foreign environments. They include things like new food, differences in how people dress, architecture, art, ceremonies, and so on.*

Deep culture: *Implicit patterns of cultural difference that are experienced more intuitively, and that are harder to analyze and explain analytically. It includes things like communication styles, cultural values, patterns of thinking, and so on. Learning these patterns requires habituation and a trial-and-error process of intuitive learning.*

Discussion Quote: *Culture shock is not a psychological ailment, but a side effect of a largely unconscious learning process.*

6.

configuration

Unless you *open your mind,* nobody *will open your mind.*

—Kenta

Some travelers believe that when abroad they will encounter people who are, deep down, the same as they are. In fact, our cultural settings are an integral part of the way our minds work. We'll look at the interface between culture and cognition, including cultural differences in cognitive processing. Plus, cross-cultural research into parenting shows that we pass on cultural patterns without being aware of it.

Thumb Pointing

During the U.S. presidential election of 2012, when Barack Obama was debating the challenger Mitt Romney, Obama used a subtle yet distinctive gesture—one seen by millions but noticed by few. In the midst of gladiatorial rhetoric, his aura of political leadership on the line, he could be seen repeatedly pointing at his opponent with his thumb. A BBC reporter mentioned it in the story "U.S. Election: 10 Oddities Explained," writing: "Featured in the three presidential debates were Romney, Obama, and Obama's thumb." The reporter described the gesture by saying "The president jabbed his hand, with his thumb resting atop a loosely curled fist, to emphasize a point." In order to explain this "oddity," a body language expert was consulted. The expert surmised that someone had coached Obama into doing this to look powerful, because, "On a subconscious level, it's phallic."[1]

Oddity, of course, is in the eye of the beholder. It turns out there was another observer who wrote about the thumb, but from a different perspective. Edward Fox had seen this gesture before—in Indonesia, where he had researched Javanese culture, and where pointing with the thumb is not uncommon. Obama, of course, spent several years of his childhood living there on the island of Java. Much has been written about Obama's multicultural background in Hawaii and his father's Kenyan roots. Fox, however, points out that it was Obama's mother—not his father—who raised him, took him to Indonesia, and encouraged him to adapt to the local culture. Using the thumb to point is seen as more discrete and reflects the Javanese cultural ideal of serene self-composure.

Fox goes on to explain that, traditionally, Javanese with high status should embody *halus*, a code of noble behavior characterized by inner serenity and quiet power. *Halus* is an inner moral quality that counterbalances the chaotic forces of evil, providing a solid foundation of calm self-assurance. The ideal Javanese ruler doesn't engage in histrionics or macho posturing. Instead, he (leaders were traditionally male) absorbs the attacks of his enemies. He triumphs without seeming to make any effort at all, as a natural result of his command of the forces in play.[2]

Obama has, of course, become famous for his calm, "no drama" political style. His role as the first black president makes it easy to forget, however, that the first political foes he faced were not from Chicago; they were the neighborhood children in the streets of Jakarta who taunted him for being dark-skinned. He went to an Indonesian-speaking school and "spent his boyhood playing with the sons and daughters of rice farmers and rickshaw drivers."[3] In Janny Scott's biography of Obama's mother, we hear, "This is where Barack learnt to be cool . . . if you get mad and react, you lose."[4]

Obama himself talks about learning his manners in Indonesia, and apparently he became so adapted to local norms that his friends accepted him as one of their own. Fox argues that Obama took these Javanese ideals back to the United States, where they formed the tectonic plates of his political identity. Did the Javanese value of *halus* work its way into his character? Could his cool, composed demeanor be not simply a personality trait, but represent cultural influence from his childhood? Did Obama's thumb express, in a subtle yet profound way, these Javanese ideals?

We are all shaped by the values and habits we grow up around. It's not hard to believe that the ideals of *halus* live on in Obama's body language. How could a child growing up in Java *not* be shaped in some way by values there? For that matter, how could a Luo growing up in Nairobi not be affected by his tribal identity? How could a Korean girl from Pusan not be influenced by the culture of Confucian deference? How could a young Saudi not be informed by Islam? How could *any* of us claim to be the simple result of our individual preferences and choices?

We sometimes think that our cultural and ethnic background is what makes us unique. There is truth in this assumption, of course, but also a degree of cultural bias. North Americans in particular have fetishized individualism to such a degree that one's cultural background is often seen primarily as a shaper of individuality, rather than as a marker of shared community. In Obama's case, it's easy to overlook how *typical* his distaste for the dramatic is in Java—his "no drama" style is something he *shares* with the Javanese he grew up around. While it makes Obama unique in the U.S., for Javanese it's simply normal.

In Java, *halus* remains in the background of daily life. As part of the social fabric, it is barely noticed at all. In the same way, Americans do not think of themselves as being "influenced" by the values of individualism, self-determination, entrepreneurship, and so on. Foreign experiences remind us, however, that our cultural background is more than a heritage that we can be proud of. It provides the initial building blocks that we use to create our worldview and a starting point for finding our sense of self.

Plasticity

Understanding how our mind is shaped by culture is not easy—culture and individual self are intertwined and can't easily be separated or measured. We can, however, approach this from the perspective of cognition by looking at the *plasticity* of the brain. Plasticity refers generally to the idea that cognitive processes are not fixed and static—like the levers and gears of a machine or the electrical pathways of silicone computer chips. Neural function develops and changes over one's lifetime; it is responsive to the environment, affected by changes in behavior, and often can adapt and reconfigure in response to injury.[5]

The prevalence of neuroplasticity is one reason why computers are *not* an accurate metaphor to talk about brain function. Most computers, once programmed, function in a preordained way, giving predictable results corresponding to their initial instructions. The brain not only acquires new information from the environment, but also changes in terms of physical structure—anatomical change—and functional organization.

Like some sort of shape-shifter from a science fiction movie, our brain operates in interactive union with the world around it, modifying itself with activity as mundane as, for example, reading a novel.[6] Research subjects who read a novel over a period of nine days were found to have increased connectivity in areas of the brain associated with perspective taking and story comprehension. Some of these changes persisted for days after the novel was read. This is a tiny example of a broader principle—our brain changes in accordance with many external factors, including experience and learning. Some of those changes can be long-term or perhaps even permanent.

While the brain has a great deal of plasticity generally, to understand the deep impact of culture on our minds, we need to look at plasticity early in our lives—the period, for example, when the young Barack Obama was running through the streets of Jakarta. Newborn babies clearly have a lot of learning and growing to do, and their cognitive systems depend on input from the environment to fully develop. In that sense, our childhood social environment doesn't really *influence* us; rather, it is central to a fundamental configurative process. As neurocognitive researcher Bruce Wexler explains, "The chemical mechanisms of neuronal growth and learning that are so active during childhood are much less evident in adult brains, and learning in adults depends largely on different cellular mechanisms. On the psychological level, established perceptual, attitudinal, and cognitive structures resist change."[7]

In other words, our early experiences are formative. While we continue to learn later in life, our cognitive systems are configured in important ways by the world that surrounds us as we grow up.

Critical Periods and Developmental Programs

There's another world leader whose experience can teach us something about the brain's plasticity. In September 2012, Vladimir Putin was photographed flying over the Yamal Peninsula in Russia. He wasn't in a jet, however. He was dressed in a white jump suit and piloting a motorized hang glider in an attempt to lead a flock of young Siberian White Cranes.[8] Birds hatched in captivity have no mentors to show them migratory routes, and Putin was participating in an attempt to do so.

Ethologists—most famously Konrad Lorenz—have long known that such birds can be trained to follow people or even inanimate objects.[9] This process is referred to as *imprinting* and involves exposing the birds to a particular stimulus—Lorenz famously imprinted geese to follow his boots—during a "critical period" of developmental plasticity—typically twelve to seventeen hours after hatching.[10] After this critical window closes, they are no longer trainable in the same way. Wildlife specialists have learned to use this imprinting process to help wild birds return to the wild using hang gliders.

A critical period makes a lot of evolutionary sense for social animals. Ducks and geese need to learn migratory routes—a feature of their environment—and need the example of other ducks and geese to do so. Imprinting allows for information about the environment to be passed on to the next generation in a stable way. Other social species share and pass on information as well, including dialect variation of songbirds, synchronized changes in the songs of humpback whales, seed gathering practices in rats, and shared knowledge of water and salt sources in elephants.[11]

A period of high sensitivity to input from the environment allows for a configurative process in which critical information becomes a functioning part of the animal's behavioral repertoire. In the case of ducks and geese, once they are imprinted, their following reflex is fixed. They will then follow their parent—or a hang glider—for the rest of their lives. Environmental information is thus "soft-wired" and becomes a permanent cognitive and behavioral feature. This doesn't mean that these animals stop learning, of course. The critical period allows for initial formative input, whereas more general learning capacities allow for learning from day-to-day experiences.

From the perspective of evolutionary biology, the difference between humans and other social animals is only one of degree. Humans cognitive abilities require a great deal of social input. The most obvious example of this is language acquisition—our cognitive capacity for language is built in, but it requires social and linguistic input in order to develop. Just as wild geese are imprinted to follow their parents, we acquire our native language through exposure and practice as children. It then becomes—for all practical purposes—a permanent feature of our cognitive and behavioral repertoire. We are not aware of this, of course. We simply use language and know what "sounds right" grammatically, as we effortlessly pronounce sounds that many foreigners will struggle in vain to reproduce.

There is no clear separation between what might be considered "innate" and what is "learned." Some interpretive abilities, for example, seem to be built into the very architecture of our brain. Newborn babies, for example, will look longer at figures that resemble a face compared to similar figures assembled randomly.[12] By two months of age, babies distinguish between objects and people, and by seven months they seem to understand that people, but not objects, can move on their own. Despite this universality, there is increasing evidence that our cultural environment has a long-term impact on cognitive processes.[13] Many things once considered to be universal cognitive functions, such as how we use numbers, may be more influenced by cultural configuration than we realized.[14]

Cognitive processing also seems to be shaped by the patterns of the language we use.[15] One area of research looks at tonal versus non-tonal languages. Tonal languages use pitch to distinguish words; for example, the word "ma" in Chinese means *mother* when spoken with a high pitch, while it means *horse* with a different pitch. This difference in language structure significantly affects the neural mechanisms of language processing. Recent findings suggest that the neural mechanisms engaged by our native language form stable cognitive patterns that are not easily modified. Researchers are also trying to understand the neural processes involved in second-language learning. It is possible that there is both an assimilation process, in which the brain processes the second language as though it were the first language, as well as an accommodation process, in which the brain's processing network adapts to the structure of the new system.[16]

I bring up these details of language learning because it's easy to forget just how complex our cognitive systems are, as well as how much configuration they require. Our brain does not simply work "out of the box." As it grows and develops, it incorporates the patterns from the environment that will be needed to function in society. Linguists refer to this process as *language acquisition* (as opposed to the *language learning* that we do in school later in life). This process also involves what sociologists refer to as *enculturation*—the acquisition of cultural knowledge and competencies necessary for social functioning. This process of cognitive development and learning takes time. After five years we've mastered only the fundamentals of our native language and even at fifteen we have an incomplete understanding of the social worlds that surround us. This involved developmental process is so natural, so taken for granted, however, that in everyday life we simply call it "growing up" or "learning to talk."

Language learning and cultural adaptation can be challenging and even threatening precisely because they touch upon cognitive settings that are set early in life. For the same reason, they can be mind-expanding. As we develop these new cognitive capacities, we not only gain access into other social worlds, we gain a new perspective on ourselves. This provides us more options—new ways to communicate and see the world—and helps prevent us from being stuck with a limited, ethnocentric set of mental pathways, like the geese who seem to have little choice but to blindly follow Vladimir Putin's hang glider.

Embodied Culture

Talking about the configuration of cognitive processes may give the impression that the brain is an information-processing device that is simply wired a little differently depending on linguistic and cultural patterns. But language, culture, and cognition are not phenomena that occur only in some abstract realm of informational patterns. They are not cut off from our physical and emotional states. Language and culture are *embodied*, integrated with and dependent on the whole organism.

Many people have learned about this through the book *Descartes' Error: Emotion, Reason, and the Human Brain*.[17] In it, neurologist Antonio Damasio argues that the popular conception of reason and emotion being separate—symbolized by the thinking of René Descartes, who famously wrote, "I think, therefore I am"—is fundamentally flawed. Damasio presents neurological evidence that even the most abstract realms of cognition, such as the experience of consciousness, are tightly integrated with body and emotion.

Emotion permeates our mental processes at many levels of experience. To demonstrate this, Damasio introduces one patient with damage to the part of the brain necessary for experiencing emotion. On a winter day with treacherous conditions, this patient calmly explained the driving techniques he had used to make it to his appointment. He also coolly described the cars and trucks he witnessed skidding off the road. This sort of detachment allowed him to drive on icy streets without stress or fear. Yet this detachment can be surprisingly paralyzing in everyday life. This same patient was unable to choose between two possible dates for a follow-up appointment, discussing for nearly half an hour the rationally possible reasons for choosing one day over another. Damasio's point is that even everyday choices have an important emotional component, with emotion *marking* certain aspects of an experience, outcome, or action. He refers to this idea as the *somatic marker hypothesis*. For instance, you simply *know* that you want avocado on your burger because of previous positive experiences—particular choices are *marked* with positive or negative emotion.

We tend to think of emotion in terms of dramatic feelings, such as sadness, anger, and fear. But emotion is more foundational than that. It's critical in the formation of intuitions, sensations of rightness and wrongness that guide our reactions to everyday life. Damasio defines intuition as "rapid cognition with the required knowledge partially swept under the carpet, all courtesy of emotion and much past practice."[18] Intuitions, quite literally, provide us with a "feeling" for a situation. They are intimately tied to decision-making and play a critical role in social cognition.

An understanding of the embodied nature of cognition shows us that it's no accident that we talk about having a "bad *feeling*" about a situation, or say, "I *feel like* eating gnocchi for dinner," or, "How do you *feel* about this matter?"

Ideas, concepts, symbols, and language—all highly abstract phenomena—have an emotional and intuitive resonance. Have you ever been "on top of the world" when you were struck by a brilliant idea? If someone criticizes your idea, on the other hand, your "blood may boil." These metaphors capture the embodied nature of meaning, and remind us that mental phenomena have a powerful effect on our physical state.[19]

In everyday life, of course, the mind-body connection runs in the background and we may not be aware of it. When we use language, for example, our brain seems to go through a mental simulation of the actual behavior we are talking about.[20] This simulation affects us physically. When talking about the future, we tend to unconsciously lean our bodies forward. When we say, "I look forward to seeing you," or, "I look back on the past," these phrases are more than metaphors. They reflect the fact that concepts as abstract as time and space are experienced viscerally.[21] Our thoughts, our feelings and our bodily states are all integrated into an organic whole.

As researcher Nils Jostmann says, "How we process information is related not just to our brains but to our entire body. . . . We use every system available to us to come to a conclusion and make sense of what's going on."[22] And it's not just language that is embodied; cultural patterns are embodied as well, which is why an encounter with cultural difference can be experienced as an attack. We easily become angry or upset when someone criticizes some symbolic part of us—such as our ideas, our country, or our values. Even if we attempt to be non-judgmental, we aren't simply dispassionate observers when abroad. Our whole being has been shaped by the cultural world we come from—we are like culturally cogitating viscera, reacting intuitively to our experiences.

I was reminded of this tight mind-body-emotion connection when one of my French students recounted with some exasperation his feelings about Japanese bowing. He felt that lowering one's head to others was demeaning. Referring to a French symbol of equality and egalitarianism, the French revolution, he said sharply, "You know, in France, if you lower your head, it gets chopped off." While he may have thought about this in terms of universal human rights and social equality, his analysis was almost certainly colored by an emotional resonance that came from his own deep cultural configuration.

Such deeply felt cross-cultural reactions are being studied empirically. Research into symbols of dominance (such as "standing tall") and submission (such as head hanging down) has shown that when Americans viewed images associated with dominance, the reward circuitry in the limbic system was activated; whereas in Japanese participants, the reward system responded to submissive, not dominant, symbols.[23] Japanese feel rewarded when someone bows to them because they associate such behavior with politeness and smooth social relations. The French student likely had positive associations with such dominant symbols and negative associations with symbols of submission. He wasn't making a reasoned, conscious choice to oppose Japanese bowing; he just *felt* that it was demeaning.

Researchers have also tested whether Asians are culturally trained to be better at turning off their emotional responses at will.[24] They point to media coverage of the March 2011 earthquake in Japan, which devastated a large stretch of Japanese coast. Many news stories highlighted the discipline and self-control of the Japanese, with survivors not seen as angry, sad, or weeping. Such a lack of evident emotion would be inconceivable in cultural communities that are more expressive. This raised the question of whether the Japanese survivors were simply suppressing the expression of their emotion—bottling it up inside—or whether they were somehow able to tame those feelings.

Researchers assessed a neurophysiological marker for emotion—called LPP (late positive potential)—while subjects looked at unpleasant images, such as pictures of mutilation and threats (human and animal). Participants were told to "suppress any emotional response you may have" and "try to remain calm and diminish" any response they might feel. Compared to American subjects, Asians showed a clearly greater ability to "down regulate" their emotional responses, such that their emotional levels quickly returned to a baseline state. This suggests that people in certain cultural communities may learn a form of unconscious emotional regulation—with the ability to intentionally stop experiencing negative emotion.

The embodiment of culture reaches down even to the level of genetics. Researchers have found that, compared to people from individualistic societies, people from collectivist societies are more likely to have a serotonin transporter gene—called the "S-allele"—that has been correlated with higher levels of anxiety, depression, and negative affect.[25] In spite of this, however, people in collectivist communities do not suffer from higher levels of depression. The researchers speculate that, in fact, collectivism coevolved with the S-allele, mitigating the genetic tendency towards depression through an emphasis on close community bonds and social support. If so, this would mean that biological evolution was a driver of cultural evolution, and that genetic tendencies produced a particular kind of social structure.

We know that the opposite happens—that culture speeds up biological evolution.[26] As human populations settled into fixed communities, diseases became more virulent. Genes that were advantageous in these new circumstances—those that gave protection against malaria, or the ability to digest milk—could spread rapidly. We are used to thinking that genetic change only happens over millions of years, but social factors often have a powerful impact. A mere 10,000 years ago, for example, no one on the planet had blue eyes, since the OCA2 gene that causes them had not developed yet. These macro trends remind us that culture and biology coevolve, which isn't surprising if we recognize how tight the nature-nurture connection is.

In the past, culture was sometimes thought of as a kind of informational content that is poured into the empty vessel of the mind. American children learn about the Declaration of Independence in 1776, while French children study the revolution of 1789. Culture is also sometimes seen as something we "know about"—as when we can recount the names of historical or artistic trends. Yet cultural patterns consist of more than just factual knowledge or artistic traditions. They are more, even, than a set of symbols or concepts that are shared within a community. Although symbolic thought is an important element of our humanity, culture is a bodily phenomenon as much as a mental one. It is "harder" and less abstract than many imagine—more habitual, behavioral, and physiological—and not simply some set of purely mental patterns.[27]

Fractals, the Chicken and the Egg

One of the best-known books about cultural difference is *Cultures and Organizations: Software of the Mind*. Written by Geert Hofstede, it attempts to quantify the impact of cultural patterns on the mind. Hofstede conceptualizes culture as a type of mental conditioning related to a variety of psychological domains—including, among others, the degree to which we learn to avoid uncertainty, and how people experience differences in power and status.[28] The metaphor of the computer—referring to culture as *software*—is very easy to understand. Unfortunately, it also creates the impression that the brain is *programmed* in some deterministic way—as though culture directly controls our behavior.

Common sense tells us, of course, that this isn't true. Human beings are not computers that follow a rigid set of behavioral instructions. What, then, is the influence of culture? How is it passed on? Do we somehow magically absorb it through everyday living? What's the role of parenting? These questions are tricky because they involve different scales of analysis. Culture can be talked about at the macro level of society—shared values and social practices. It can also be talked about at the micro level as something that exists within the individual. The difficulty lies in determining the relationship between these two. It's clearly not the case that society (macro-level analysis) rigidly programs the individual (micro-level analysis).

Culture is a multi-scale phenomenon. To grasp this, we must understand the relationship between (1) the broadly defined cultural patterns found in society generally; (2) the social practices found in everyday behavior; and (3) the evidence for cultural influence at the micro level of mind. We can do so using the concept of *fractals*.[29] This term, which comes from mathematics, refers to *self-similar* patterns that look the same when seen either from up close or from far away. When you zoom in on a fractal figure, you see that the larger figure is constituted by smaller versions of the same figure.

Fractal tree

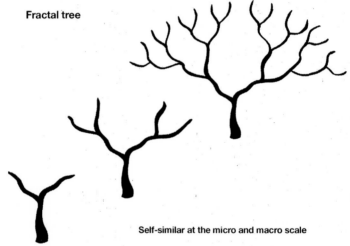

Self-similar at the micro and macro scale

Figure 6-1

While they are described using mathematical equations, fractals are evident in many natural structures and phenomena—such as the shape of certain fern leaves and species of trees. Like fractals, culture has patterns that are self-similar at different scales of analysis—from the micro level of the brain to the macro level of social practice. As Shinobu Kitayama puts it:

> Human psychological processes and functions are linked, on the one hand, to various macrolevel factors, which are involved in the pro- duction, dissipation, and adoption of a variety of cultural ideas such as values and beliefs, practices, and tasks. They are also tied, on the

other hand, to brain processes that plastically change as a function of one's engagement in the ideas, practices, and tasks of the culture.[30]

Put more simply, patterns that we find at the micro level of brain processing will be echoed at more macro scales of behavior and social practice.

Let's take as an example research that asked participants to choose whether a monkey should more properly be categorized together with a banana or with a panda. (See figure 6-2—These are not the images used in the original research.) Results showed that Asians were relatively more likely than Westerners to group the monkey with the banana, based on the fact that monkeys eat bananas—drawing a *contextual* connection between the two. Meanwhile, Westerners were more likely to group the monkey with the panda because they are both animals—identifying an *object-category* relationship. This is an example of cultural difference at the micro-scale of cognitive processing. Westerners tend more towards object-category thinking, whereas Asians show a preference for contextual thinking. This finding is interesting in and of itself, but to appreciate its larger significance, we have to see how these cultural patterns are reflected at the more macro level of social practices—how cultural patterns found in these basic cognitive functions are reflected in everyday behaviors as well.

Which go together?

Figure 6-2

We can find more examples of contextual-interdependent thinking in Asia in everyday life. For example, in Japan it's common for parents to sleep together in the same bed with their children for several years, whereas Western parents more often sleep separately from their children. This social contrast, between interdependent and independent relationships, echoes the contrast between contextual thinking and categorical thinking found in the research about the monkey, panda and banana. Put differently, the contextual-thinking tendencies in more collectivist societies are reflected not just in cognitive tasks, but also in everyday behavior such as sleeping together with children.

We can continue to zoom out to ever-higher levels of macro-level abstraction. Cultural patterns are found in broader social practices as well, such as educational systems and standards of politeness. Whereas Western children are often taught to raise their hands in class and contribute their individual point of view, Asian children are more likely to be taught to *not* try to stand out. Or, we can zoom out even further and look at broad social and historical trends—we could contrast the subject/object thinking of Greek philosophers with the relational method of thinking associated with Taoism and Confucianism.

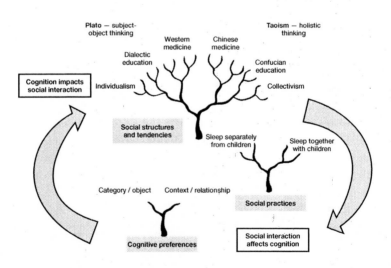

Fractal culture: The feedback loop between cognition and social systems

Figure 6-3

This fractal view of culture highlights the multi-scale nature of cultural difference. Figure 6-3 gives a visual representation of this phenomenon, in which cultural difference is found at the micro scale of cognitive preferences, the higher-level scale of social practices, and the macro scale of social structures and tendencies. There is a feedback loop between the brain's cognitive architecture and society. An individual who grows up in an Asian society that emphasizes collectivism and holistic thinking will have her cognitive preferences shaped by that environment. That person will then become part of that society, perpetuating those patterns.

Shinobu Kitayama explains it this way: "Public patterns of behavior, over a number of repeated occurrences, are likely to cause systematic changes in neural connectivity of the brain. It is thus reasonable to hypothesize that recurrent, active, and long-term engagement in scripted behavioral sequences (what we call cultural practices or tasks) can powerfully shape and modify brain pathways."[31] Culture shapes cognitive processes, which help integrate that individual into the cultural community that, in turn, shapes the next generation in an ongoing evolutionary dynamic.

Parental Ethnotheories

My wife—who was raised in Japan—was sent away to live and work on an organic farm from age twelve to eighteen. This wasn't punishment for errant behavior, but part of an attempt by her parents to provide an alternative education for their children. In high school, instead of academic subjects, she went every day to the fields, and her graduation project involved taking care of 14,000 tomato plants. Her parents disagreed with many of the values they saw prevalent in Japanese society, and got some of their unconventional thinking from American ideas about parenting. Of particular interest was the idea that a child should be treated as a unique individual. They were trying to instill a sense of individualism and independence by choosing this educational option.

They did other things to instill individualism. My mother-in-law decided to teach her young daughter to become independent by not immediately picking her up if she cried when put to bed. She even told neighbors not to worry if they heard her baby crying. In Japan at the time, the idea of a mother intentionally separating herself from her child, and not picking it up when it cried, was unconventional. Some might even feel it was akin to child abuse. My wife's family, however, decided to educate their children with values they thought were better than those of society at large.

This experiment in unconventional values raises interesting questions. How do children absorb the cultural lessons of the larger community, and what is the role of parenting? To what degree can parents choose the values they pass on to their children? Do parents pass on cultural values that are so taken-for-granted that they don't notice them? How does that happen? If culture operates at unconscious levels of self, then we must pass our culture on largely in ways that we are unaware of. For her part, my wife ended up being comfortable functioning in Japanese society, but she also has a strongly developed sense of independence and individual self. It would seem that her parents' experiment was a success.

One way to understand how cultural patterns are passed on from generation to generation is through the study of *parental ethnotheories*. These are largely unconscious mental models, held by parents, that are related to children and parenting—assumptions about what a child needs in order to develop, the proper role of the parent, and so on.[32] They are seen as the "natural" or "right" way for parents to act, and serve as ideals that guide parents in caring for their children. One study of such parental ethnotheories took data from the International Baby Study and compared ideas about caretaking among parents in the United States, the Netherlands, with additional data from Spain, Italy, and Korea. Researchers observed parents taking care of their children, interviewed them about childcare, and had them record their parenting activities in diaries. The goal of the research was to uncover implicit cultural attitudes and assumptions that parents took for granted.

Researchers found that parents in different countries expressed quite different attitudes about what constitutes good parenting, and that these ideals had a profound impact on the way they treated their children.[33] For example, American parents overwhelmingly felt that a baby's most important developmental need was stimulation. As one American mother says:

> I think he needs to be warm, to be fed, to be clean, dry, that kind of thing, but I also think he definitely needs some stimulation. There are times when he is in a chair and we're not paying attention to him or, you know . . . he needs some stimulation, something of interest to look at, something to, you know, just for him to play with.[34]

On the other hand, Italian mothers spoke about their child's development in terms of relationships, emotional development, and closeness. As one mother said:

I don't think he likes being alone, at least now, maybe because he gets bored . . . and also because he is used to having me or other people around talking to him: aunt, grandpa or this woman who takes care of my father. There's always somebody talking to him, perhaps he's more used to seeing faces than to playing. . . . He has so much fun when somebody talks to him, puts him on the couch, plays with him, or on his bed. . . . When he's in the mood, he has more fun than with his toys![35]

Italian mothers tended to look at their child's development in terms of social interaction, as opposed to the American parents who saw it in terms of cognitive capacities. It seems that from the point of view of the Italian ethnotheory, no amount of social interaction is too much—indeed, babies are seen to thrive on it. For the Americans, on the other hand, a baby is treated more like a budding thinker in need of mental challenge. In line with this, another cross-cultural study showed that Italian children expressed more affect (emotion) in their pretend play than American children. For their part, American children showed slightly more imagination in theirs.

In contrast to Italian and American parents, Dutch parents spoke at great length of the need for regular routines and getting enough sleep. This fits with a Dutch maxim about the need for the "three Rs" of childcare—*rust* (rest), *regelmaat* (regularity), and *reinheid* (cleanliness). Parents put a great deal of energy into providing their young children with a regular schedule that included plenty of rest, with the assumption that this would make them cheerful, calm, and self-regulated. Whereas American parents thought of their child's sleep patterns as being a simple result of biological needs, the Dutch parents saw sleep as a developmental tool.

Interestingly, when American parents talked about schedules and sleep, it was more often in the context of struggling with the innate sleep needs of their child, as when children wouldn't sleep through the night: "Now usually he wakes up around 4:30 a.m. and he's hanging on to the headboard, jumping up and down. So finally at 5:00 a.m., I get up." Dutch parents seemed to have few problems managing their children's sleep and emphasized the need for regularity. As one Dutch parent said, "To bed on time, because they really need rest to grow, and regularity is very important when they are so little. If she gets too little rest, she is very fussy."[36] Tellingly, at six months, the Dutch babies slept an average of fifteen hours per day compared to thirteen hours for American parents. Dutch babies were also more often left to play quietly in their playpens or infant seats.

This research shows how deeply ingrained attitudes towards parenting are. (It also shows that behavior that might seem to be fundamentally biological, such as how long babies sleep, may be more affected by environmental factors than we might imagine.) While these studies provide an interesting glimpse of cultural differences in parenting, they don't answer the question of how parents learned these mental models. Ethnotheories seem to be absorbed unconsciously in the course of growing up and living in a society, and reflect implicit cultural values in the broader society.

Research is also being done on how cultural differences in parenting and culture affect the cognitive and emotional development of children. One study looked, for example, at cultural and family influences on children's development of *theory of mind*, the ability to understand that other people have intentions and beliefs distinct from one's own. It found that Iranian and Australian children had different levels of development for particular aspects of theory of mind, although their overall scores were equivalent. Australian children showed a more developed understanding of the diversity of beliefs and desires, whereas Iranian children had a more developed sense of sarcasm and what is known as *knowledge access*—the ability to understand that, for example, someone who hasn't looked inside a box doesn't know what's inside it.

Such research is still in its early stages, but we are starting to see how parental attitudes and cultural factors shape us at an early age. Parental ethnotheories are, of course, largely invisible to the parents themselves. American parents who assume that a child needs cognitive stimulation believe these needs are universal to all children. The same is true for Dutch parents who assume that children's sleep needs to be regulated. I am struck by the differences found among cultural communities—the Dutch and Americans, for example—that might otherwise be considered relatively culturally close. It makes me wonder what we'd find out by comparing Tibetans, Turks, and Trinidadians. I assume that a broader study would reveal an enormous variety of values and assumptions held about parenting around the world.

Passing on Deep Cultural Values

Cultural values are more than a set of moral or ethical priorities and principles. They also shape interaction and provide expectations that help manage human relations. Collectivism and individualism, for example, can be seen as two contrasting unconscious assumptions about whether the common good is best served by (1) each individual being responsible for herself and thus contributing to collective well-being, or (2) a shared responsibility for each individual within a collective.[37] Cultural values can be seen to rest on hidden, unconscious assumptions. Thus, they emerge from, and contribute to, particular styles of interaction. Different starting assumptions leads to differing values, which in turn leads to divergent social practices and priorities.

If, for example, the common good is assumed to require individuals taking personal responsibility for themselves—an unspoken tenet of individualist thinking—then creating independence and self-reliance becomes a priority. In contrast, if the common good is seen primarily as shared responsibility for each other—an unspoken tenet of collectivist thinking—then close social ties will be prioritized. Seen in this way, *cultural values do not reside primarily within individuals as a set of explicit notions. Rather, they act as implicit guidelines that shape interaction and collaboration between members of a community.* This view of cultural values would seem to predict, then, that we learn values not through maxims or explicit instructions, but through relationships and interaction. In effect, the structure of human relations provides us with a sense of what is valued and prioritized.

Research by Sheena Iyengar provides a glimpse of how contrasting cultural values shape relationships between children and their parents.[38] In order to test the impact of cultural values on motivation in children, she had a group of Anglo American and Asian American children do word puzzles. Under one set of conditions, children were allowed to choose which puzzles they wanted to do, as well as the pens they wanted to use. Under another set of conditions, children were told that their mothers had chosen the puzzles. There was also a third, neutral set of conditions, under which the children were told that the researcher, Ms. Smith, had chosen the puzzles. Can you guess which condition motivated the children more?

You may guess that American children were more highly motivated when they chose the puzzles themselves. You would be right—they completed three times as many. When told that their mothers had chosen which puzzles to work on, they performed much more poorly, with one child even exclaiming incredulously, "You *asked my mother?*" Clearly, the Anglo American children resisted having to follow someone else's choice—even their mother's.

The Asian American children, however, scored quite differently. When they chose themselves which puzzles to solve, they scored nearly as high as the Anglo

American children. But when told their mothers had chosen the puzzles, they scored even higher, completing nearly four times as many puzzles as the Anglo American children under the same conditions. How can we explain this? Iyengar proposes that Asian American children identify more closely with their parents—they don't see themselves as existing separately and in opposition to their parents, but rather as being cared for by them and intimately connected to them. In short, they implicitly trust and want to please their mothers, feeling intuitively that they know and do what's best for them.

This research highlights how cultural values are internalized through our interactions with others—in this case, through the relationship between parents and their children. The Asian American children were developing what is sometimes called an *interdependent self*, an identity formed in relation to others—something typical of more collectivist societies. The Anglo American children, on the other hand, felt the need to separate from their parents in order to feel self-actualized, typical of an *independent* construal of self.[39] The parents of these children didn't plan it this way, of course. American parents don't instruct their children to resist guidance that they might give, nor do Asian parents tell their children that independence isn't important. Children are shaped by the interactive patterns they are exposed to, and the relationships they must navigate as they grow up.

This helps explain why we are largely oblivious to culture's role in shaping our values and relationships. It also implies that measuring cultural values will be quite difficult, as they rest on unspoken assumptions. Recently, I found an example of this in data from the World Values Survey.[40] One item, which asked what qualities were important when raising children, found that only 23 percent of Americans emphasized the need to encourage children to be independent, compared to 29 percent of Japanese and 47 percent of Chinese. On the face of it, this seems like a contradiction. If Japanese and Chinese societies tend towards collectivist values, and the US is supposed to emphasize individualism, why wouldn't Americans emphasize independence more strongly?

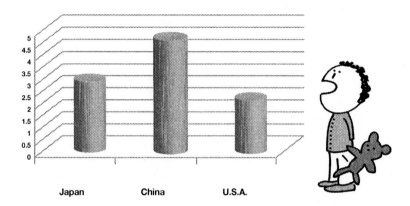

Importance of encouraging children to be independent

Figure 6-4

I suspect it's because the Chinese and Japanese parents take strong social bonds more for granted than American parents, and thus tend to value independence as a sign of maturity. American children, on the other hand, are socialized to be more individualistic from a young age, and parents don't feel the need to emphasize it. On the contrary, American parents may be so used to seeing their children express their individual self that they'd like them to learn to be more cooperative. Simply asking parents what values they want to pass on to their children may miss the largely unconscious cultural values that they take for granted.

Configuration and the Intercultural Mind

The research we've seen provides evidence of a very deep kind of cultural configuration—one that is built into people's worldviews and is easily overlooked by the individual. Obama's thumb gesture during his debate was most likely unconscious, performed automatically in accordance with his unique personality, but also related to cultural values he absorbed as a child. This is a reminder that our individual development necessarily happens within the context of our social and cultural community. As we've seen, we gain vast stores of tacit cultural knowledge that help us communicate with and understand others. We have also seen that culture has fractal qualities, exists at many levels of abstraction, and is passed on largely unconsciously through human interaction.

All of this paints quite a complicated picture of the relationship between culture and the individual, one that takes us beyond simple dichotomies—such as "nature vs. nurture." Nature and nurture are intertwined and inseparable. This view is supported by a growing body of research related to what is called *dual inheritance theory*. This refers to the notion that "Certain genotypes may predispose people to create particular features in their environment, thus influencing cultural selection. . . . Concurrently, aspects of the broader culture may act as environmental pressures that ultimately affect genetic selection."[41] Put more simply, genetic factors may affect culture, and culture may have an impact on our genetic makeup.

One straightforward example of this is the development of lactose tolerance—an increased ability to digest milk—among communities that keep cattle. Cultural and genetic factors are intertwined and depend on each other. This effect extends to the realm of mind as well. A large body of research "points to psychiatric symptoms such as depression and anxiety as a result of certain interaction between genes and social or environmental factors. Yet, a significant source of environmental influences is culture, raising the possibility that cultural influences might also vary as a function of particular genes."[42] In other words, genes may predispose particular populations for particular forms of cultural community. One gene that has been pointed out as potentially important in terms of cultural evolution is the dopamine D4 receptor gene. More prevalent in Asian communities, it may have played a role in the development of collectivist values and interdependent thinking.[43]

My point in bringing up such specialized research is simply to highlight some of the profound questions about human nature that intercultural experiences can raise. As Shinobu Kitayama, a pioneer in cultural psychology, states, "It has become increasingly sensible to conceptualize human nature as interactions between genes, environment and the brain."[44]

The research we've seen here, as well as intercultural experiences themselves, reminds us, above all, that human nature is complex and the interface between biology and culture is still not fully understood. They also help us see that the influence of culture on the cognition and values of any given individual is diffuse—and thus not easy to measure or describe. It seems clear, however, that these patterns are found at a very deep level of self. This depth renders such influence largely invisible, but provides our intercultural experiences with a rich potential for subtle discovery.

KEY CONCEPTS

Embodied culture: *Language, culture, and cognition are not phenomena that occur only in some abstract realm of informational patterns. They are not cut off from our physical and emotional states. Language and culture are embodied—integrated with and involving the whole organism.*

The fractal quality of culture: *Cultural patterns are reflected at different scales of analysis, from the micro level of the brain to the more macro level of everyday social practices, all the way to the highly abstract level of social structures and philosophical traditions.*

Parental ethnotheories: *The largely unconscious cultural models that parents hold related to children and parenting—assumptions about what a child needs to develop, the proper role of the parent, and so on.*

Discussion Quote: *Cultural values are more than a set of moral or ethical priorities and principles. They also shape interaction and provide expectations that help manage human relations.*

7.

the architecture of bias

Don't judge the gravity. Each planet has its own way of
regulating the ecosystem.

—Heeyeon

We have the impression that when we go abroad, we are objective observers. Yet our reactions and interpretations are subjective, influenced by cultural conditioning and subject to mental shortcuts and bias. Being mindful of these tendencies helps us get more out of intercultural experiences.

Like It Used to Be in the States

On her first visit to Japan, I took my mother to the retro-modern Tokyo Tower, the Edo museum, with its walk-through diorama of a feudal-era Tokyo neighborhood, and the swarming maze of Shinjuku station—a human beehive used by 3.5 million passengers *per day*. We saw pachinko parlors with flashing lights and clanging cascades of shiny metal balls, as well as the pebbled walkways and sculpted gardens at the Meiji Shrine. Nothing impressed her more, however, than the table service she received at dinner on one of her first evenings here.

The Japanese wait staff called out a greeting *irasshaimasse* (Welcome!) the moment we stepped in the door. Menus were placed gently in front of each diner (not passed out like a deck of cards). Unlike in California, there was no chitchat with the waiter. ("Hi, I'm Justin. How are you folks doing today?") A nod was enough to get the server's attention, and he held his free hand behind his back while pouring the wine. Each stage of the meal had corresponding honorific phrases, such as *Go yukkuri dozo* (Enjoy leisurely), or *O sage shitemo yoroshii deshoka?* (May I do the honorable clearing of the table?)

Impressed, at the end of the meal my mother asked about leaving a tip. I told her if we left money on the table, staff would come after us to return it. She was effusive in her praise. Searching for words to describe her impressions, she proclaimed, "The service is wonderful in Japan. It's so dignified . . . just like it used to be in the States."

Reporting the Facts

Everything we see and experience abroad is interpreted through the filter of our previous life experiences. We use that filter to make sense of things—to turn an event into a meaningful experience. Often, however, we don't notice this interpretive process.[1] My mother, for example, probably felt that she was simply reporting the facts about what she witnessed. She wouldn't have felt that she was passing judgment or coming to idiosyncratic conclusions. Unavoidably, however, her impressions about service in Japan were not a simple reportage. They were a personal interpretation based on her particular point of view.

Perhaps the actions of the wait staff in Japan activated memories of her mother, who was born in 1885 and was quite proper. My grandma Kerrigan believed in etiquette: *Use the outside fork first. Put the napkin on your lap before beginning. Wipe the bottom of your spoon on the back edge of your soup bowl.* It's not hard to see why my mother saw restaurant service in Japan as a throwback to another era in the United States—one characterized by more formality and concern for public decorum. These associations were not wrong, of course, but neither were they objective in any scientific sense. The subjectivity of cultural interpretations calls to mind the words of Milton Bennett, who I have heard saying, in one of my favorite quotes: "An American tourist in Tokyo is not having a Japanese experience; he is having an American experience in Japan."

While we may *feel* we are simply witnessing and reporting, sojourners tell stories that are full of judgments. We have a powerful tendency to take the difference we find personally—as though someone has asked us to grade the behavior of the locals and give them a report card. Listen to Andy's reaction to a perceived attack on one of his favorite foods:

> In America I always loved pizza. Thick crust, tomato sauce, loads of cheese, and maybe some pepperoni or peppers on top. A dorm full of guys could order and each receive a fourteen-inch, one-topping pizza for five dollars. In Japan, I went searching for this beloved food, and was astonished at what I found. Thirty-centimeter pizzas for four thousand yen?! Corn, mayo, and tuna? Gross! I felt that Japan had bastardized my favorite food, and wanted to charge me an arm and a leg for the monstrosity.

Andy's rant is a partially tongue-in-cheek reminder that reactions to difference are necessarily subjective. The pizza that Andy saw as normal was, in fact, simply what he was used to. Pizza was imported to the United States, as it was to Japan. Andy wasn't complaining that pizza in Japan wasn't *authentic*—something an Italian might more understandably feel. His sense of what a pizza should be was grounded in his direct experience—a reminder that our interpretive systems often create the impression that what is familiar is *normal*, and that what is normal is *right*.

Figure 7-1

Making Sense

Making sense of foreign experiences is a core challenge of cultural learning, so an awareness of our cultural subjectivity is important for developing an intercultural mind. That's not easy, though, because our common sense tells us that we see things "as they are" and that our own conclusions are unbiased. Bias, after all, is considered a sign of prejudice or narrow-mindedness, and the word *ethnocentrism*, which refers to the tendency to judge things from our own cultural perspective, sounds overwhelmingly negative. While most people recognize that they are not completely objective in all things, we tend to trust our own judgments and find our perspective reasonable.

A closer look at cognition, however, reveals that our confidence in our own judgments is largely misplaced.[2] Subjectivity and bias, far from being a sign of limitation, are normal parts of our cognitive functioning. Our eyes are not cameras that simply record images for later retrieval, and our minds are not encyclopedias from which we can simply pull out facts and knowledge. Our mental processes did not evolve in order to reach painstaking empirical conclusions about the external world—that's the goal of the scientific method. Instead, they developed the ability to think quickly and accurately enough to ensure our survival.

As research illuminates hidden cognitive processes, we are having to accept that normal cognition involves mental shortcuts and a reliance on faulty intuitive judgments. For example, we are unconsciously affected by our mental and emotional states and overgeneralize from our own experience. We assume bad things about others and good things about ourselves, while judging outsiders harshly. We are comforted by the familiar and habitually interpret things in our own favor.[3] From the perspective of cognitive neuroscience, bias is so pervasive in our interpretive processes that it's reasonable to call it a structural feature rather than a flaw.

The fact that bias is natural doesn't, of course, make it desirable—cancer and heart disease are natural too. And not everyone is culturally biased to an equal degree. Certain people will naturally be more empathetic and open-minded while others will be more prejudiced and narrow-minded. And while it's true that travel, education, and a multicultural background can make people more cosmopolitan, tolerant, and open to difference, even open-minded people will react negatively to cultural difference sometimes. Andy's reaction to Japanese pizza was not a reasoned conclusion based on a thoughtful analysis of cultural culinary trends—it was a gut reaction: *They put mayonnaise on pizza?* With that in mind, let's look at some of the pitfalls we face when trying to make sense of foreign experiences.

Heuristics

Intercultural settings are full of ambiguity. For obvious evolutionary reasons, our brain doesn't like loose ends or unexplained phenomena. (Unfamiliar things are more likely to be threats.) Our intuitions favor quick answers that make sense based on previous experience. This desire for coherence—a *coherence bias*—is so strong, however, that we not only fill in blanks; we may ignore contrary information, jump to conclusions, or take other mental shortcuts.[4] To get a sense for how this works, read the following three sentences:

Martha came home late.
Ted was angry.
Ted decided to watch TV.

Most likely, these three sentences created a story in your head. You may assume that Ted was angry about Martha coming home late and responded by pouting in front of the TV—perhaps a whole scenario played out in your mind. But that's not what those sentences say. They are simply three statements of fact—it was you who filled in the gaps to create a coherent narrative. Reading that Martha came home late creates the impression that this caused Ted's anger. But Ted might have been angry already, about something else, or maybe Ted doesn't even live with Martha.

The tendency for the mind to take such shortcuts is referred to as *heuristics*. Heuristics can be a problem across cultures because the easiest interpretations—such as, "The people in this country are lazy!"—may be ethnocentric. Different types of heuristics include the *availability heuristic* (a tendency towards explanations that easily come to mind) and the *familiarity heuristic* (assuming that the circumstances of past behavior holds true for our current situation). Social psychologists also talk about the *representativeness heuristic*—the tendency to judge based on prototypes we have in our mind.[5] These heuristics make it easy for our intuitive mind to make fast, loose, generally accurate judgments. Unfortunately, they may short-circuit the intuitive learning process. Once our attentive mind endorses these sort of interpretations, they can easily become the default interpretation.

Familiarity Bias

Our mind has a love/hate relationship with novelty. The new and exotic stimulates us and piques our curiosity—it's why we love travel and foreign adventure in the first place. At the same time, the unconscious machinery of interpretation and judgment is, broadly speaking, biased against the unfamiliar. Interpretations of events that are familiar to us come to mind easily—the *availability heuristic*. In effect, it takes more mental energy to form a new set of conclusions than it does to simply call upon previously developed patterns—which makes it easy to jump to hasty conclusions.[6]

In line with this, magnetic imaging research suggests that we use different areas of the brain when reasoning about familiar and unfamiliar situations.[7] This bias towards the familiar manifests itself in a variety of ways. The *mere exposure effect* refers to the intuitive mind's tendency to positively evaluate things that we have previous experience with, even if we have no conscious memory of that experience. In one typical study, psychologist Robert Zajonc exposed subjects to meaningless Chinese characters, some more frequently than others. Told that the characters represented adjectives, participants were asked to guess whether the symbols had positive or negative connotations. Not only were the most frequently seen characters rated as more positive, subjects who had been repeatedly exposed to these characters reported being in a better mood.[8]

Zajonc believes this result reflects the basic need of all organisms to be cautious when experiencing novelty. From an evolutionary perspective, it makes sense that a familiar stimulus should be experienced more positively since familiarity implies previous safe encounters. To test this hypothesis, he exposed unhatched chicken eggs to two different tones. After hatching, chicks made fewer distress sounds when they heard the tone they had been exposed to before hatching.

Another way in which we are biased towards the familiar is related to the degree of strain a task has on the attention and resources of our mind. We experience *cognitive ease* when doing familiar tasks in a non-threatening environment. It's associated with fluent processing by the intuitive mind, little need for active attention, positive mood, and a lack of perceptual interference. We experience *cognitive strain*, on the other hand, when a task requires active attention and problem solving. Cognitive strain also occurs when you are in a bad mood or are faced with uncertainty, ambiguity, or unfamiliarity. You become vigilant and more suspicious. As you start to feel uncomfortable, you become less intuitive than usual. Familiarity increases our cognitive ease, and novelty and uncertainty increases cognitive strain. You can experience the difference simply by reading the two sentences below:

The novelty of travel creates increased cognitive strain.
The familiarity of home creates more cognitive ease.

Reading the first font—it's called Braggadocio—requires more attention and thus reduces cognitive ease. The second font, the more familiar Arial, costs us less cognitive energy to process. This highlights the fact that attention is a limited cognitive resource; when cognitive strain becomes too great, we feel tired, irritable, and overwhelmed.

Daniel Kahneman calls the attentive mind—he uses the term *System 2*—the *lazy system* because it seeks to conserve its limited resources.[9] The idea that our mind has resources is not simply a metaphor. Our brain depends on glucose for energy, and when exerting ourselves mentally, we deplete our supply. Replenishing glucose has been shown to improve cognitive performance after activities that deplete the attentive mind, such as suppressing emotion. Disturbingly, judges have been shown to approve more parole requests just after lunch, when they were more focused.[10] Once we are mentally tired, we tend to revert to default judgments—in this case, denial of the prisoners' requests.

Needless to say, foreign experiences place high cognitive demands on travelers and often lead to *ego depletion*—the negative judgments and irritability that comes from too much cognitive strain. Wandering the streets of New Delhi for a few hours can overload anyone not conditioned to a similar environment. One of my students, Sayuri, for example, says: "I visited some towns and met many local Indians. There are a lot of things that are [very] different from Japan. Many cows, dogs, beggars, garbage on the street, curious people, always delaying train. . . . At first, it was new and interesting for me. But gradually it became [stressful]."

If you find yourself in such highly stimulating situations, be sure to monitor your mental and emotional state. The food stands that seemed charming and exotic at first may lose their appeal. You will become increasingly distrustful and impatient, and less willing to give people the benefit of the doubt. Many travelers feel this cognitive fatigue at some point during a trip. You'll find plenty of presumably adventurous backpacker travelers in exotic places such as Kathmandu and Bangkok . . . downing pizzas and hamburgers. I'm sure they feel a rising tide of cognitive ease as the familiar food is set before them and as the glucose hits their brains.

I tell sojourners that the best defense against the negative reactions that come from ego depletion and cognitive strain is simply not to overtax your mental systems. International business travelers are sometimes guilty of overscheduling themselves and missing meals. Backpackers may seek an authentic experience and feel that eating familiar food or seeking physical comfort is a form of selling out. Expatriate employees may try to "hit the ground running" only to become crabby and burned out. Their cognitive strain may contribute to critical judgments about the locals, which can degenerate into cynicism. If you find yourself in any of these settings, remind yourself that an intercultural mind requires that our mental systems don't operate too far beyond capacity. Sometimes the best way to move forward is to slow down.

Ingroup Coherence

The raiders arrived at night, having darkened their skin "commando style." *Rattler* boys invaded the cabin of the sleeping *Eagle* boys, turning beds over and ripping mosquito netting, taunting their enemy to come out and fight. Mason, the leader of the Eagles, jumped out of bed to try and rouse the others, but they mostly sat stunned. Earlier the Eagles had won the tug-of-war, but the Rattlers groused that the Eagle tactics were unfair and planned for revenge.

Relations between the two groups had been deteriorating. During their first days at Robbers Cave Camp, the two hadn't even known about each other, since they stayed at opposite sides of the campground. Once they found out, however, each set of boys had become increasingly pack-like. They became competitive—each belittling and challenging the other group. When organizers set up a tournament, the animosity escalated.

The conflict between the Eagles and Rattlers may sound like typical pre-adolescent hijinks, but the whole drama was played out under the watchful eye of psychologist Muzafer Sherif as part of a research program at the University of Oklahoma in 1954.[11] Two groups of boys took part in a summer camp that was actually a psychology experiment. Sherif wanted to learn about how groups are formed, how conflict between groups develops, and how it can be overcome.

One important finding was that the two groups quickly developed a competitive animosity *even before they had met*. No actual competition was necessary for a feeling of competiveness to emerge. This suggests that social cohesion within a group can create the conditions for denigration of a different group. In the experiment, the boys spontaneously chose a name for themselves and made flags. They became territorial regarding shared facilities. Though all the boys were from the same age range, race, and social class, members of one group saw the others as cheating enemies, called them names, such as *stinkers* and *sissies*, each feeling that the other group needed to be taught a lesson. Organizers tried improving relations by bringing the boys together in getting-to-know-you activities, like the showing of a film or bean-gathering. This didn't work. In the end, the researchers were able to create good relations between the two groups only after presenting superordinate problems—such as trouble with a water tank—that required the efforts of both groups to solve.

This research highlights the sometimes surprising power of *social cohesion*. Humans have a natural desire to interact with others and form unified social communities. Bruce Wexler, a research scientist in psychiatry, explains that:

> People selectively affiliate with like-minded individuals, and forget and discredit views and information inconsistent with their existing beliefs. On the level of subjective experience, people like things

more simply because they have seen them more and they more closely match established internal representations. Because of this, individuals generally try to surround themselves with familiar objects and people, and resist intrusions of foreign elements into their environment.[12]

This desire for coherence leads us to tune in and adapt to the mental and emotional states of others and take on the opinions of others as our own. In another classic experiment, Sherif brought test subjects into a dark room in which there was a single point of light projected on the wall.[13] In this situation, because the eye has no frame of reference, the point of light appears to move (the *autokinetic effect*). Participants were asked to guess how far it was moving and each settled on their best guess, which ranged from twenty to eighty centimeters. Yet when these same people were brought together and asked to guess as a group, the guesses converged on a common point—individuals adapted their guesses to the opinions of others. Participants were not, however, consciously aware of this process. This demonstrates the common tendency to adopt collective attitudes and judgments—what social psychologists refer to as *conformity*.[14]

Adapting to the perceptions of others is natural. It is a normal part of social relations that allows us to stay in tune with the mental states of the people around us. (Imagine if it *weren't* that way!) When we travel, our desire for conformity and social cohesion motivates us to follow local customs, which helps explain why many would be horrified if they inadvertently did something to give offense when abroad. Yet a desire for coherence doesn't always work in our favor. It can lead to exclusivity, as immigrants congregate in particular neighborhoods, expatriates frequent the same bars, and travelers quickly form connections with their compatriots when on vacation, reinforcing their cultural judgments by spending time with people with a similar background. For years I worked on university entrance exam committees split nearly evenly between Japanese and American/British professors. At meetings we all worked together, but at break time there was an inexorable tendency for people to clump together in groups of compatriots, despite the fact that everyone was bilingual and quite international.

It's easy to overlook the degree to which we need other people and how automatic it is to create social bonds. Many people think of excluding outsiders—including prejudice and discrimination—as fundamentally *learned* sets of attitudes or behaviors. The human tendency to identify with those around us is, however, a foundational element of our evolutionary psychology. Unconscious distrust of difference is so basic to us, in fact, that researchers find we even tend to distrust information given to us by non-native speakers of our language.[15] This, and the other biases we've seen, suggests that anyone interacting in foreign environments is subject to any number of limitations and barriers, which many of us never become consciously aware of.

Unconscious Bias, Associations, and Stereotypes

In addition to our natural tendency to favor the familiar, our attitudes towards foreign experiences are shaped by unconscious associations—in effect, our unconscious mind remembers experiences that our attentive mind does not. In a famous experiment from 1911, the Swiss neurologist and psychologist Édouard Claparède was researching memory with a patient who suffered from short-term amnesia. She recalled her past but couldn't form new memories, such that each time Claparède met her, he had to introduce himself all over again. On one occasion, he hid a tack in his palm when they shook hands, giving her a painful prick. The following day, although the patient had no conscious memory of Claparède, she refused to shake hands with him, despite being unable to explain her resistance.[16]

Patient later refuses handshake despite no conscious memory

Claparède pricks amnesia patient when shaking hands

Figure 7-2

In a sense, we are all like Claparède's poor patient. Throughout our lifetimes we accumulate implicit memories about all manner of things. These associations then influence our later reactions, even if we aren't aware of where they originate. If you pass food to a Saudi friend using your left hand, he may need to suppress a disgust response, since in Saudi Arabia the left hand is associated with using the toilet. In Thailand, if you sit in front of a temple, you should be careful not to point your feet towards the altar, as the feet are associated with defilement. These sorts of negative associations also explain why many Westerners find the idea of eating dog meat disgusting, though it's not so rare in Korea.

Kanchana, from Thailand, says of her stay in the United States: "The [praying] before the meal was not as [shocking] as when they let their dog lick the plates we finished before putting them in the dishwasher. The first moment I was so [shocked]!" It was relatively easy for her to feel good about different customs regarding praying—something with positive associations—but dogs, which are seen on the streets in Thailand, are considered dirty and rarely allowed inside. Likewise, in the Middle East, to call someone a dog is a powerful insult, so seeing Americans allow dogs in their homes, on their furniture, and even *on their beds* can provoke genuine disgust.

In addition to such implicit associations, our mind also relies on existing schema to make sense of novel phenomena. We easily fall back on simple and accessible schema—stereotypes. Stereotypes exist in every society because categorization comes so naturally to us. They also exist because we often lack a detailed understanding of foreign people and places, and thus can only call to mind simple images to refer to or make sense of them. Most travelers, at one point or another, run into stereotypes that people in foreign countries have towards them. Those categories may be positive (*French people are sophisticated!*), have a grain of truth to them (*Italians talk with their hands*), or prejudicial (*Elbonians are dishonest*).

Much of the research into stereotyping and bias is done in the United States in the context of race relations, and the use of stereotypes is commonly associated with racial prejudice.[17] From a cognitive perspective, however, stereotyping is a form of categorization—using existing mental drawers to organize our experiences or make sense of something. Travelers often come across simple schema in the form of seemingly naïve statements—Australians are asked about kangaroos and Germans hear comments about Oktoberfest and beer. In Mexico, I told someone I lived in Japan, and she replied, "Everyone knows karate there, right?" I have heard of a Kenyan asking a Japanese, "In your country, do people eat goats or keep them as pets?" If goats are a ubiquitous part of life, and you are accustomed to thinking of them as either food or pets, it may be hard to conceptualize a place that is different. Stereotypes about faraway people and places are unavoidable. The danger, however, is that negative stereotypes can hijack the interpretations of our experiences. In other words, we don't take the time to think things through because certain associations are so readily available. In such cases, we don't *feel* that we are jumping to conclusions based on faulty premises, but we do because certain answers come to mind quickly and with little cognitive effort. In this way, negative stereotypes can shape our interpretations without us noticing.

I found this tendency in David, a commercial airline flight instructor. I was interviewing him about cultural difference he encountered in his work training commercial pilots from different countries. The interpretations of behavior he witnessed seemed to lean, for example, on stereotypes about Asians "not valuing human life." He told stories to "prove" how true this was, talking about, for example, Chinese trainees who made poor decisions in critical situations. One Chinese trainee, for example, insisted on trying to land at an airport that was fogged in, even though he hadn't been trained for it. Instead of guessing that perhaps this particular student showed poor judgment, David constructed an interpretation that leaned heavily on stereotypes:

> Never fly with those people. They just don't understand anything, not even what can hurt. I mean if you fly into terrain, it's gonna hurt. They don't get it. They don't understand it. It's just like they have no clue what can happen. [It's] indoctrination . . . they have no survival instinct—from what I felt in the training.

David would probably deny that he was being influenced by stereotypes. Probably, however, the idea that Asians lack respect for human life was an image that he had picked up unconsciously, and it worked its way into his interpretive schema.[18]

Neuroscience has given us new tools to research such hidden bias. Brain imaging, for example, is used to research stereotypes and social identity threat.[19] Another common tool to study hidden bias is *implicit association testing* (IAT). IAT measures the amount of time it takes our unconscious mind to assign images to different mental categories. It is premised on the understanding that frequently used neural networks are more accessible—they light up more easily—than those we use rarely.

IAT uncovers negative associations about people of different races or body types. A participant might, for example, be asked to sort negative words and positive words, like "danger" and "caring," together with white or black faces. Unconscious bias would be found if it took longer for participants to categorize positive words with black faces as compared to white faces. This would show that at the level of their unconscious associations, "black" = "negative." These kinds of biases are widespread but can be hard to interpret. A significant percentage of blacks, for example, also have negative associations with black skin.[20] Some research has shown, however, that IAT can successfully predict behavior, such as how implicit racial bias affects election outcomes.[21] Researchers are also trying to predict who might injure themselves or attempt suicide by testing for the unconscious associations between self and injury.[22] Not only are we sometimes unaware of unconscious bias, it's not unusual for our conscious values to conflict with unconscious attitudes.[23] The important lesson is: *We may genuinely believe that humans everywhere are equal, yet still respond negatively to cultural, ethnic, or racial difference.*

Recent research suggests that negative associations and stereotypes should be thought of as separate kinds of mental processing.[24] This implies that overcoming implicit bias and going beyond stereotypes may require different strategies. The psychologist David Amodio suggests that getting over unconscious biases involves a form of humanizing the threatening other, and that social interaction may accomplish this. Stereotypes, on the other hand, require a form of self-regulation—we need to be aware of our own tendency to think in stereotypical terms.[25] Amodio's suggestion for guarding against stereotypes matches my experience as well. When we have limited experience with a foreign environment, our mind naturally relies on simple perceptual categories. But once we become aware of that tendency, we can consciously examine our own stereotypes in light of our experiences. A traveler who went to Morocco told me that he was aware of his own ignorance of Islam, and of negative stereotypes about Muslims he had been exposed to in the United States. He said he looked at his trip to North Africa as a way of moving beyond those simple notions and negative images. He made a conscious decision to open his mind to novel ways of seeing. This sort of meta-cognition helps us avoid stereotypical thinking, and makes us aware of the most pervasive cultural bias of all—ethnocentrism.

Ethnocentrism

Ethnocentrism refers broadly to *judging another culture by the standards of one's own culture*. Ethnocentrism relates to how we interpret the world; it is the cultural lens that we use to make sense of our experience. Ethnocentrism is a natural outcome of our reliance on previous experience to interpret current phenomena. As Anaïs Nin has been quoted as saying, "We don't see things as they are; we see them as we are." Ethnocentrism may also involve prejudicial attitudes towards outsiders, stereotypical thinking, and ingroup bias—more favorable attitudes towards people who are perceived as being similar to oneself.

Ethnocentrism is such a natural part of how our mind works that it's somewhat misleading to call it a bias. Until we have intercultural experiences, it's difficult to even become aware of our cultural worldview. Consider these quotes taken from a survey of dissatisfied customers by a travel agency:

> "There are too many Spanish people. The receptionist speaks Spanish. The food is Spanish. Too many foreigners now live abroad."

> "I think it should be explained in the brochure that the local store does not sell proper biscuits like custard creams or ginger nuts."

> "On my holiday to Goa in Indi, I was disgusted to find that almost every restaurant served curry. I don't like spicy food at all."[26]

These quotes show a narrowness of vision that is familiar to all of us. The first person is dismayed to find so many *foreigners* in Spain—when in fact in Spain *this tourist* is the foreigner. This inability to shift cultural frames of reference is at the core of ethnocentrism. We see the situation from our own perspective and can't put ourselves in the perceptual shoes of cultural others. Ethnocentrism creates an *inability to empathize* as a result of cultural difference. Foreigners seem, well, *foreign*, and we have trouble seeing things from their point of view.

Anyone who has traveled or lived elsewhere knows that we are *all* guilty of this kind of thinking to some degree. The first memory I have of discovering my own ethnocentrism occurred while living in Mexico. I had grown up with the idea that people all over the world wanted to come to the United States as the land of opportunity. Living in Mexico, however, I regularly met people who had little interest in the United States and no apparent desire to go there—it simply wasn't something they thought about very much. For the first time, I realized that the view of the U.S. as a "promised land" was an *American* cultural narrative, and that it wasn't universal.

Ethnocentrism comes naturally to us because our cultural background provides us with a set of habitual ways of construing events, something referred to as *framing*. You can think of frames as a sort of mental box that we use to categorize phenomena. For example, two people can look at the same object and frame their understanding differently. A tree can be seen as either a resource to cut down and use, or a sacred living thing that should be protected at all costs. Both of these frames are reasonable, but they represent fundamentally different starting points for thinking about trees. Naturally, the "trees are sacred" frame can easily lead to different behaviors than the "trees are a resource." The former may be formalized with a ceremony while the latter is put into action using a chainsaw.

Seen in this way, ethnocentrism involves an assortment of frames that we share with others who were raised in a similar environment. As Timothy Wilson puts it: "Our unconscious minds develop chronic ways of interpreting information from our environments; in psychological parlance, certain ideas and categories become chronically accessible as a result of frequent use in the past."[27] Chronic accessibility has been described as a "permanent screen or filter through which the person's world is experienced."[28] In other words, if you grow up in a place where trees are mostly seen as potential lumber, that framing can become automatic and it can become difficult to experience trees in a different way. Wilson explains that, "We all have implicit frames of reference that produce habitual thinking and behavior. Our experiences and actions always *seem* to be rooted in conscious thought . . . but hidden forces . . . exert a powerful pull."[29] While he is referring to cognitive processes generally, *cultural patterns* also influence our interpretation of events, the way we construe situations, and our gut-level emotional responses to daily experiences.

Let's look at an example in which contrasting cultural frames can produce cross-cultural misunderstanding. In this example, one person framed a situation in a collectivist manner, while the other used a more individualist frame. The story comes from a Japanese university student living in the U.K. with a British roommate:

> When I washed my dishes, I found her dishes left unwashed there. So I washed them at the same time. After that, I was told by her that I shouldn't wash her dishes. I was shocked by her words because I [had washed them out of kindness to her].

The Japanese student went on to explain that she washed the dishes as an act of solidarity. As a group of people living together, they should all help each other out. This corresponds with a more collectivist framing of the situation. Her roommate, however, seems to have framed the situation in terms of personal, not shared responsibility. This framing is based on the more individualist assumption that overall well-being depends first and foremost on taking responsibility for oneself.[30] In this way, cultural values are affecting how these two young women are making sense of this situation—each is using different mental frames to interpret the behavior of the other.

Misunderstandings that result from different ways of framing a situation can be doubly tragic because both sides may have good intentions but each end up feeling aggrieved. The British roommate may not have wanted to burden her roommate with a task she recognized as her own responsibility. The intended message may have been, "Don't wash them for me. It's my responsibility, and I don't want to you to have to pick up the slack for me." Viewed from the collectivist perspective, however, the British woman's behavior is a clear rebuke. She's not only refusing the support and consideration of her roommate; she's implying that she wouldn't help out if the situation were reversed. "Leave me alone!" the message seems to be. "And if you ever need help, you're on your own!" Such interactions produce behavior that is diametrically opposed to what we expect. In such cases, our intuitive mind may simply find people rude or unreasonable. If we generalize that to whole groups, we can end up with negative stereotypes that have been confirmed by experience (e.g., "When I lived in Britain, I was surprised how self-centered people are. My roommate would leave dirty dishes then get mad at me if I tried to wash them.").

Interactions like this are a fork in the road of intercultural learning. If we can make sense of the other person's perspective, we end up better understanding different cultural frames. This requires a willingness to not react too impulsively, to suspend judgment and give people the benefit of the doubt. If the British roommate had paused for a moment after seeing that her dishes had been washed for her, she might have had the presence of mind to soften her message and explain her thinking a bit more fully. ("I know you're trying to be helpful. Thanks. I'm sometimes lazy, but I realize I need to do dishes myself. So next time, please just leave them.") In order to do that, of course, it's necessary to pay attention to how the *other* person is experiencing the situation.

While ethnocentric frames of reference are natural, they can easily provoke negative judgments when we encounter cultural difference. A strong handshake is common in Russia but may create the impression that Russians are strong-willed. A Finn told me that Americans are "friendly but shallow" because of their tendency to talk to strangers. We've already seen how my American students see Japanese as "shy." In such cases, our intuitive mind offers up interpretations based on the familiar interpretive categories that easily come to mind. If our attentive mind validates them, they may harden into negative judgments or stereotypes. These sorts of experience-based stereotypes are hard to counteract once formed. People whose biases have been confirmed by firsthand experience will say, "I know what those people are like because *I've seen for myself.*" Here's Philippe, for example, a French man talking about his attitudes towards Germans after having lived in Germany for several years:

> What I do resent about German culture that's very different from French or American culture is telling on other people, minding other people's lives. They pay attention to what you do even if they don't know you. They will always make sure that you obey the law, that you are a perfect German. And [this happened to me on] many occasions [with] people that I didn't even know—if I parked my car bad or if I took my garbage out on the wrong day. It's very hypocritical, but this is the way they live.

How can we describe Philippe's attitude? He certainly has some negative attitudes towards German culture. But his conclusions are more than ignorant stereotypes or negative associations. They originate in cultural differences found between Germany and France. In Germany, *universalistic* values are common. People more commonly accept that order and systematic procedures create fairness and efficiency for everyone. In France, *particularism* is a strong value. Particularist thinking emphasizes flexibility and adapting to unique circumstances. From the French perspective, it's presumptuous to remind strangers to follow rules, whereas Germans may find the same behavior to be conscientious.

Because ethnocentrism is so foundational to our perceptual processes, so easily influenced by stereotypical thinking and cognitive bias—so "natural," as it were— it's hard to overcome it completely. Milton Bennett, who has written extensively about the process of combating ethnocentrism, puts it this way: "Intercultural sensitivity is not natural. It is not part of our primate past, nor has it characterized most of human history."[31] Bennett sees ethnocentrism in terms of shared patterns of interpretation. A key organizing principle of his view is *differentiation*, taken in two senses: "First, that people differentiate phenomena in a variety of ways and, second, that cultures differ fundamentally from one another in the way they maintain patterns of differentiation, or worldviews."[32] I see this as another way of saying that ethnocentrism reflects the natural tendency to frame things using the patterns we are familiar with.

To me, the most striking thing about ethnocentrism is its invisibility. As Edward Hall wrote more than thirty years ago, "It is frequently the most obvious and taken-for-granted and therefore the least studied aspects of culture that influence behavior in the deepest and most subtle ways."[33] Simply being in a foreign country does not automatically give you access to the shared worldview there, nor does it automatically take us beyond ethnocentrism. We can spend years in a foreign country and yet never enter into the perceptual world of our hosts. When I asked Jack, a long-term expatriate in Tokyo, about the challenges of adapting to life in Japan, his outsider's perspective was obvious:

> The biggest thing is knowing that the Japanese—not that they've told me this . . . [but] you could learn the language fluently, do everything to be accepted, but they never really would . . . according to what I heard from other foreigners. So that was enough for me to not try. . . . I [felt like] it wasn't even worth trying to break that barrier down. I'm happy on this side. If the culture was accepting and open, and not this "us versus the outsider," then I'd be more apt to get closer to them, because I'd feel wanted. I don't accept the fact that they are not accepting.

Jack seems unaware of the self-justifying nature of his reasoning. He decided not to try to fit in *based on what foreigners have said* about Japanese society. He senses a barrier of differing worldviews—one that keeps him on the outside—but can't, or doesn't want to, enter into this other perceptual world. This is the elemental challenge of ethnocentrism. How do we escape the comfortable zone in which we blame others for not understanding us, rather than trying to step into that worldview and see ourselves in a new light?

The Fundamental Attribution Error

The *fundamental attribution error* (FAE) is a common mental bias that causes us to evaluate the behavior of others as though it is caused by essential qualities, such as personality or character, while evaluating our own behavior in more situational terms. If a job applicant arrives late to an interview, for example, we easily conclude that he or she is irresponsible, whereas when we are late, we blame the traffic.

This topic was first explored in a study that asked students to evaluate the political attitudes of authors of political essays. As expected, when researchers told the participants that the author had freely chosen what opinion to express, the participants assumed that the opinions in the article reflected the author's overall political philosophy. But there was an unexpected result as well. When told that the content of the articles was determined by a coin toss—introducing the possibility that the writers were assigned an opinion to express—the study participants still believed that the opinions in the article reflected the author's true political opinions. They were unable to prevent themselves from feeling that behavior was a reflection of an essential inner quality.[34]

Fundamental attribution error

Overestimating the effects of situation for ourselves and overestimating the effects of internal dispositions in others.

Figure 7-3

Humans are highly sensitive to the intentions of others. Perhaps this is why we tend to think that other humans have essential qualities—their character or personality—that largely determine what they do. The FAE is a form of over-generalizing about such intentions. This type of essentialist thinking may be influenced by culture as well, as people raised in individualist cultures have been shown to be more susceptible to the FAE.[35] This is supported by research in cultural neuroscience that finds that Asians have a preference for contextual explanations even when explaining physical phenomena (like friction slowing down movement). Meanwhile, Americans are more likely to prefer explanations related to the characteristics of an object (such as weight or density).[36] It's as though the cognitive preference for objects and categories makes Westerners more likely to assume essential—as opposed to situational—causes for the behavior of both people and objects.

The fundamental attribution error is extremely common in cross-cultural settings. We often return from a short visit to a foreign place full of proclamations about the essential qualities of the locals. We use words that are more properly descriptions of personality or character, such as, "The people were so friendly!" or, "People are always smiling! They are so happy!" Or if we get cheated, "Be careful! The people are dishonest!" Visitors may overlook any number of situational factors, such as different standards of politeness. (Smiling may be simply a reflexive courtesy.) It's also easy for travelers to forget that they may be seen as high-status, thus provoking deferential behavior. (*The people are so helpful!*) Likewise, the behavior of airport taxi drivers is not a good guide to making generalizations about the population of a country in general.

One of my Japanese students went to a bar with an American friend, who decided to approach some young women by buying them a drink, something that's not common in Japan. As my student recounts:

> All of sudden, Clyde asked me if three girls sitting at the table were beautiful. I took a look at them, and I nodded. He said that he would show me how to make a chance to talk to them. After that, he asked a bartender to give them drinks from us. While Clyde was ordering, I was trying to stop it; however, he said, "It's normal in U.S. Don't worry!" . . . I was really shocked because I had never seen these scenes before except films. So, I feel embarrassed to do it. I learned American guys are more *charai* (immoral and not serious) than Japanese.

This student seemed to miss the obvious fact that behavior in a bar while drinking may not be a sufficient sample to draw such sweeping conclusions. In this way, based on limited experience, the fundamental attribution error can lead us to the conclusion that we have understood the essential qualities of the foreigners we meet.

Bias and the Intercultural Mind

The biases we have seen are not exclusive to cross-cultural situations. Foreign environments do, however, provide plenty of opportunities to fall into such mental traps. Developing an intercultural mind includes recognition that *bias, stereotypes, and ethnocentrism are normal elements of our humanity.* This helps us guard against them within ourselves and not be too shocked when we encounter them in others. An understanding of the pervasive nature of bias also helps us take the narrow-mindedness we find in others less personally. Tolerance for our own foibles, as well as those of others, is yet another key that unlocks our potential for a more intercultural mind.

KEY CONCEPTS

Familiarity bias: *We are, broadly speaking, biased against the unfamiliar. Interpretations of events that are familiar to us come to mind easily—something called the* availability heuristic. *We have a natural tendency towards social cohesion and mistrust of out groups.*

Ethnocentrism: *Refers broadly to judging another culture by the standards of one's own culture. It's true that ethnocentrism may involve prejudicial attitudes, but it's also a natural product of interpreting phenomena based on previous experience.*

Fundamental attribution error: *Causes us to evaluate the behavior of others as though it is caused by essential qualities, such as personality or character, while downplaying situational factors. It can lead people to think about culture in terms of internal essential qualities.*

Discussion Quote: *Intercultural sensitivity is not natural. It is not part of our primate past, nor has it characterized most of human history.*[37]

8.

cultural intuitions

What?! Oh well.

—Fumitaka

Our intuitive mind is an expert at reading the cultural patterns found in our everyday interactions. Our expert intuitions may not work, however, when interacting in foreign environments.

Reading the Air

One December evening, I found myself on a street corner near Shibuya station, shivering with cold. I was underdressed, as often happens in climate-controlled Tokyo. Even with an icy wind invading from Siberia, you see men outside with no overcoats and women delicately navigating slush in skirts and high heels. I stood exposed to the chill, standing with a group of students who attended classes at the English conversation school where I worked. Class was over, and we were attempting to decide on a restaurant for dinner together. Somehow, however, it was taking a long time. The students mulled the options with long pauses, tentative suggestions, and half opinions.

"Where shall we go?" asked Keiko.

"Well, last time we went to Tsubohachi," offered Masaki through cold-clenched teeth.

"Tsubohachi was good," replied another.

"Hmmmm."

"Well, we could try Tengu."

I kept silent and scrunched my shoulders to protect my ears from the wind. Finally, consensus emerged in a subtle dance of shared intention. I, however, was in a bad mood—frustrated with what seemed to be the glacial pace of decision-making. The turn-taking seemed slow, the opinions tentative—some people didn't speak at all—and there was precious little debate. As an American, I was accustomed to decision making more akin to an open marketplace—one in which people *put in their two cents' worth, put their cards on the table, have an open give and take* in order to *exchange views* and *weigh one's options*. Japanese decision making was clearly following a different cultural logic. But what was that underlying logic? It felt slow, inefficient, awkward, and hard to interpret.

At this moment, I felt the limits of analytic thinking and problem solving of the attentive mind. Intellectually, I knew that this interaction was typical and reflected Japanese communication norms. I was *paying attention* to my students' behavior and *thinking about* what it meant. Yet still it didn't *feel* right or natural. It didn't provide me with the ability to "read" the subtleties of what was going on or anticipate what would happen next. It would take many more such interactions for me to not only feel comfortable with such interaction, but to see its advantages and find it normal.

I knew that my Japanese students faced the opposite frustration when learning English. Used to a more deliberative pace in meetings, for example, they had trouble keeping up with the rapid back-and-forth of English speakers throwing out opinions and quickly rebutting ideas they didn't agree with. Learning to speak English well required not only linguistic skills, but the ability to play a whole new communication game. The rules of these interactive games, of course, are not spelled out. You have to get a *feel* for such things through a long process of trial and error. These things cannot be learned by memorizing etiquette rules or reading books. When diving deeply into another cultural community, you have to learn to *read the air*.

Social Cognition

In Japan, the art of picking up on social cues is sometimes referred to as *reading the air*. Someone who can't read the air is considered naïve, boorish, or clueless. The ability to read the air is a crucial element of *joshiki*—the commonsense social knowledge required for polite behavior. People without *joshiki* bumble along in their social interactions, clueless about what others are thinking or expecting and leaving irritated people in their wake. Standing on that freezing street corner in Shibuya, I was a foreigner who had no *joshiki*. I was unable to read the air or smoothly participate in the decision-making process.

The Japanese aren't the only ones who read the air, of course. We all do. Reading the air involves what social scientists refer to as *social cognition*, the cognitive knowledge and capacities that allows us to function socially.[1] To get along with others we must accurately interpret social situations, infer what things mean, and follow appropriate social protocol. When we are in familiar social environments, we are mostly unaware of social cognition. We know how to politely interrupt someone or make a point without seeming pushy. We are familiar with the routines for ordering in restaurants or making small talk with a check-out clerk. In foreign environments, we are less competent.

Social cognition involves a lot of unconscious knowledge about our social world—often called *schema*—and an understanding of behavioral expectations—often called *scripts*.[2] Schema is the background knowledge that we need to function in a community—everything from knowing what a toothbrush is to the knowledge that blowing your nose at the dinner table may be considered rude. Scripts, on the other hand, refer to expectations about behavior—knowledge of how to introduce yourself, wish someone a happy birthday, or say "bless you" when someone sneezes. Scripts and schema are closely tied together. Knowing which glass is for wine and which is for beer goes along with knowing how to clink glasses when making a toast.

Perhaps the most striking thing about our social cognition is how second nature it is. The intuitive mind acts as a kind of social autopilot, reading social patterns based on its store of schema and scripts. In a foreign environment, we may falter because we misread situations, don't pick up on social clues that locals take for granted, or are oblivious to the intentions or communication subtleties of our hosts. We need to get a *feel* for how things work and what things mean. My ability to *read the air* in Japan was limited because I hadn't developed the *intuitive expertise* to do so.[3]

Reading the Air Across Cultures

Our ability to read other people's intentions and interpret their behavior is a mix of innate capacities and culturally conditioned intuitions. Our most innate cognitive social skills—such as recognizing faces—involve pattern recognition abilities that are built-in and universal. This implies that some things can be communicated unambiguously in spite of cultural difference. Psychologist and facial expression expert Paul Ekman, for example, has argued that there are six or more expressions recognized universally across cultures: *anger, fear, disgust, surprise, happiness, sadness,* and perhaps *contempt*.[4] There is certainly some truth to the idea that a smile can communicate pleasure anywhere in the world. That doesn't mean, of course, that we can always read the faces of people everywhere, and some research suggests that culture shapes the expression of even basic emotions.[5]

One experiment that looked into this question compared the facial expressions of blind athletes from the 2004 Olympic and Paralympic games. The study found that facial expressions related to winning and losing were the same for both sighted athletes and those blind from birth, meaning that they couldn't have learned them from seeing others.[6] Of course, functioning socially requires much more than reading basic emotions. While a smile is universally associated with positive feelings, its use in communication varies widely—it may express amusement, hint at embarrassment, or mask rage. In everyday life, we read facial expressions in the larger context of expectations for that situation.

If the only interaction we have abroad is shopping at a marketplace or ordering in restaurants, our innate abilities to read basic emotions and judge friendliness or threat may well be enough to get things done and create positive interactions. The longer we stay, however, and the more we attempt to adapt to local norms, the more we must read subtle and intricate social patterns. Like me, Rebecca, from Norway, struggled with patterns of Japanese decision-making:

> I was going to go out for dinner with a couple of Japanese friends and a Danish friend of mine. After an event at our university, we stopped to decide where to actually eat, and the decision-making was being made in Japanese. . . . They were asking each person what they wanted and kept on going like this, in circles, for over twenty minutes. . . . As the both of us are Scandinavians, we are more used to being straightforward and . . . it did feel different and to some degree a bit uncomfortable. . . . Something I understand is that they didn't notice or even think that they were using a different set of communication patterns compared to the two of us.

Rebecca talks about being *uncomfortable*. I wonder, however, if what she really means is *irritated*. When cultural patterns don't match our unconscious expectations, it can easily provoke frustration.

Confronting foreign social expectations creates adaptive dilemmas as well. Is it always better to try to fit in? What if doing so goes against norms and values that we hold dear? Communication is not simply a matter of technique; it touches us at deep layers of the self. Sally, who went to live in the U.K. from Romania, struggled with standards for politeness:

> Initially in the U.K., I found it very difficult to address people who were clearly more advanced in age than me by their first name. It all

sounded very rude to me, and I could not bear to hear myself speaking to them, which sometimes [in a silly way] lead to me not socializing, in order to avoid embarrassment. Over the years it has become more and more easy to address elderly or teachers in the U.K. by their first names, without a feeling of guilt, but it still surprises me how easy it is to change back to the polite style when visiting Romania.

Notice that it took Sally *years* to become comfortable addressing her elders by their first name and that she easily reverts once back in Romania. Our scripts and schema are deeply integrated into our identity—and changing the way we act can feel like a betrayal or negation of self.

Cultural Empathy

A large part of learning to read the air in a foreign environment involves learning to view the situation from more of an insider's perspective—in effect, to develop a more local perspective. The capacity to look through the eyes of our cultural hosts relies on the broader human capacity for *empathy*. The word *empathy* was introduced in English in 1909 by the psychologist Edward Titchener as a translation of the German word *Einfühlung*, meaning "feel in."[7] In everyday usage, empathy refers to the ability to understand or experience something vicariously through the experience of another. This is, of course, harder to do across cultures since the way people make sense of things, or what they value, can vary widely. The general human capacity for empathy is not always enough to create mutual understanding.

Within neuroscience, empathy has gained attention through research into *mirror neurons*, which fire both when observing an action and when doing that action oneself. Researchers first discovered mirror neurons when studying neural functioning in macaque monkeys. They were surprised to find that certain neurons fired not only when a monkey performed an action, but also when the monkey observed that same action.[8] This discovery provided an important key to understanding the brain's ability to tune into the behavior of others—to experience the actions of others as though performing them oneself. This capacity is so critical for social behavior that some believe empathy is a fundamental building block of human nature.[9] In this view, we have, so to speak, an "empathetic brain," which shapes our learning, behavior, and social organization in very important ways.

The economic and social theorist Jeremy Rifkin argues that a need for increased empathy is a primary challenge of a globalized world.[10] He believes that humans are fundamentally empathetic, but that we must extend our empathy beyond those we know best into a wider and more encompassing circle of people. In his view, our hunter-gatherer ancestors empathized primarily with members of their own family, tribe, or group. As society became more complex, people started empathizing with others in the same kingdom, country, or religious community. The great challenge of the twenty-first century, Rifkin believes, is the development of an *empathic civilization*, in which we are conscious of our connection to all of humanity, and can thus go beyond narrow national, ethnic, or sectarian self-interest. By doing so, he hopes we can create a more inclusive and harmonious global community.

There are barriers to empathy, of course. While empathy is a fundamental human capacity, the intercultural theorist Milton Bennett points out that we extend empathy primarily to people we feel are fundamentally similar to us.[11] When people are perceived as different, we have more trouble empathizing with them. This creates profound problems for intercultural relations. If we perceive immigrants or foreigners as fundamentally different from ourselves, for example, we may easily start to denigrate them. In times of war, the enemy is dehumanized so that normal empathy is not extended to one's opponents.

Bennett also warns against a naïve empathy that too strongly assumes that people around the world are similar to ourselves. In our attempts to empathize across cultures, we may unintentionally project our cultural viewpoint on others. As an approach to intercultural understanding, he argues, the *Golden Rule*—"Do unto others as you would have them do unto you"—has a fundamental flaw. It assumes that all people want to be treated in the same way, which is often not true in intercultural situations. Bennett makes a distinction between *empathy* and *sympathy*. He describes sympathy as imagining ourselves in the situation of another: "How would I feel in that situation?" This approach to cross-cultural relations is risky because we end up projecting our own viewpoint onto others. Bennett's conceptualizes *empathy*, on the other hand, as the ability to look at a situation through the eyes of another person, *even if his or her perspective is different from one's own.*

The ability to look at a situation from the perspective of a person dissimilar to oneself is the critical component of empathy as Bennett describes it. Empathy, as opposed to sympathy, is important when people have fundamentally different positions, interests, or perceptions. When a psychologist is providing counseling, for example, she needs to be able to see the situation from the perspective of the patient. Likewise, cultural empathy is required when attempting to understand a situation from a new cultural perspective. Just as a psychologist doesn't take on the personality of her patient, developing cultural empathy doesn't imply that we *become* a different person or transform our way of thinking. Rather, it involves the ability to see things from the local perspective *regardless of how we may feel about that perspective.* This takes time, of course, but without cultural empathy, our attempts to read the air across cultures will always be limited by our outsider point of view.

Expert Intuitions

In chapter seven, I highlighted the pitfalls of unconscious bias, particularly as related to intercultural experiences. This can give the impression that our intuitive mind is rather inept and that we need to constantly stand conscious guard against it. One person whose research inclines in this direction is Daniel Kahneman.[12] His work—which features, for example, statistics professors who suffer from unconscious biases about statistics—provides ample evidence that unconscious cognition can and does lead us astray. He's not the only one who looks at unconscious cognition in this way.[13]

Yet for interculturalists, focusing too much on bias and misunderstanding risks missing large swathes of forest for the trees. Despite occasional misunderstandings and confusion, we often *do* read cross-cultural situations successfully. Not all interactions are full of ambiguity about hard-to-interpret phenomena. In addition, while our intuitive mind may get tripped up at times, it is also capable of learning from its experiences. Over time, we get *better* at interpreting behavior, even if we aren't consciously focused on doing so. Learning new patterns is as much a part of our cognitive psychology as taking shortcuts is. Intuitive cognition is as much about mastery as it is about folly.

To learn about the mastery of the unconscious mind, we can turn to Gary Klein, whose research focuses on decision-making and what he calls *expert intuitions*.[14] Klein views intuition not as some special ability possessed by particularly sensitive or spiritual people, but as a cognitive capacity that is developed with practice. Expert intuitions give us a *feel* for a situation or problem. Klein studies the intuitions of experts such as firefighters, pilots, and doctors—people who are highly trained and must make high-pressure split-second decisions.

Whereas Kahneman admits to finding pleasure "in the come-uppance of arrogant experts who claim intuitive powers," Klein is in awe of the power of the human mind to read subtle patterns.[15] He recounts the story of a fire commander who orders his team out of a burning building without knowing why—only to have the floor they had been standing on collapse from a hidden fire. The commander credits his decision to "a sixth sense," but Klein argues that his decision was based on unconscious intuitions.[16] Klein's work reminds us that the unconscious mind has a remarkable capacity to learn to read subtle patterns, and to use that knowledge to skillfully guide our behavior, almost like magic. Expert intuitions are *felt* rather than understood consciously.

Klein defines an intuition as "an emotional reaction to anticipated consequences of good and bad decisions."[17] Intuitions involve the vague, but often powerful, feeling of rightness or wrongness and "recognizing things without knowing how we do the recognizing."[18] Intuitions are produced by the intuitive mind and influence our behavior in ways that we ourselves can't explain—this contrasts with what is sometimes referred to as *declarative knowledge*, which refers to knowledge we can articulate and explain.[19] And though they feel spontaneous, expert intuitions are the result of a hidden process of evaluation and pattern recognition. Expert intuitions develop over time, as we learn to "recognize familiar elements in a new situation and to act in a manner that is appropriate to it."[20]

Expert intuitions abound in everyday life—mechanics identify engine problems based on the subtle clicks and vrooms of an engine; cooks add just the right pinch of spice; baristas get a feel for pulling a good shot of espresso; a quarterback instantly reads the coverage downfield; a comic sharpens her routine until it looks effortless. These abilities have been written about in books such as *Blink: The Power of Thinking Without Thinking*, in which we hear about art appraisers who immediately and intuitively spot forgeries, for example, or about a tennis coach who could spot double faults before a player had struck the ball on his second serve.[21] The psychologist Gerd Gigerenzer talks about intuitions in terms of gut feelings that are indicative of the intelligence of the unconscious mind.[22]

An important element of our expert intuitions is the ability to recognize patterns. To get a sense for this, take a look at figure 8-1. If you are a novice chess player, these boards will look nearly identical. A skilled chess player, however, can instantly recognize two standard opening sequences: one is the Najdorf variation of the Sicilian defense and the other is the Ruy Lopez opening. When chess players do this, they are not going through a step-by-step analysis of the individual pieces on the chessboard. They have a holistic, intuitive grasp of the patterns involved, including the sequence of moves that bring about each of these positions, and the risks and advantages of each. (The Ruy Lopez, on the right, is a standard, safe opening, while the Sicilian defense involves an aggressive attack by the black pieces.) They have a *feeling* for these patterns and may have a favorite opening or one they dread seeing.

Pattern recognition...

Which is the Sicilian defense Najdorf variation?

Figure 8-1

Our expert intuitions develop as a result of our familiarity with patterns. They provide us with quick responses and guide us when we come across similar patterns in the future. They may involve very complex and abstract tasks and problems. The French mathematician Henri Poincaré recounts an important intuitive insight that occurred as he got on a bus:

> [W]e entered an omnibus to go some place or other. At the moment when I put my foot on the step the idea came to me, without anything in my former thoughts seeming to have paved the way for it, that the transformations I had used to define the Fuchsian functions were identical with those of non-Euclidean geometry. I did not verify the idea; I should not have had time, as upon taking my seat in the omnibus, I went on with a conversation already commenced, but I felt a perfect certainty. On my return to Caen, for conscience' sake, I verified the result at my leisure.[23]

This feeling is familiar to everyone, of course, because we all rely on expert intuitions. Who *hasn't* had the experience of awaking in the middle of the night with an insight into an intractable problem, an idea for a new business, or a plot twist for the story we've been writing? Our intuitive mind is not some simple generator of emotions; it generates complex algorithms of cognition that we draw upon in every aspect of our lives.

Cultural Intuitions

Klein calls expert intuitions "the power to see the invisible," and he points out that novices are blind to things that experts see as quite obvious.[24] The idea of expertise rendering things visible—implying the ability to recognize patterns—also describes the difference between a cultural insider and a foreigner who hasn't learned to read local behavior. In other words, *in our home cultural environment, intuitive expertise is the norm and foreigners are novices who have yet to develop accurate cultural intuitions.* I have quoted Klein below, but substituted *locals* and *outsiders/foreigners* for *experts* and *novices*:

> **Locals** see the world differently. They see things **foreigners** cannot. Often **locals** do not realize that **outsiders** are unable to detect what seems obvious to them. . . . That is why they can move freely in their domain while **foreigners** must pick their way carefully through the same terrain. There are many things that **locals** can see that are invisible to **foreigners**:
>
> Patterns that **outsiders** do not notice.
> Anomalies—events that did not happen and other violations of expectancies.
> The big picture (situation awareness).
> The way things work.
> Opportunities and improvisations.
> Events that either already happened (the past) or are going to happen (the future).
> Differences that are too small for **foreigners** to detect.
> Their own limitations.[25]

Seen in this way, deep cultural understanding requires more than conscious knowledge or analytic ability. Deep culture knowledge is intuitive and requires long practice to develop. Sometimes, vague words such as *cultural awareness* are used to describe the desired goals of intercultural education or foreign experiences.[26] An understanding of expert intuitions, however, points to an *unconscious* learning process that may or may not be experienced in terms of conscious awareness or the ability to analyze a situation rationally.

Intuitive expertise is gained through practice.[27] Just as a chess master, a firefighter, or a surgeon may hone their intuitive skills over a period of years until they gain mastery in a burning building or an operating room, sojourners develop new cultural intuitions through foreign interactions. Here, for example, Klein describes the feeling of a fire commander reacting intuitively to a fire, but this description could just as easily be applied to someone struggling to make sense of an intercultural encounter:

> [His] experience had provided him with a firm set of patterns. He was accustomed to sizing up a situation by having it match one of these patterns . . . relying on the pattern-matching process to let him feel comfortable that he had the situation scoped out. Nevertheless, he did not seem to be aware of how he was using his experience because he was not doing it consciously or deliberately. He did not realize there were other ways he could have sized the situation up. He could see what was going on in front of his eyes but not what was going on behind them . . .[28]

Klein refers to the sense of mastery that comes from expert intuitions as feeling "comfortable that he had the situation scoped out." This is precisely the feeling we get from familiar patterns of social interaction. We know where we stand, what things mean, and how to interact successfully.

It should be pointed out that many superficial cross-cultural encounters don't rely on expert intuitions. Buying gasoline in Istanbul is a relatively concrete task that doesn't require reading subtle cues from the gas stand employee. The more involved our interactions, however, the more important our cultural intuitions become. Klein's work helps us understanding the difference between the more superficial cultural learning involved in being a tourist, and the deeper, more intuitive expertise entailed in learning a foreign language, adapting to life in a foreign country, and so on.

Intuitive judgments are based on a situation's typicality. Experienced decision makers are better able to make proper decisions because their mental models are more accurate. In Figure 8-2, we can see how Klein conceptualizes this process. We recognize intuitively if the situation is typical—it matches patterns we've experienced in the past. If not, we go through a diagnostic process. We go through mental simulations to evaluate potential actions and behave in ways we feel might be effective. To deal with anomalies, we try to clarify through feature matching and story building—we attempt to identify patterns and create a coherent understanding of the situation. Though this process is complex, it happens quickly and in the moment.

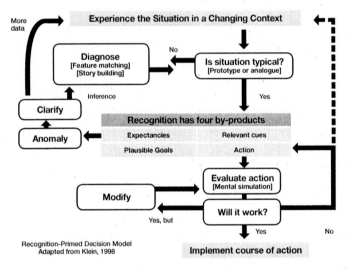

Figure 8-2

Expert intuition requires mental models that allow us to read situations, predict what will happen next, and evaluate options. The mental models that we develop in a foreign environment help us decipher local behavior. When our mental models are incomplete or don't match the situation, we may get flustered, as in the case of this Chinese student in Japan:

> When we decided where to go, it would take a lot of time, and everybody stood in the corridor but nobody would give suggestions. After talks about weather, clothes, and homework, some people would give suggestions, but they also claimed humbly that the restaurants may

not be so good and hoped other people also give their suggestions—but other people would also say the same thing, that the restaurants may not be good. The communication like this would continue for about half an hour. . . . [The] first time we stood in the corridor and spent one hour to decide the place, I got so angry and I shouted in my heart "Couldn't you decide now?! What you are discussing is nonsense!!" But now I can stand with them together and look at the meaningless discussion continuing for one hour because this is just their way to do things. It is the Japanese style of decision-making.

This student describes Japanese decision-making as "meaningless discussion." But Japanese discussion is not meaningless. It simply follows a different set of patterns. This student had not yet, however, developed the expert intuitions that would have allowed her to decipher those patterns.

Mindfulness, Modeling, Trial and Error

Developing an intercultural mind involves developing new sets of expert intuitions. It's not enough to know a set of cultural facts, or have a general awareness of cross-cultural issues. As I see it, developing new cultural intuitions involves *intuitive learning* joined together with more *analytic learning*. Cultural learning needs to be experiential—giving our intuitive mind a chance to learn new patterns and generate new insights. It also needs to be informed by critical thinking, reflective analysis and intentional problem-solving.

How, then, can we encourage this sort of two mind cultural learning? I tell the sojourners I work with that it includes: (1) a state of *mindfulness*, (2) conceptual *modeling*, and (3) a *trial-and-error* process of testing the mental models we create. This is part of an ongoing experiential learning cycle that engages both our intuitive and attentive minds. You can see a visual representation of this process in figure 8-3.

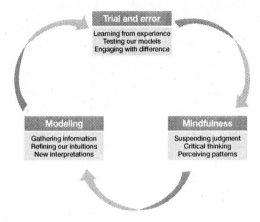

Figure 8-3

As I use it, "mindfulness" refers to an increased awareness of our own cognitive processes, including the sensations, feelings, interpretations, and reactions provoked by our experiences. This greater awareness allows for *critical thinking* that includes a *suspension of judgment*. We need an awareness of the thoughts and feelings that we experience, and the ability to leave open questions in the "back of our minds." This provides our intuitive mind more opportunity to absorb and make sense of new patterns. It also allows our attentive mind to take its time working through problems. Mindfulness acts to slow us down; to provide extra time to notice things we wouldn't have otherwise.

The second step—*modeling*—involves a conscious effort to inform and enrich the unconscious mental models we use to interpret cultural phenomena. The more *information, experience,* and *reflection* dedicated to understanding a given phenomena, the richer our intuitions will be. A Wikipedia article about a country you visit may contain information that sheds light on what people there are doing. Actively observing behavior, asking cultural informants, or learning about cultural values and customs are other ways to gather information and experience. Since intuitions are holistic, it's important that we gain cultural knowledge from varied sources, including not only factual information, but lived experiences. As our mental models are enriched, our intuitive mind can generate increasing numbers of novel interpretations.

The goal of gathering cultural knowledge and experience is not, however, to come up with cause-and-effect explanations for behavior. We should try to add to the bank of explicit and implicit knowledge that informs our cultural intuitions—our *intuitive reading* of a phenomenon. This is different from the way in which historical information is sometimes misused as a way of "explaining" why "those people" act in a particular way. People sometimes say that Americans are friendly, for example, because they come from a country of immigrants, or that the British are reserved because they have an "island mentality." Such statements are not, however, explanations for specific behaviors. Improved modeling comes not from seeking causal explanations, but from the increased ability to understand cultural context, and thus a more fully developed sense for the local perspective.

The third stage of improving cultural intuitions is a trial-and-error testing of our interpretations of situations. This simply means that we focus on the ongoing process of refining our intuitions. There's no substitute for lived experience, of course, but even if we have limited opportunities to visit a foreign place, or can stay for only a short time, we can still engage in an active process of trying to test our understanding. A commitment to trial and error implies that we always leave room for modifying our view of cultural worlds we are exploring. I have seen study abroad programs, for example, that have students come up with cultural research questions before heading off to a foreign country, which they must report on when they have come back home. In this way, the mental trial-and-error process starts before they leave and continues even after they have come back.

Developing cultural intuitions takes time. When I was standing on the corner in Shibuya, irritated at Japanese decision-making, I had already spent six months living in Tokyo. I wasn't very mindful. I quickly allowed my thoughts to degenerate into negative reactions and judgments. This meant that my mental models were slow to evolve and didn't help me much in my ongoing interactions. My experience wasn't unusual, of course. We all get frustrated and jump to ethnocentric conclusions. If we know the importance of the more hidden intuitive mental processes that go into cultural understanding, however, we can provide conscious support to our intuitive mind's struggle to read the air in foreign places.

KEY CONCEPTS

Social cognition: *The implicit knowledge and abilities, including schema and scripts, that allows us to function socially.*

Expert intuitions: *The ability to recognize familiar patterns and respond accordingly. They are experienced as a sense of "rightness" or "wrongness" about a situation. These sensations are generated by the intuitive mind.*

Cultural intuitions: *The intuitive ability to read and respond to the cultural patterns in a given situation. Locals in a cultural community have expert cultural intuitions, while outsiders do not.*

Discussion Quote: *Reading the air across cultures can be frustrating.*

9.

catching culture

Every individual is unique, while our cultural back-
ground drives us to the same wide path.

—Dino

It's natural to want to quantify and compare culture—but it's not easy to do so.
Fortunately, there are new ways to research and contrast cultural patterns. While we
remain far from the dream of Edward Hall—an all-inclusive cultural grammar—
we have new tools at our disposal.

A World-Class Gathering

Aworld of intercultural experience gathered for the plenary address of David Matsumoto—a highly accomplished cross-cultural psychologist, researcher, expert in reading emotions across cultures, seventh-degree black belt in Judo, former coach of the U.S. Olympic Judo team, fluent Japanese speaker, author of numerous books and hundreds of academic articles, entrepreneur and business owner, and—as if this weren't enough—a generous, warm-hearted person. The audience members were intercultural trainers and educators—specialists working on the front lines of globalization; helping expatriates understand cultural difference; teaching intercultural communication; preparing students to study abroad; teaching foreign languages and cultures. Even among these experienced interculturalists, however, Matsumoto was in a class of his own.

As he spoke, however, some members of the audience shifted uncomfortably in their seats. He began by talking about research into *individualism* and *collectivism*—terms his audience was certainly familiar with. His PowerPoint slides showed bell curves laid across one another, each representing results of cross-cultural studies. Countries like India, China, or Japan are often spoken of as more *collectivist* societies, and are contrasted with countries such as the United States, the U.K., or Germany, said to be more *individualist*. Many trainers and educators use these terms in their work as a way of describing and quantifying cultural difference. What Matsumoto said, though, went against much of the conventional wisdom in the room. Instead of accepting that such research represented important elements of cultural difference, he used the same data to argue for the *unimportance* of the difference found by such studies. Without saying so directly, he called into question the whole notion that research into cultural difference reveals meaningful differences between peoples.

Matsumoto's talk touched upon a fundamental question faced by intercultural educators and researchers, and by thoughtful interculturalists in general: What is cultural difference, and how can we quantify it? In his talk, and in an article on this topic, he raises some tough questions about the usefulness of the most common type of cross-cultural research. He says, for example, that: "Statistically significant differences in culture means may or may not reflect practically important differences between people of different cultures."[1] He does not claim that cultural difference doesn't exist; rather, he points out that *just because standard quantitative testing methodology produces statistical differences on cross-cultural measures, those differences aren't necessarily meaningful in practical terms.*

In his talk, Matsumoto questioned whether cultural generalizations about groups of people—typified by statements such as "Americans are individualistic"—are actually meaningful. He argued that just because there is a statistical difference between the total scores of two groups doesn't necessarily mean you can predict behavior based on that difference. To give a more mundane example, knowing that Americans drink less tea on average than Indians doesn't allow you to accurately predict whether a particular Indian or American will chose coffee or tea in a Café in Aleppo.

For the trainers and educators in the audience on that day, this was a provocative thesis. Many people who work in the intercultural field take for granted that cultural difference, as conceptualized and measured using terms such as *individualism* and *collectivism*, is important and meaningful. Many people have powerful *experiences* of cultural difference, and thus assume that such research captures some essential element that they know through their own experiences. This raises a difficult point. How is it that cultural difference can feel so significant when we travel or spend time abroad, yet be so hard to measure or quantify? At the end of the talk, an audience member brought this up, asking, "If statistical measures of cultural difference are so unreliable, then why do sojourners report such powerful experiences of cultural difference?"

Matsumoto's response: "That's an interesting question. You should do some research about it."

Describing Cultural Difference

It can be hard to answer even the most basic cross-cultural questions. After my first trip to Tokyo, my brother asked me, "What's Japan like?" This question looks simple, but it's not. If someone answers such a question using facts—things that can be measured and agreed upon by people everywhere—it will sound like a Wikipedia entry:

> Japan is an archipelago with four main islands and thousands of smaller ones. 126 million people live there, with 30 million in the Tokyo metropolitan area. Japan's economy is highly developed. There is a low crime rate and near universal literacy. The country is highly homogeneous, with 95% of the population belonging to the Yamato ethnic group.

This is not, of course, what people want to hear. They don't want to know *what a foreign place is*; they are curious about *what a foreign place is like.* They want to know how it's *different* from back home. Our foreign experiences are meaningful because they contrast with our previous experience. To satisfy the folks back home, a visitor would need to provide a more personal narrative that draws attention to particular elements of their experience, something more like the following:

> The trains in Tokyo are packed. During rush hour, when the doors open people flood from the cars, flow down steps, wash through the ticket gates, then pour out into the streets. It's efficient but strangely impersonal. Faces are polite and deferential, with no emotion—numb from rubbing shoulders with strangers. In traditional Japan, the nail that stuck out got hammered down. Now they just make you ride the subway.

This description gives a stronger sense of what it's like to be in Tokyo, yet it's clearly subjective and even judgmental. Are Japanese people really numb? Has traditional culture been lost in Japan? Is politeness in modern Japan simply conformity? The passage reveals as much about the writer's biases as about Japan. It's not, for example, how I would interpret Japanese behavior on trains.

Is there a way to somehow split the difference between dry facts and highly subjective narratives? How can we talk about or measure cultural difference in a balanced way that captures something essential? Is there, for example, such a thing as *Italianness*? Anyone walking the streets of Rome and interacting with Italians will experience cultural patterns, and may have an impression that they have experienced "Italian culture," but trying to define or measure just what that means is difficult. For starters, Milan is not the same as Rome, though both are still formally "Italian." Obviously, too, each resident of Rome has his or her individual personality and eccentricities. Stereotypes of Italians being passionate or talking with their hands are certainly oversimplifications at best.

At the same time, there are obviously commonalities in cultural communities. The communication patterns found in Finland really *do* vary in meaningful ways from those in Italy or China. To discover that, we can ask Finns about the adjustments that they have to make when living and working among Italians or Chinese. If cultural difference was negligible or unimportant, it would be easy to blend in to other cultural communities. The fact this often isn't the case hints at important elements of cultural difference, even if those elements are hard to quantify or describe. Evidence for cultural difference is found not only in explicitly contrasting behaviors, but also in the difficulty of adapting to the behaviors, values, and lifestyles of foreign places.

Cross-Cultural Comparison

Most sojourners recognize that they can never be completely objective about their cross-cultural experiences. They may not realize, however, just how hard it is to define, quantify, or compare culture. With that in mind, let's look back to Edward Tylor's famous definition of culture as "that complex whole which includes knowledge, belief, art, law, morals, customs, and any other capabilities and habits acquired by man as a member of society."[2] Tylor helped turn the study of human diversity into a more scientific pursuit by developing approaches to conceptualize and systematically research culture. He is considered a founding father of the field of anthropology. His work marked an increasing interest in understanding human diversity. In the twentieth century, culture became a key concept explored in many fields, including sociology, psychology, and linguistics. The concept of culture seems to turn up everywhere.

This universality, however, hints at a problem with Tylor's definition: it's extremely broad. Anything that is "acquired by man as a member of society" falls within the bounds of culture. Just what "acquired" means—what it means to *share* in a culture—is not clear. Does it refer to professing similar beliefs? To acting in the same way? To looking at the world in a similar way? If we want to quantify or compare elements of culture, we need to have more precise answers to these questions.

In 1959, Edward Hall lamented that eighty years after Tylor's influential definition of culture, it still lacked "the rigorous specificity which characterizes many less revolutionary and useful ideas."[3] Hall felt the study of culture lacked a solid theoretical foundation and spoke specifically for the need to: (1) identify the building blocks of culture; (2) tie these building blocks to a biological base that would provide a foundation for cross-cultural comparison; (3) build up a fundamental grammar of culture so that its components could be researched objectively, without a need to rely on vague qualities such as empathy; (4) build a unified theory of culture; and (5) find a way to make the study of culture useful to non-specialists.[4] Hall hoped to find universal elements of culture that could serve as starting points for cross-cultural comparison, such that intercultural relations might become smoother.

This is an important goal. It would be great if we could provide travelers with shortcuts to understanding patterns of cultural difference. If, when a Finnish student arrives for a study-abroad program in Italy, he has learned useful information about what to expect in Italy, his experience will likely be more positive and enriching. Yet even today, as hinted by David Matsumoto's lecture, we still have not reached a consensus on how to describe or quantify culture even in relatively straightforward cases like this. Specialists still disagree about our ability to make valid cross-cultural comparisons and on what constitutes useful information for sojourners. Culture may be a more complex and diffuse phenomenon than even Edward Hall anticipated.

I think, however, that we're making progress. As we've already seen, we are starting to better understand the interface between our biological systems and our mental experience of the world, including culture.[5] Research has advanced to the point where neuroscientists and cognitive psychologists are finding ways to quantify and compare the effects of culture on our brain.[6] The kind of research that Dr. Matsumoto was calling into question is now being supplemented by new approaches to understanding cultural patterns. This is good news for sojourners. While in 1959, the study of culture was the near exclusive domain of specialists, in the twenty-first century, we are all de facto anthropologists trying to make sense of the world's diversity. And we need all the help that we can possibly get.

Collectivism and Individualism

During his presentation, David Matsumoto's criticism centered on the most extensively researched areas of cross-cultural comparison: *individualism* and *collectivism*. The best-known researcher in this area is Geert Hofstede, who carried out highly influential cross-cultural studies starting in the 1980s.[7] He was asked by IBM to research the attitudes of employees around the world towards their working conditions. His research provided him with a data set that could be compared country by country. He did statistical analysis of his results in an attempt to identify key elements of cultural variation.

As an example, in certain countries, a relatively larger number of people wanted jobs that would give them (1) time for themselves, (2) freedom to adopt their own approach to their work, and (3) the opportunity to achieve a personal sense of accomplishment. These answers clustered together—people who tended to choose one of those items were statistically more likely to choose the others—and were associated by Hofstede with *individualism*. The respondents in certain other countries, on the other hand, tended to look relatively more frequently for (1) training opportunities, (2) good working conditions, and (3) the full use of one's abilities. Answers like this that clustered together were interpreted by Hofstede to reflect a more *collectivist* orientation towards work.

Based on this, Hofstede created an *individualism index*, in which the U.S., Australia, and Great Britain ranked first, second, and third. Panama, Ecuador, and Guatemala ranked as the least individualist among countries sampled. Hofstede went on to identify other categories of cultural comparison, including *power distance, masculinity/femininity, uncertainty avoidance*, and then *long-term orientation*. Most recently, he has been working with the concept of *indulgence vs. self-restraint.*[8] Hofstede's research is hugely influential and widely cited in academic literature, with nearly 100,000 scholarly citations, according to Google's citation index. His work has been incorporated in cross-cultural training and taught in universities around the world, particularly in international management courses.

But this kind of approach attracts plenty of criticism, too.[9] You may have noticed that Hofstede used a pretty narrow set of questions—about workplace preferences—to draw conclusions about an extremely broad concept: *individualism*. In addition, using questionnaire items in order to extrapolate a numerical ranking for a whole country—which will undoubtedly have lots of variation within its borders—has also been criticized. Such an approach may also encourage people to think of culture as a quantifiable essence—a kind of national character—that resides within each individual. For his part, that doesn't seem to be Hofstede's intent. I have heard Hofstede say during a presentation that, "Culture doesn't exist." By this, he means that labels such as *individualism* and *collectivism* are not intended to describe qualities that reside predictably in all the individuals in a cultural community.

From the sociological perspective, of course, terms such as *individualism* and *collectivism* are constructs—convenient labels that describe a group-level phenomenon. They wouldn't be expected to predict individual behavior any more than knowing that the Super Bowl is popular would be expected to predict whether a particular individual is a football fan. There's a reasonable concern, however, that listing countries by cultural characteristics encourages stereotypical thinking, such as: "Oh, people from Guatemala are collectivists!" And, as David Matsumoto points out, cultural value orientations can be poor predictors of actual behavior. Knowing how people answered on a workplace questionnaire may tell us little about their behavior or preferences in other areas of their lives.

This highlights some of the challenges of quantifying culture. Until recently, the dominant methodology used to measure cultural difference came from the social sciences. Sociological research—such as the massive World Values Survey, an international research project measuring attitudes from people from around the world—uses value questionnaires that are then analyzed statistically.[10] Culture is also studied by psychologists who measure it as a *trait*—a stable internal characteristic that can be shown to influence behavior at the individual level. Measuring cultural traits requires that you define the cultural element you want to measure (the cultural *dimension*) and the realm in which that element might manifest itself (the *domain*).[11] The starting assumption of such an approach is that culture is a form of shared behavior and attitudes. As David Matsumoto himself explains:

> Culture exists in each and every one of us individually as much as it exists as a global, social construct. Individual differences in culture can be observed among people in the degree to which they adopt and engage in the attitudes, values, beliefs and behaviors that, by consensus, constitutes their culture. If you act in accordance with those shared values or behaviors, then that culture resides in you; *if you do not share in those values or behaviors, then you do not share that culture.*[12] [Emphasis added.]

The idea that I've highlighted here—that if you don't share a community's values or behavior, then you don't share in its culture—is a cornerstone of much cross-cultural research. If we follow this line of reasoning to its natural conclusions, we may conclude that because individual behavior varies widely in any community, and is *not* easily predicted by cultural traits alone, then culture's role in our lives is very limited and perhaps even inconsequential.

Yet this brings us back to the dilemma faced by the intercultural educators at the conference. If culture has so little predictive value, if it has supposedly so little influence on behavior, then why is the *experience* of cultural difference so powerful? Why, then, would cultural difference create significant amounts of misunderstanding? As we'll see, the answer to this question may lie in the fact that culture—and by extension cultural difference—functions at a level that is deeper and more diffuse than can be measured using traditional methodology.

Deep Culture Difference

During lunch after Matsumoto's plenary address, I asked other audience members what they thought about his ideas. Many were skeptical of the idea that statistically measured cultural difference does *not* represent any meaningful difference between peoples. Their lived experience told them that *cultural difference is powerful.* They had seen it cause misunderstanding and miscommunication. Many had faced challenges adapting to life in foreign countries—gradually understanding what had initially seemed like exotic or puzzling behavior. At the same time, Matsumoto's arguments were statistically and intellectually convincing. All of this creates a complicated and contradictory picture of cultural difference. It feels real, yet it's hard to define or quantify clearly.

I believe that a view of culture that explicitly takes into consideration out-of-awareness cognition can help us move forward beyond this seeming contradiction. Rather than seeing culture primarily as a factor that influences behavior—*He did that because of his culture*—we are learning how cultural knowledge operates in the background of our minds. This reminds us that culture is not only manifest in our actions and choices; it can also be found in our ability to interpret the behaviors of others. This flips Matsumoto's argument on its head. He proposes that when people choose different behaviors, they cannot be said to share in a cultural community. From the perspective of expert cultural intuitions, however, *the mark of shared cultural knowledge is not the degree to which our be-*

havior is typical or non-typical; it is the degree to which we are capable of successfully interpreting behavior in accordance with community standards.

Seen in this way, what makes me culturally American is not whether my behavior or personal values are typical of other Americans, but whether I can successfully predict how other Americans will perceive the behavior that I choose. If I break a convention, I do so knowingly, and as an expression of my intentions. A foreign tourist in Paris, for example, may neglect to say *bonjour* when entering a shop because of ignorance—unintentionally breaking a convention—whereas a French person may do so because she is angry at the poor service she received during a previous visit. While the behavior is the same, the communicative intent is different. The angry French individual is not less culturally French because she chooses not to say *bonjour*—in fact, she is breaking cultural conventions in order to express her state of mind. She can only do this skillfully with accurate cultural intuitions. The tourist, on the other hand, is simply bumbling.

My larger point is that we need to keep intuitive knowledge in mind when trying to understand cultural difference. As a largely unconscious, multidimensional phenomenon, we shouldn't expect cultural difference to be easily pinned down. As David Amodio says in a discussion of unconscious bias:

> Implicit processes are like the dark matter of social cognition. We have strong reason to believe they exist, given that so much of our behavior is unexplained by explicit beliefs and intentions. But because implicit processes are defined by the absence of awareness, they excel at eluding concrete description.[13]

Any study of cultural difference must take implicit processes into account. This means that while some elements of culture would seem to be accessible to conscious reflection and traditional research, we will need new approaches to these questions if we want to more fully understand the cultural dimensions of cognition and behavior.

New Paradigms

In 1991, Hazel Markus and Shinobu Kitayama published a landmark paper: *Culture and the Self: Implications for Cognition, Emotion, and Motivation.* In it, they articulated a new approach to understanding and studying cultural difference, arguing that our cultural environment can have an important impact on largely unconscious cognitive processes.[14] They attempted to identify principles that could be considered the building blocks of a neuro-cognitive approach to studying cultural difference. Their goal was to look at cultural difference not just in terms of behavior, but also in the architecture of the mind.

Their overall thesis is that cultural difference can be found in patterns of cognition that affect the way we process information, make sense of situations, and even think about our identities. As a starting point for their analysis, they introduce the idea of *independent* and *interdependent* construals of self. They point out that Westerners often take it for granted that a person is made up of a collection of relatively stable internal traits that mark them as a unique, autonomous entity. In this view of self, you have an inner core that should be expressed and developed. The idea of self-actualization and "finding oneself" is part and parcel of this way of thinking. Markus and Kitayama refer to this as an *independent self-construal*.

They argue, however, that people who grow up in more collectivist communities are more likely to have a more *interdependent self-construal*. This refers to a sense of self that is more contextual, based on relationships and social setting. You are a father at home and a subordinate at work. People still have unique identities, but they express those unique qualities in the context of their relationships with others. You can see a visualization of these contrasting construals in figure 9-1. The solid lines in the figure represent clear identity boundaries, while the dotted line represents a self that is more construed in relation to others.

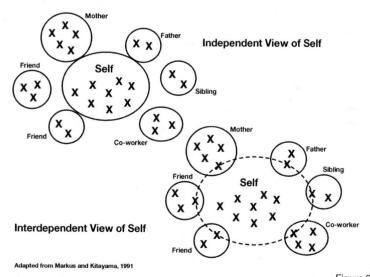

Figure 9-1

Adapted from Markus and Kitayama, 1991

In the *independent* view of self, internal traits are emphasized (the Xs in bold) and form the central organizing principle in how we conceptualize ourselves.

The bold Xs in the *interdependent* view of self, on the other hand, rest *between* individuals. Each individual has distinct internal qualities, but the starting point for self-construal is one's relationship with others. This means that we know others by the company they keep, and by whether they are a good friend, colleague, mother, cousin, and so on. Mental and emotional health comes not so much from having a positive self-image, but rather by building positive relationships with those around us. Being overly self-concerned is unhealthy since it takes away from the relationships that nurture us.

People with independent self-construals tend to think of individuality in terms of standing out, being unique, marching to a different drummer, and so on. I sometimes ask students in what situation they feel that they are most purely "themselves." My Western students regularly recount scenarios in which they are doing something alone, or something that is particular to them, such as listening to music by their favorite band. Asian students often recount scenarios in which they are with other people—particularly their friends or family. From the interdependent point of view, you are never more *yourself* than when you are among the people who know and care about you. That's when you can really let your hair down and fully express what's special about you.

The differences between these two kinds of self-construals can be heard in the story of Mohamed, an African who lived for more than twenty years in Germany before returning to visit his family in Mali. After all his time in Europe, he had become accustomed to more private space and a more independent construal of self. At one point he left the family's living room and went into a different room to be by himself, closing the door behind him. This worried his family members, and his brother came to ask him if he felt sick. Mohamed explained that he just wanted to be alone with his thoughts. His brother left, but came back a few minutes later and said, "Mother sent me back to help you with your thinking." For Mohamed's family, the desire to be separate and cut off from those who know and love you was a worrisome sign.

Figure 9-2

Markus and Kitayama's approach represents a fundamental shift in how cultural difference is being conceptualized. Rather than looking at cultural *values* as the building blocks of culture, they seek to identify culturally modified cognitive organizing principles.[15] These are said to reflect structural differences of our cognitive systems, with implications for our ways of thinking, our self-image in relation to others, what motivates us, and when and how we regulate emotion. Put more simply, our cultural environment shapes our cognitive systems in multiple, interrelated ways. For example, they propose that self-independent thinking is not only associated with seeing ourselves as discrete people with internal qualities; it means looking at the world in general that way, too.

This new approach is taking us beyond lists that compare or rank countries based on cultural values, and opening up new avenues of cross-cultural research. Independent–interdependent thinking has been studied, for example, using neuroimaging. A new generation of brain scanners, and in particular functional magnetic resonance imaging (fMRI) scanners, have allowed researchers to see what parts of the brain are activated during various cognitive tasks, providing a visual representation of cognitive patterns. The relatively new field of cultural neuroscience has put these tools to use in an attempt to unravel the relationship between cultural background and brain function.[16]

Research has largely supported the idea that culture shapes our cognitive processes in ways consistent with Markus and Kitayama's view. In one line of research, for example, participants are asked to think about a person and then judge whether a particular personality trait matches that person. Researchers found that when Chinese subjects were asked to think about their mothers, they exhibited brain patterns similar to when thinking about themselves. When Westerners thought about their mothers, on the other hand, the result was similar to when thinking about a stranger.[17] It was as though the Chinese subjects experienced people close to them *as part of themselves*, whereas the Westerners experienced selfhood as being more separate, even from the people they are closest to.

These contrasts are found not only in the relationship between the self and others, but in other cognitive tasks as well. Below is a sample of this sort of research, as summarized by Shihui Han and Georg Northoff:

> *Westerners generally think in an analytical way, whereas East Asians generally think in a more holistic manner.* For instance, during a perception task, Americans were better at detecting changes in salient objects than East Asians and were less affected by contextual information.

> *Cultural differences are also evident in social cognition.* In a game that involved two individuals interacting, *Chinese participants were more in tune with their partner's perspective than Americans.*

> Furthermore, *Chinese people were more likely to describe memories of social and historical events* and focused more on social interactions, whereas *European Americans more frequently focused on memories of personal experiences* and emphasized their personal roles in events.

> *Westerners were better at remembering trait words that they associated with themselves* than they were at remembering words associated with people close to them, whereas Chinese people remembered both equally well.

> *Americans tended to explain behaviors in terms of people's dispositions* (for example, a person's gender and education), whereas *East Asians showed a preference for attributing behavior to situational factors* (for example, environmental events), and were more likely to use situational information to predict other people's behavior.

> *Chinese people endorsed contextual explanations of physical events* (for example, friction influencing the movement of an object) more often

than Americans, who were more likely to attribute physical events to dispositional factors (for example, an object's weight or composition).

Culture influences category-based classification of objects: Compared to European Americans, Chinese people organized objects in a more relational way (for example, grouping a monkey and a banana together because monkeys eat bananas) and less of a categorical way (for example, grouping a monkey and a panda together because both are animals).[18]

Research like this makes it clear that we are just at the beginning of a long road to understanding cultural difference. As we shift our focus from behavioral measures of cultural difference to examining contrasting patterns of cognition, we undergo something of a paradigm shift. Instead of attempting to measure the affects of culture on behavior—as though our actions are the truest measure of our essential qualities—we are now examining more directly the machinery of perception, emotion, and thought. It's like transitioning from the intuitively straightforward Newtonian worldview to the much more complex world of Einsteinian physics.

This is both good and bad news for interculturalists: the study of culture, long a diffuse and elusive phenomenon, is becoming more grounded in an empirical understanding of the brain. The old dichotomy between biological sciences and social sciences is being breached. Yet we still lack simple answers to basic questions, such as *How does culture affect the way we experience the world?* And current research looks only at the tiniest fraction of the myriad cultural differences that we find around the world. So far, population samples are highly limited—often focused on people from East Asian and Western countries. And the effects being found are highly diffuse—they are spread out over a number of different cognitive functions.

Still, this represents real progress, though Markus and Kitayama predict challenges with this new approach. First of all, we are forced to recognize that conscious introspection is insufficient to understand cultural difference, since we may be unaware of the very cognitive processes we are attempting to measure.[19] That implies that the effects of culture will be hard to define and measure. And a neurocognitive approach hasn't answered some fundamental questions, such as the *depth* of culture difference—whether cultural differences are primarily behavioral, or whether people experience situations differently as well.

For a traveler who is packing a suitcase for Tallinn or Toledo, the primary lesson of all this is that cultural difference is more complex than it might appear.

Culture is not an invisible hand that makes people act in a particular way. Cultural influence on behavior is indirect, multifaceted, and complex. The doubts that Dr. Matsumoto raised in his lecture are indicative of the limitations of traditional approaches to measuring cultural difference, and to an overly simple view of what those differences might be.

The Culture of Honor

As I've said, new research methodology is allowing us to measure culture's impact on the cognitive processes of the brain. Yet as a phenomenon, culture also exists out in the world, as patterns of interaction and social organization—how we educate our children, the norms that we follow in everyday life, the values we aspire to, and so on. How then, do the culturally influenced patterns of cognition in our brain relate to the cultural patterns found in society at large? Can we analyze cultural difference at these different levels—the more strictly biological level of brain and body, together with the more abstract level of behavior and social systems? To do so, we would need to draw on biological sciences, cognitive science, social psychology, sociology, and anthropology. Cross-cultural research that attempts to make a connection between cultural patterns inside the individual, and the patterns in a cultural community, would be complex indeed.

There are researchers who are taking on this challenge. Richard Nisbett took a multidimensional approach in researching the cultural value of *honor*. In one experiment that drew from the methodology of social psychology, for example, he set up an elaborate scenario in which participants were sent to drop off a questionnaire at the end of a hallway. On the way, however, a male confederate of the researchers opened a file cabinet, blocking the subject's path. The confederate eventually closed the drawer and let the subject pass, but when the subject returned, needing to pass again, the man slammed the drawer shut, bumped the subject with his shoulder, and muttered "Asshole" before walking away.

Honor in the hallway...

Asshole!

Nisbett and Cohen, 1996

Figure 9-3

The purpose of this manufactured conflict was to test how people respond to being insulted in public. Nisbett wanted to know if this confrontation would provoke signs of violent thought patterns, a stress response (elevated cortisol levels), or an aggression response (a spike in testosterone). Also, observers in the hallway pretending to study took notice whether the subject's facial expression more resembled anger or amusement. The subjects, naturally, had no idea they were being tested.[20]

Researchers hypothesized that someone raised in an environment that places a cultural emphasis on honor—the defending of one's public reputation—would respond more strongly to a public insult. They had a hunch that on average, men from the American South would react more strongly to being bumped in this way. They chose subjects that were all of a similar age (young) and level of education (well-educated), and from families that were well-off. Results showed that the Southerners were indeed more likely to react with anger, accompanied by a spike in their levels of cortisol and testosterone. In a variation on the experiment, Southerners were more likely to challenge a large football player who refused to give way when passing them in the hallway.[21]

Surprising? Is there truly an *honor culture* of some sort in the South that can provoke these physiological responses? Does this sound stereotypical or just like common sense? To find out more, the researchers looked at a wide range of data from other sources—including social psychology experiments, crime statistics, immigration patterns, and anthropological data from honor-based cultures around the world.[22] One interesting facet of their research involved sending out job applications from people who had supposedly been convicted of a crime in which they had defended their honor. Companies in the American South were more likely to look beyond that and express an interest in the applicant. With this multipronged approach, Nisbett was able to quantify the existence of an "honor culture" that influences bodily responses and behavior.

We tend to associate *culture* with the past: tradition, ceremonies, and beliefs passed on from previous generations. This research takes that idea a step further by tracing honor back through history. Its premise is that the emphasis on honor in the American South has its roots in the Scottish Highlands, where many immigrants from the southern United States come from. Anthropologists have long known that herding societies, such as those found in Scotland in the past, commonly value honor—defined as giving importance to public reputation. Animals kept in plain sight are tempting targets, so having a reputation as a fierce defender of one's own interests can help safeguard one's flock. The cultural logic of defending your honor, then, is as a means of protecting your assets by defending your reputation. The rush of testosterone felt by the young Southerners in the hallway may well represent an embodied form of cultural cognition passed on from previous generations across the ocean.

Cultural Difference and the Intercultural Mind

The testosterone spikes in that hallway in Michigan—and other research into cognition, emotion, and motivation—remind us that culture is not simply an idea, symbol, historical fact, or customary behavior. Our cultural configurations affect our perceptions and physiological reactions to the world, meaning that we can find cultural difference at the deepest levels of self. In addition, it reminds us that cultural difference is manifest in interaction—the way that the Southern and Northern gentlemen reacted in that hallway, made sense of their encounter, and decided on what course of action to take.

Cultural difference is related to the shared patterns of communication and interaction that we use every day. This *everydayness* highlights the intuitive nature of culture—we act and react based on our unconscious evaluation of a situation. And culture is symbolic: abstracts concepts, values, and symbols—such as ethnicity, honor, and national flags—are meaningful and experienced as part of our identity. People regularly die defending such symbols. And finally, cultural phenomena exist at multiple scales—from the micro level of associative networks in the brain to the macro scale of civilizations and philosophies.

It's hard to wrap one's head around the big picture of cultural difference. It would be nice if researchers had found some straightforward grammar of cultural difference—the kind of thing Edward Hall was looking for. We're not even close to doing that. Richard Nisbett believes that in order to get there, we need to draw on insights from evolutionary psychology to differentiate between universal problems that all societies face (how to raise one's young, for example) and problems that are more local in nature (such as the Dutch needing to collaborate to build dykes).[23] Having this sort of metatheoretical base could help guide our efforts to identify areas of universality and variation in culture.

What does this sort of research mean for those of us grappling with the challenges of intercultural living? Primarily, it is a reminder of the depth and complexity of cultural difference. Cross-cultural research is like a very narrow beam of light that we can only shine on tiny features of a dark and complex landscape. As we look around, highlighting different elements of our surroundings, we become more consciously aware of patterns in the cultural landscape. Even the best cross-cultural research, however, can only take us so far. A deep understanding of cultural difference requires an intuitive, experiential learning process. We need to grope around in the dark in order to explore and move forward. While the abstractions and analysis presented in this chapter can help us conceptually, we also need to allow our minds to detect cultural patterns intuitively—stumbling around and bumping into unexpected cultural topography, and thereby sharpening our intercultural mind.

KEY CONCEPTS

Independent construal of self: *A sense of self as a collection of relatively stable internal traits that mark you as a unique, autonomous entity—you have an inner core that should be expressed and developed. This construal is associated with a more analytic cognitive style, a focus on self as opposed to relations and situation, and a tendency towards category-based classification.*

Interdependent construal of self: *A sense of self that is contextual and based on relationships and social setting. People express their unique identities in the context of their relationships with others. This construal is associated with holistic thinking, sensitivity to context, an emphasis on the perspective of others, and a tendency towards relational thinking.*

Discussion Quote: *Implicit processes are like the dark matter of social cognition. We have strong reason to believe they exist, given that so much of our behavior is unexplained by explicit beliefs and intentions. But because implicit processes are defined by the absence of awareness, they excel at eluding concrete description.*

10.

the language-culture connection

Wearing different color glasses!

—Marina

It's easy to agree that there's a connection between language and culture, but it's difficult to tease apart the relationship between the two. New research into embodied simulation, however, shows us that linguistic meaning can be seen as a form of simulated experience. This can help us better understand the language-culture connection in our minds.

The Monolingual American

After fourteen years living in Tokyo, Paul's Japanese language ability is still limited. He can handle the simple needs of daily life—shopping, ordering food, asking for directions—yet can't connect simple ideas into an ongoing conversation or narrative. He can introduce himself and tell you that he works as a university instructor, yet he doesn't get far beyond the basic facts he needs to convey. Though he's open and engaging, he can't really express his personality in Japanese, so with strangers he switches to English if possible. He feels somewhat embarrassed by this lack and recognizes that it fits the stereotype of the ignorant American abroad.

The reality of daily life, however, is that Paul gets by quite well with only foreign language basics. He vacations in Hawaii, streams American movies and news, and has plenty of foreign friends. His Japanese wife speaks excellent English. Paul is happy and does not feel isolated—he knows Tokyo well, and is knowledgeable about food and the customs of daily life. He can order food and drink, shop, ask for directions and make basic small talk. The administrative documents at his university are mostly translated into English for the benefit of foreign staff members. He's happy as a mostly monolingual expat. He seems to have found an equilibrium abroad that doesn't depend heavily on using the local language.

Paul's story raises many questions, but I want to focus on the relationship between language and culture. More specifically, I'm curious about the relationship between linguistic ability and intercultural understanding. How important is learning a foreign language? Is it a critical part of cultural learning? Does it provide us with an insider's view that can't be obtained otherwise? Or is language learning primarily a way to meet practical needs?

I regularly meet people like Paul who live in a foreign country for long periods without learning the local language. I meet expatriate executives who simply decide that they are too busy to focus on language learning. Some study-abroad students in Asia find that a year abroad may not be nearly enough to make them fluent in Japanese or Chinese and give up trying. Most agree that language learning adds to a foreign experience, but many still don't make it a high priority. It takes years and the payoff is not always clear. Paul told me that he has enough language ability to get his needs met, and thus improving his Japanese really wouldn't help him that much. Is that true? As travel and communication become more convenient—you can get a translation app for your smartphone—is foreign language learning worth all the effort?

Language-Culture-Cognition

Your attitude towards Paul, and towards foreign language learning in general, hinges at least partly on your view of the relationship between language and culture. Does speaking a new language give us access to a new way of looking at things? Is Paul missing out on a unique Japanese perspective because of his limited language ability? Does speaking a new language involve learning to inhabit a different perceptual world? Or is language just a set of labels for thoughts? Perhaps language is simply a code that allows us to communicate concepts and ideas that don't fundamentally depend on language. Perhaps Paul can learn about Japan by having Japanese things explained to him in English. If the answer is closer to the former—a more *relativistic* view—then Paul is really missing out on whole worlds of meaning. If the truth is closer to the latter, more *universalistic* view, then perhaps Paul doesn't need Japanese that much after all.

This distinction is important because it shapes how we approach our intercultural experiences. Broadly speaking, a more relativistic view emphasizes the importance of language learning when in a foreign environment. Language is seen as unlocking a door that helps cultural learners gain entry into a new cultural world—one that can only be fully accessed through the insider's perspective of language. Relativism implies an important distinction between insiders who share a linguistic and cultural worldview, and outsiders who do not. Language learning becomes a sort of pre-requisite for cultural learning, implying that Paul is really missing the boat. How could someone live in Japan so long and *not* have learned more Japanese?

Others, however, find Paul's case more understandable. A more universalistic stance lends itself to a pragmatic and functional view of language ability. Language is about communicating ideas and accomplishing tasks. It is seen as less central to thinking and perceiving. Language, in this view, is simply a tool for communicating ideas. What's important is not the language we use, but the ideas we communicate. In this view, Paul's attitude is not so hard to understand. Japanese is, after all, a difficult language. He has functional language skills and is respectful of Japanese people. There are, it must be added, many different ways to learn about Japan. From a more universalistic perspective, speaking the local language may be useful, but it's not necessarily essential for cultural learning.

There is no consensus on this question. Cognitive linguist Steven Pinker expresses this more universalistic position when he writes, "People don't think in English or Chinese or Apache; they think in the language of thought."[1] He says that mistaking language for thought is a "conventional absurdity"—something that goes against common sense but that people repeat because they've heard it before.[2] This view represents a kind of "thought first" view, which holds that the human capacity for thought, advanced cognition, and consciousness evolved first and was a starting condition for the development of language.[3] The neuroscientist Antonio Damasio argues along those lines when he says, "The idea that self and consciousness would emerge *after* language, and would be a direct construction of language, is not likely to be correct. Language does not come out of nothing. Language gives us names for things."[4]

There are those, however, who think the opposite—that the development of language led to our ability for abstract thought. In this view, words allowed us to express thoughts not related to the here-and-now, and this spurred the development of more abstract thinking.[5] It allowed us to live more fully in a world not just of physical objects and immediate concerns, but of ideas and meaning, speculation and fantasy. If so, then language may well have a big impact on our ability to conceive of the world in new ways. In this view, language, as a symbolic system to express thought, is seen as a central element of our cognitive processes.

At the root of this conundrum is our ignorance about the nature of *meaning*, and how it is related to thought and language. For Pinker, meaning is independent of language. He hypothesizes what he calls *mentalese*—meaningful thoughts, existing *independently* of language, that consist of "symbols for concepts, and arrangements of symbols that correspond for who did what to whom."[6] This view sees meaning primarily in terms of concepts that we hold in our mind, and that can then be transmitted, using language, to others. Or, as Pinker puts it, "Language conveys news." This view implies that meaning is a product of general cognitive capacities, and thus not likely to be affected in important ways by linguistic and cultural differences. In other words, because we have similar cognitive systems that we use to experience the external world, linguistic differences will likely only reflect superficial variation in how we experience things.

There are others who take a more relativistic stance, arguing that language is an artifact or tool of culture—something developed in response to particular environments and thus reflecting wide variations in human experience.[7] People who see language as an important shaper of our thoughts typically argue for some degree of *linguistic relativity*, popularly known as the Sapir-Whorf hypothesis. Edward Sapir stated his position way back in 1929:

> Human beings do not live in the objective world alone, or alone in the world of social activity as ordinarily understood, but are very much at the mercy of the particular language which has become the medium of expression for their society. It is quite an illusion to imagine that one adjusts to reality essentially without the use of language and that language is merely an incidental means of solving specific problems of communication or reflection.[8]

Since then, linguists have attempted to prove or disprove this idea in a number of ways. Studies supporting linguistic relativity looked at, for example, the ability to classify colors, categorize objects, and make hypothetical interpretations.[9, 10, 11] Other researchers, however, have challenged such results.[12] Studies like this seemed to go out of fashion for a time, but new research is emerging and encouraging those who speak in favor of linguistic relativism.[13] One study that I enjoyed showed that when Spanish speakers describe the qualities of a key, for example, they tend to use more feminine adjectives (such as "lovely" or "little"), whereas German speakers tend to choose more masculine words (such as "jagged" or "serrated"). Researchers propose that this is because the word for "key" is a feminine noun in Spanish and a masculine noun in German, and that this affects the way people perceive these objects.[14]

Though interesting, this sort of research seems only distantly related to Paul's situation. It's hard to imagine Spanish speakers having distressing intercultural conflicts with German speakers over miscommunication about keys. It's not clear how such differences could create barriers to intercultural understanding. The issue for intercultural learners is not *perception* in the sense of processing visual stimuli in relation to colors or shapes, it's about *perception* in the broader sense of *how we look at things*. It's possible that language has little or no affect on the perception of colors and physical objects, yet still is closely related to one's view of a situation. For sojourners, the question is the degree to which ignorance of a foreign language will prevent us from understanding others. If we had highly skilled translation technology, for example, would mutual understanding be relatively easy? Or are there many things that would still get lost in translation?

Lost in Translation

It's often said that certain things can't be translated into another language. Some will say that reading Tolstoy in Russian is different from doing so in translation, or that the novel Don Quixote by Cervantes can only be fully appreciated in its original Spanish. The nuances of Japanese are purported to be notoriously difficult to capture and put into English. Looking at such translation difficulties may bring us closer to understanding the relationship between culture and language, because translation attempts not only to transmit individual ideas, but to also to provide entry into other times and places; other social worlds. With that in mind, let's look at examples of translation difficulties and see what lessons they might hold for interculturalists.

One famous example of a cultural product that is considered difficult to translate accurately is Japanese haiku poetry. One of the most famous poems is one by Matsuo Basho, which, in a total of only 17 syllables, evokes a scene of a frog jumping into a pond. For these 17 syllables, there are more than 100 different published translations, including:

Old pond – frogs jumped in – sound of water.

Pond, there, still and old!
A frog has jumped from the shore
The splash can be heard.

An old pond
The sound
Of a diving frog.

Breaking the silence
Of an ancient pond,
A frog jumped into water –
A deep resonance

Of the above translations, the first one is perhaps the most literal. Even so, there's some ambiguity, as the Japanese doesn't make clear whether "frog" is singular or plural. What's missing from this translation is the atmosphere, or the nuance of the scene as would be imagined or experienced by a Japanese speaker. Other translations try to capture the mental imagery that might occur to a Japanese speaker using turns of phrase like *breaking the silence*, or *a deep resonance*. Those words are not directly in the poem, but they are part of the linguistic experience for Japanese speakers.

As you can see, the difficulty here is not so much communicating facts—the facts of what happens in this haiku are very straightforward. The challenge is in capturing the mood and symbolic associations. A pond is more than a body of water, and the silence is more than a lack of sound. This is a reminder that language is about more than "concepts" that can be objectively represented using different linguistic codes. Language captures something of human *experience*. The images and associations that this haiku generates for Japanese speakers is, in some hard to quantify way, different from any approximation created in English.

From the intercultural perspective, then, language learning is not so much about acquiring information as about gaining access to shared experience. Words that are difficult to translate are often related to shared experience. The word *furoshiki*, for example, is a Japanese word that refers to a piece of cloth used to wrap things in. In Japan, where there is a tradition of using cloth to wrap things, this word calls up memories and associations related to the *experience* of using *furoshiki*. Likewise, the word *saudade* is a Portuguese word for the feeling we have towards something that we love and have lost. While this is an experience that may be common to people everywhere, Portuguese focuses our attention on that experience. In the Yagan language of South America, *mamihlapinatapei* refers to the silent, meaningful look exchanged by two people who are ready to initiate something, but hesitate. We can see that language has, at the very least, the power to focus our attention on particular aspects of our experience.[15]

Sometimes, an understanding of a word hinges on having experience *within* a cultural community. For example, a friend of Barack Obama's mother in Indonesia, Elizabeth Bryant, described him during his childhood in Java in the following way: "He has the manner of Asians and the ways of Americans—being *halus*, being patient, calm, a good listener."[16] As we saw in chapter 6, *halus* refers to a Javanese ideal of restraint, dignity, and calm command. Bryant seems to have used this Indonesian word because she felt it was impossible to accurately express it using the conceptual universe of English. You have to experience *halus* in the Indonesian context to have a clear understanding of how a Javanese might understand this word.

Likewise, the psychologist Takeo Doi wrote a whole book about the Japanese word *amae*—meaning a sort of nurturing dependence—which he argues is a central organizing principle of Japanese social relations, and thus untranslatable.[17] *Amae* assumes a hierarchical social world in which those in higher positions care for and nurture those below, and those in a lower position depend on and are guided by those above. Depending on the context, it can be used as a verb to refer to seeking indulgence or special treatment (as when an employee presumes that it's no big deal to come back late from lunch), to seek affection or reassurance (of a child towards a parent, for example), or even to let one's guard down (as when a strong man rests his head on the shoulder of his girlfriend in a gesture of trust and intimacy). As with the word *halus*, understanding the word *amae* is contingent upon having a sense for how people relate to each other in a particular cultural community.

If language reflects shared experience, then it follows that language and cultural communities that are more closely related will have fewer problems with shared understanding. For my part, I remember only occasionally feeling that it was difficult to grasp culturally laden concepts in Spanish. One example was the word *macho*, which seemed much more complex in Mexican Spanish than the way I was used to using it in English. When learning Japanese, on the other hand, I struggled more often. One example is the word *nakama*. A Japanese–English dictionary provides a long list of more than fifty possible equivalents, including: associate, buddy, chum, cohort, colleague, companion, comrade, cohort, coterie, crew, crowd, family, fellow, friend, good buddy, helpmate, homie, mate, neighbor, pal, peer, sidekick, tribe, and yokemate.[18] With time, I figured out that *nakama* refers to the particular social connections that come from sharing an ingroup—a kind of ingroup feeling. To get an intuitive sense for the word *nakama*, though, I needed more than a list of translations. I needed lived *experience* with Japanese ingroups.

The extensive list of possible equivalences for *nakama*, and the roundabout descriptions necessary for communicating words like *halus* or *amae*, provide clues to the relationship between language and meaning. If we think of meaning in terms of *mentalese*—symbolic thought separate from language—we run into difficulties. How could a single word in one language require so many possible translations in another? The word *nakama* had more than fifty possible equivalents! If meaning exists independently of language, and thus independently of culture, it seems like it should be easier to create clear, concise translations. An idea that can be expressed with one word in one language shouldn't require so much roundabout description and contextual information to label in another. This hints that linguistic meaning not only exists as universally definable concepts, but is also closely tied to situation and shared social experience, and thus culture.

Embodied Simulation

Recent research in the field of cognitive science and neurolinguistics is giving us new tools to look at the questions of language, thought, and meaning. New theoretical models—supported by empiric research—are taking us beyond the simple cause-and-effect conceptualization of Whorfian thinking about language and meaning.[19] We are starting to be able to test these models using more empirical methods. We can ask the question: How is the experience of meaning generated by cognitive processes? And How is the experience of meaning related to our use of language? What, in other words, is the relationship between language, thought, and meaning?

From the intercultural perspective, I am particularly excited by recent research related to the theory of *embodied simulation*. This research attempts to understand how the brain produces meaning, and how this process is related to language use. Neurolinguist Benjamin Bergen, for example, argues that linguistic meaning does not simply consist of abstract concepts or symbols that are somehow stored in our brain, as would be the case with mentalese. Instead, when we hear a word, our brain *simulates the experience that is associated with that word.*[20]

Let's take a look at some of the implication of this idea. According to this theory, if I say to you, "The dog jumped over the swimming pool," your brain responds by creating a mental simulation of what it would be like to actually see this. This means that the word *dog* doesn't exist in our mind only as a disembodied prototype or construct. Rather, the meaning we construct when understanding this sentence is a direct result of our experiences. Thus, someone who has a Chihuahua and lives in a big house with a full-sized pool would call to mind a different image than someone with a Great Dane and an inflatable kiddie pool.

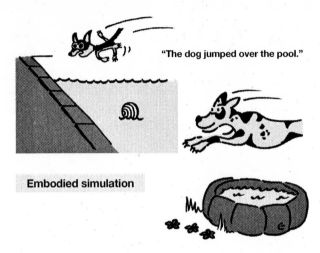

"The dog jumped over the pool."

Embodied simulation

Figure 10-1

This view provides a new approach to asking questions about meaning and language. It allows us to make predictions that can be tested, taking the debate from the realm of philosophy more fully into that of empirical research. For example, if meaning is produced in a non-linguistic way as images that exist as abstract *concepts*, one would expect the images in our minds to be fairly prototypical—say, an idealized dog jumping over an idealized swimming pool. If linguistic meaning is more closely tied to actual experience, however, then the images this sentence provokes in our head should vary more widely based on individual experience, and by extension, on cultural background.

Bergen points to many studies that he feels support the view that linguistic meaning is tied to actual experience. In one, volunteers were exposed to words accompanied with either a picture or an audio recording—with the word *cow* they might see a picture of a cow, whereas with the word *rooster* they might hear *cock-a-doodle-doo*. The next day, they were asked to recall whether they had learned particular words together with a sound or picture. An fMRI scan showed that when remembering the words they learned with the picture, the parts of the brain used in seeing were activated, while the words paired with audio activated the part of the brain used in processing sounds. In other words, recalling a word reflected the experience associated with that word.[21] It's also been shown that recalling actions activates parts of the brain responsible for those actions. When recalling the action of making a fist, for example, PET brain imaging showed activation in parts of the brain associated with that behavior.[22]

The idea of embodied simulation jibes with other common experiences. Research has shown that picturing the perfect tennis serve in your mind can help you attain one on the court because there is a cognitive connection between imagining a behavior and performing it.[23] Another interesting finding is that hearing a word can interfere with our ability to perceive that object, a phenomenon known as the Perky effect.[24] Think, for example, how hard it is to pay attention to our surroundings when speaking on a cell phone. If the embodied simulation hypothesis is correct, this is because language processing uses up mental resources that otherwise would be used for physical perception. Embodied simulation could also be what allows us to mentally rotate an image in our mind to see it from a different perspective—something that would seem more difficult if meaning existed as pure abstraction.[25]

This line of research accords with the phenomenon of embodiment in general—the idea that our mental experience entails integrated mind-body processes. Daniel Kahneman talks about this in terms of *associative activation*, the way in which one meaning in our mind will trigger another, and another, and so on.[26] He explores this by asking readers to look at the following two words:

banana   vomit

Simply seeing these words creates a cascade of images and physiological effects in your mind and body. A rather disgusting scenario pops into mind—one associated with vomiting—such as getting drunk or being sick. Your body will have an embodied reaction as well, with a slight grimace on your face and a rise in your heart rate. Your mind has also now been *primed* (made more sensitive) to other things that are yellow or that might make you feel nauseous. This range of reactions begins instantaneously at the level of the intuitive mind, before you've fully registered the meaning of these words consciously. As Kahneman puts it, "Cognition is embodied; you think with your body, not only with your brain."[27]

Seeing linguistic meaning in terms of embodied simulation seems relatively straightforward when talking about objects and actions—like seeing, hearing, and eating. But what about our ability to think about things that don't exist in time and space, such as *company*, or *joy*, or *quadratic equation*? One answer is that we think metaphorically. We *shed light* on a problem, *move forward* with our lives, have it *up to here* when losing our patience, and even *feel down* when depressed. In this view, we experience the meaning of abstractions in ways that correspond to more concrete experience. The linguist George Lakoff argues that metaphor also structures our thinking and interactions, and that "our ordinary conceptual system, in terms of which we both think and act, is fundamentally metaphorical in nature."[28]

In Lakoff's view, metaphors are powerful shapers of experience. He believes that "Our concepts structure what we perceive, how we get around in the world, and how we relate to other people." When English speakers talk about arguments, for example, they use expressions associated with competition and war—such as *scoring points, winning an argument*, not *giving ground*, or *yielding an inch*. In chapter eight, I talked about how decision-making in English can be conceptualized metaphorically as a marketplace of ideas—as reflected in expressions such as *give and take* and *putting our options on the table, weighing our options*, and so on. This can be contrasted with metaphors for decision-making in Japanese. Words such as *nemawashi* (root binding) or *uchiawase* (strike together) are metaphorically related to fusion or coming together. Lakoff and some other linguists argue that such metaphors are more than just turns of speech; they can provide clues to the thinking of that language's speakers.[29]

In an attempt to test these ideas empirically, Benjamin Bergen has done research related to the metaphorical properties of the words *joy* and *happiness*. He wanted to find out if words that represent abstract qualities such as these also trigger embodied simulation. He points out that though these words are close in meaning, there are metaphorical differences between them. Joy is more often talked about as though it is a liquid—we are *full of* joy or *overflow* with joy. Happiness, on the other hand, is typically talked about as though it is an object, as when we refer to *finding, sharing*, or *searching for* happiness. These tendencies aren't absolute, but *joy* is used twice as often with a container metaphor, and happiness ten times more often with the metaphor of searching.

Bergen was curious whether—all else being equal—people would more likely use the word *joy* in situations associated with liquid, and *happiness* in situations with searching. To test this, he showed people a smiling face and asked them whether the person seemed to be experiencing joy or happiness. He asked this question to three different groups: people who were filling themselves with liquid (in a bar); people actively searching for something (in a library); and people who were doing neither (sitting in a classroom). He found, in fact, that those in the bar chose *joy* more often, that those in the library chose *happiness* more often, and that the control group scored between the two. He argues that the state of the respondents' bodies affected their answer, and that this provides evidence that relatively abstract words are embodied simulations of more concrete things.[30]

Embodied Cultural Knowledge

If we experience meaning as a form of mental simulation of previous experiences, it becomes easier to see why some words are so hard to translate. As Bergen explains:

> The embodied simulations we construct when understanding language depend on the experiences that we've personally had. When those experiences differ systematically across cultures, this can in principle lead to the same words being interpreted differently—the same words can drive different embodied simulations for different populations of people.[31]

From this perspective, the words and expressions of language are more than symbols that encode information—they are mental simulations that we experience holistically. People who share the same language and culture have in common a rich body of experiential details about the world. Take, for example, the following sentence:

The Fourth of July is celebrated on July 4.

For Americans, the *Fourth of July* is more than a day on a calendar. It's a holiday associated with the American Declaration of Independence. It calls to mind images of fireworks, picnics, and hot dogs. Americans may associate it with the aged parchment of the Declaration of Independence, and be able to picture its loopy handwritten script in their mind. They may have affective associations with this word—a positive sense of national pride or nostalgic feelings about setting off firecrackers as a child. Even Americans who have never watched fireworks on the Fourth of July understand this rich set of associative meanings and experiences, as long as they've had enough lived experience in the cultural world of Americans to understand these associations.

Herein lies the power of language and its connection to culture—*sharing a language allows us to share a world of linguistic and, by extension, cultural experience with other speakers.* For those who learn English as a foreign language, and thus don't share this rich assortment of embodied associations, the *Fourth of July* sounds simply like the day that comes after the *third of July.* The more cultural experience one has in the United States, the more foreigners will be able to share the intuitive resonance of words like *The Fourth of July.* That is, not coincidentally, what would allow for more involved interaction with Americans. In a similar way, learning the word *halus* provides an entry point for understanding Javanese values and relationships with Indonesians, just as gaining an intuitive understanding of *amae* is part and parcel of an attempt to understand a Japanese worldview.

Patterns of Collective Simulation

There are other ways in which a cognitive perspective clarifies the relationship between linguistic meaning and cultural meaning. For one thing, the way that our brain processes meaning differs fundamentally from the way that a dictionary lists meaning. In our brain, linguistic meaning doesn't exist in discrete chunks with a list of explicit definitions. It is always connected to a network of meaningful associations. The word *bird*, for example, is associated with a particular category of animals (a category that includes animals with feathers, that lay eggs, and so on.) It is also associated with *qualities*, meaning that we can experience something as more or less *bird-like.* A penguin, for example, falls within the category of bird, although it is not very bird-like. A bat, on the other hand, has many birdlike qualities yet belongs to a different category.

In terms of cross-cultural understanding, this means that even words for an identical object can have vastly different sets of cultural associations, or belong to different categories. The word *pork*, for example, while referring to the meat of a pig, can be categorized as a forbidden food in one community and a luxury in another. It may be associated with impurity, or, on the contrary, with a wholesome breakfast (think bacon and eggs). This is a reminder that *dictionary definitions of words are not enough to communicate the network of meaningful associations found within a language or cultural community.*

The connection between linguistic meaning and cultural meaning can also be found in the patterns of associations *between* words or ideas. For many Americans and Europeans, for example, the word *wedding dress* sets off a particular cascade of images, such as the color white, the exchange of vows, veils, the procession down the aisle of a church, and so on. The white of a wedding dress has symbolic associations as well: virginity, purity, and tradition. This network of meaning, in turn, is associated with a Christian worldview—the idea that life is a struggle between good (white) and evil (black). We recognize that same symbolism in old Western movies, in which the good guy wears a white hat, and the bad guy a black hat.

Naturally, we don't normally think about the forces of good and evil when we see a wedding dress in a department store window, but people who share in these associations respond to them, and recognize them when they are pointed out. This isn't dependent on *agreeing* with these associations—it's not a question of whether people feel white *should* symbolize purity. Such associations simply exist as part of the pool of shared linguistic and cultural meaning. You may choose to break convention and wear a brown wedding dress, but you do so at your own peril, since people will not necessarily understand what you intend by it. The sum total of these associated networks is cultural meaning itself.

To take a contrasting example, Japanese Shinto wedding dresses are also typically white. But the associated networks of meaning connected to them are different. They signify purity of a different sort. White cloth is pure in the sense that it is undyed, and thus can take on the colors of the husband's family. Traditionally, marriage means that the wife incorporates herself into the husband's household—essentially taking on the "colors" of that family. White is also associated with death, as the bride dies to her family and is born into a new family. A wedding is a joining of two families and the transfer of a member from one to another. So while the white of Shinto and Western wedding dresses can both roughly be said to symbolize purity, a map of cultural associations reveals a very different set of underlying cultural patterns.

submission

天真炯没
new-born innocence

virginity

家内
in-house wife

pure soul

死 death
(leave family)

sin

Christianity

素直
sweet, genuine

clean conscious

家に入る enter household

good vs. evil

染まっていない un-dyed cloth

Figure 10-2

The schemas that English and Japanese speakers share for wedding dresses are both linguistic and cultural. Cultural schemas can be seen as the *collective simulation that unifies communities in shared mental experience,* while linguistic meaning is *the shared code that activates those shared simulations.* In other words, hearing the words "wedding dress" activates a culturally based simulation of a wedding dress. If we are cultural outsiders speaking a foreign language, our linguistic simulations are more impoverished. They may allow for communication, but they won't align as well.

The associative networks that I am describing are not simply abstractions. They are tied to everyday behavior as well, since language usage is closely tied to the behavioral scripts that govern human relations. Cultural scripts provide templates both for how to act and what to say. In the example above, it means that cultural knowledge of wedding dresses includes knowledge of wedding ceremonies, how one should dress when attending one, and so on. Cultural outsiders may learn English, but not know that "I do" is a key phrase when people get married, or have an idea of what "popping the question" refers to. Linguistic meaning, without a body of cultural associations, may serve to communicate relatively concrete facts, but will not make one fully functional in a community.

The need for these cultural schemas and scripts was discovered first hand by a student raised in New Zealand. She discovered that gaining a certain mastery of the Japanese language—how to tell people your name, for example—didn't mean that she would understand the scripts for getting to know people and make friends in Japan:

> Since I play guitar and am very interested in Japanese rock and indie bands, I joined several music circles. But despite playing with bands and going to events regularly, it was very difficult to form friendships. At the time, I thought it was purely a language barrier, but I realized that perhaps my struggle to fit in was because I didn't know the rules of interaction. I was behaving in those circles exactly as I would behave back home.

In a contrasting example, a Japanese student at an American university told me he was baffled to be invited to a *party*, only to be shown the beer keg and left on his own. He saw Americans standing around and talking, and had no idea what he was supposed to *do*. He expected a *party* to be more structured. For their part, the Americans there *were* partying—but the poor foreign student couldn't recognize the script, and didn't have the cultural and social skills to have a good time.

Language and Culture Learning

Stories like this are one more reminder of the close connection between language and cultural learning. For some people, however, it can be hard to get a sense of the benefits of taking on the challenge of foreign language learning. Beginning language learners often think of a foreign language primarily as words and rules to memorize—a new code for exchanging information. This information-centric view of language and culture affects how Paul thinks about learning languages too:

> I don't have a chance to use Japanese. I've made some attempts at times, joining language schools. I guess there are other things I've been interested in. . . . I would have to create opportunities. For example I could go to the store, and even though I don't need tuna fish, I could ask for the tuna fish. I could call a department store on the phone and ask for something.

It doesn't occur to Paul that using Japanese not only allows him to exchange information, it also creates relationships and provides a starting point for a more fully shared cultural experience. This may be why some expatriates don't feel the need for the local language. In the information age, we can get limitless information from electronic devices, so why bother interacting with unpredictable biological data systems (aka human beings)?

Many other people, of course, recognize the shared-experience aspect of foreign language learning—particularly those who have made it beyond the beginner level. Neil, an American who has spent far less time in Japan than Paul, says:

> Once you demonstrate that you have some ability to speak the language, people treat you more as an ordinary person. Maybe you won't get the special treatment, but at the same time you feel more part of the group instead of always being outside.

Neil's statement that you will be treated "more as an ordinary person" when speaking the local language captures quite nicely the way in which language provides an entry point into another cultural community. And as you share more fully in new linguistic and cultural communities, you may feel shifts in your identity as well. You may even feel an expanding intercultural self. As Robert, highly fluent in three languages, says:

> You are as many people as languages that you speak. When you speak a different language, your thought patterns change and your gestures change. And when people tell jokes in that language, you understand but you couldn't necessarily explain that to people in another language. The reference points and assumptions are just so different.

Robert's experience is not rare, though certainly not everyone who gains proficiency in a foreign language finds it to be transformational or deeply satisfying. At the very least, however, a cognitive perspective—as well as stories like this—can help us understand just how deep the culture and language connection can be.

Language, Culture, and the Intercultural Mind

Learning to speak a foreign language helps us develop an intercultural mind in several ways. First of all, it allows us to go to new places and see new things—it gives us new freedom of movement. Even a few words of Thai can give you the courage to approach a street stall and eat dinner elbow to elbow with the locals in Bangkok. Foreign language ability provides an entry point into new experiences. It gets us invited into people's homes, increases our level of interaction, and allows us to relate to people we might be cut off from otherwise. Ultimately, a foreign language opens a door into new worlds of shared cultural experience.

KEY CONCEPTS

Embodied simulation: *The hypothesis that the brain generates linguistic meaning by simulating lived experience.*

Embodied cultural knowledge: *The idea that cultural knowledge involves shared mental experiences. This includes schema (networks of meaning association) and scripts (patterns of behavior associated with particular situations).*

Discussion Quotes

Sapir: It is quite an illusion to imagine that . . . language is merely an incidental means of solving specific problems of communication or reflection.

Pinker: People don't think in English or Chinese or Apache; they think in the language of thought.

Bergen: The embodied simulations we construct when understanding language depend on the experiences that we've personally had. When those experiences differ systematically across cultures, this can in principle lead to the same words being interpreted differently.

11.

the intercultural mind

It takes a long time to be a bridge person.

—Yukino

How can we develop a more intercultural mind? Given the complexity of our cognitive systems, there's not likely any single, discrete quality that will make us interculturally competent or aware. There are, however, important cognitive capacities that seem to be important, including cultural frame shifting.

Americans in Paris

When I lived in Paris, I sometimes jumped on the high-speed Thalys train for a quick trip to the "Low Country," as the Netherlands is referred to in French. On one such occasion, as I settled into my crimson seat, I noticed a couple who had settled their substantial girth across the aisle from me. I immediately thought, "They're Americans." They wore oversized T-shirts and had two large suitcases. The man wore baggy, squared-off shorts with expandable pockets on the thighs; his head was topped off with a blue-and-white cap with a sport-fishing theme. The woman carried an enormous daypack and had sunglasses pushed up above her forehead. They spoke with an American Southern twang—as though with rubber bands in their mouths. They fit the stereotypes of Americans abroad—big-voiced, expansively casual, and unselfconscious.

Curious, I introduced myself to them. I learned they were from Texas and were enjoying their trip—first time to Europe—immensely. The architecture in Paris was, of course, beautiful. They spoke of their amusement of how things were "different," which they pronounced as if in quotations. They reported surprise at being served a hot drink when they ordered "tea." In Texas restaurants, *tea* means *iced tea*, while in France they had received *hot tea*. They were bemused to see French fries served with mayonnaise, and chuckled at the sight of a French diner eating a hamburger with a knife and a fork. They were friendly and sincere—as though we had struck up a conversation in a small-town diner in their home town.

As they compared things in France to what they knew in Texas, they seemed to assume that I, as an American, shared their perspective. There was a "Gee whiz!" quality to them that reminded me of Mark Twain's account of naïve American tourists in his book *Innocents Abroad*. I cringed inwardly a bit as I listened, but I also knew that I myself was once an "innocent abroad." On my first trip to Mexico years ago, I also noted the "quaint" differences there, such as jalapeños on hamburgers and people drinking sodas from plastic bags through a straw. Meeting these Americans reminded me of myself—and how wide-eyed we *all* are on our first trip abroad, and how much wiser we feel when we come home.

Innocents abroad...

Figure 11-1

Do foreign experiences make us wiser? If so, how? It seems safe to say that global living changes us in some way. We learn many things. This American couple now knows how to navigate the Paris metro. Perhaps they learned how many years it took to build Notre Dame, or what it's like to sit at a sidewalk café in the Marais. They will have become worldlier in some ways, and will tell stories of their journey to their friends back home. This trip might inspire them to see more of the world, or maybe convince them that they really like things back in Texas. Perhaps, like many sojourners, they will talk about the impact of their journey by using the language of vision, saying things like: "It was great to see things with my own eyes," or "This trip expanded my horizons," or "My view of both France and Texas really changed."

Developing an Intercultural Mind

This last chapter will focus on the long-term cognitive impact of intercultural living—the *changing perspective* of an increasingly intercultural mind. This perceptual shift is both easy to understand and hard to define precisely. We know *intuitively* that we become more international, develop a more global mindset, become interculturally more sensitive—whatever you want to call it—thanks to leaving home and seeing the world. At the same time, it's hard to pinpoint precisely what is changing. In addition, not everyone gains a new, more intercultural perspective to the same degree. Some sojourners may have their stereotypes reinforced, become cynical, or deny that there's anything to learn from being in foreign places.

So just what is an intercultural mind? What is the learning goal that we are striving for? What is the wisdom we are chasing? This is the hardest question that this book asks and it's one that specialists struggle with too. While it's easy to agree that some people are more insightful or successful in intercultural situations, there's no agreement on just what the eventual goals of intercultural learning should be.

One term that is commonly used to describe a successful outcome of intercultural experiences is *intercultural competence*. Intercultural specialist Janet Bennett writes that there's an "emerging consensus" about the nature of intercultural competence, which she describes as "a set of cognitive, affective, and behavioral skills and characteristics that support effective and appropriate interaction in a variety of cultural contexts."[1] Yet such broad definitions edge close to a circular logic—intercultural competence being defined as qualities that result in competent intercultural outcomes. It's easy to agree that some people are more competent interculturally than others, but it's difficult to define that ability in more detail.

There's plenty of research in this area. One overview lists more than 250 factors and concepts associated with intercultural competence, including: political astuteness, realism, ability to create new categories, openness to others, mindful reflexivity, social bonds, facework management, stress tolerance, conversational skills, coping with feelings, social sensitivity, articulation, and on and on.[2] There have also been attempts to define these qualities under the rubric of *intercultural intelligence*, which also produces elaborate taxonomies of cognitive, behavioral, and attitudinal aptitudes.[3] If anything becomes clear from research like this, it's that successful intercultural outcomes depend on countless factors. Attempting to explain such a complex phenomena as a result of a single essential characteristic is at best difficult, and at worst a misleading oversimplification. A similar tendency has been criticized in the realm of intelligence testing.[4]

Despite these difficulties with terminology, educators—and interculturalists in general—do need ways to talk about the goals of intercultural learning. In this book, of course, I have been using the term *intercultural mind*. My intention isn't to propose this as a substitute or improvement on terms such as *intercultural awareness, intercultural competence,* or *intercultural intelligence.* I don't believe an intercultural mind can be reduced to a single key cognitive ingredient. Instead, I have been trying to make two broad points:

(1) *By learning about the largely hidden structures and processes of the intuitive mind, we can better understand intercultural experiences.* I've argued that sojourners benefit from learning about culture's impact on cognition, how the intuitive mind works, the role of expert intuition, the pitfalls of bias, and so on. I've said that cultural learning happens largely at the intuitive level—it's a two-mind process—and thus sojourners need to understand hidden cognition.

(2) *The intercultural mind as a goal of intercultural learning.* I believe we can consciously develop a more insightful and cognitively flexible mindset. I've discussed, for example, awareness of Oz moments, being mindful of bias, developing expert cultural intuitions, and developing cultural empathy. I have delineated just a few of the cognitive capacities that can provide us with more interculturally insightful, more satisfying experiences, and more successful interactions. These aren't the only ones. One recent study, for example, looked at metacognitive strategies for making sense of cross-cultural encounters.[5] It showed that the type of reasoning cross-cultural experts used when making sense of cultural surprises was similar to the reasoning processes exhibited by expert scientists. I believe that continued research will show that there are any number of cognitive capacities that can contribute to intercultural understanding.

With this in mind, let's look back at some of the points I've laid out in this book. First, I'll focus on how a cognitive perspective can inform our understanding of intercultural interactions (point number 1 above). After that, we'll look at some research that may help shed a bit of light on point number 2 and the hard-to-define perceptual shifts that accompany intercultural learning.

A Bench in Brunei

The anthropologist Donald Brown tells the story of an encounter he had in Brunei, seated in front of the house where he lived while doing research in that country. He was in the company of three young men, all ethnic Malays, two sharing a bench with him and another seated on a ladder nearby. Tiring of the hard surface, Brown decided to sit down on a walkway. This, however, put him at a lower level than the young men, who immediately changed positions to avoid being higher than him, which Brown understood would have been rude according to Malay customs. Using gestures and imperfect Malay (he refers to it as "broken"), he told them he didn't mind them sitting higher. He wanted to be treated "as they would treat each other" and explained that he wouldn't be offended by such behavior. Despite his entreaties, however, the young men preferred not to, pointing out that it "wouldn't look nice." Brown says "the clear implication was that he and his fellows weren't about to let anyone see them apparently breaking one of the important rules in the etiquette of rank, even though they knew they wouldn't be offending me."[6]

Brown introduces this episode to illustrate an evolution in his thinking about cultural difference. Earlier in his career, he told this story to illustrate the importance of rank in Southeast Asia. Later, he became more impressed by the number of things that he and these young Malay men *could* understand about each other *despite* cultural differences. It was intuitively obvious, for example, that sitting in a higher position could indicate increased status. This is not an unfamiliar concept for Americans. The Malays' concern for how their behavior might be perceived was also something that people everywhere could relate to. Brown goes on to argue for the importance of *human universals*, including the idea that humans everywhere share important qualities that can be understood intuitively.[7] His work has been cited, notably by Steven Pinker, in arguments against linguistic and cultural relativism.[8]

Brown came to believe that we share so much with people around the world that intuitive understanding across cultures is not only possible, but unsurprising. Throughout this book, of course, I have been making a different case. I've said that culture affects us deeply, but in subtle ways. I have highlighted the risk of naively believing that people around the world are the same as we are. I bring up Brown's story because I think it illustrates some of the points I have been making. In particular, I think it illustrates that feeling good about cross-cultural contact is not the same as successfully collaborating across cultures. I think it also shows that understanding the cultural perspective of others requires an awareness of our own cultural conditioning.

Brown seems to trust his intuitive interpretation of this situation. He declares that he understood the feelings and thoughts of these young men. But we don't know if this is true. Did they see their behavior as a refusal to break rules of etiquette? The word *etiquette* implies expectations about social niceties. We break a rule of etiquette if, for example, we lick our plate at the end of a meal. Perhaps, instead, they saw their own behavior as a genuine desire to show respect or deference to elders. Or perhaps they found his request bizarre. Without hearing their side of the story, however, we don't know. This is a reminder that it's possible to intuitively feel we've understood, or that we've succeeded in an interaction, without ever learning the cultural perspective of the other side.

A second point relates to the difference between *intercultural contact* and *intercultural adaptation* or *collaboration*. Let's assume that Brown *did* accurately intuit what these young men were thinking and feeling. That understanding, however, does not seem to have led to a mutually agreeable approach to resolving the impasse. Both sides preferred to maintain their own cultural standards. Brown tried to convince them to change their behavior on his behalf, but they declined. For his part, Brown seemed disinclined to adapt himself to their cultural standards (by simply acceding to their desire to remain in a lower position). In this case, mutual understanding did *not* lead to successful collaboration. While feeling we have something in common with foreigners is relatively easy, adapting, collaborating, and reconciling differing cultural perspectives is much harder.

Finally, Brown's story raises questions of cultural *self*-awareness. Brown never mentions the possibility of simply going along with local customs. I wonder if he was uncomfortable with the idea that these young men would adjust their sitting position on his behalf. Such behavior certainly reflects a rather "un-American" emphasis on explicit hierarchy. Many Americans have an intuitive distaste for rank and formality and might feel similarly in this situation. For people in many places in the world, however, showing deference and respect to others—even strangers— on the basis of age, or title, is seen as a natural part of smooth human relations. To some extent, then, Brown was trying to get these young men to follow *American* norms and values. Was Brown aware of how typically American his reactions were?

My point is not to accuse Brown of a lack of cultural sensitivity. I believe that he was making genuine efforts to get along with and understand the Malay men he was dealing with. My point is that barriers to successful intercultural relations are often subtle—we *all* are conditioned by deep culture in ways that are hard to notice. This is also why superficial contact—even a lot of it—may *not* contribute that much to a more deeply intercultural mind. Experiencing diversity from a safe distance, or in a setting where we never have to adapt to others, may not be enough to bring these more hidden cultural issues into the light of our conscious awareness.

So what can lead to deeper intercultural understanding? Just what cognitive capacities are characteristic of an intercultural mind? While there's no single answer, I think one area worth exploring is research into our mind's capacity to shift between differing cultural perspectives and worldviews.

Cultural Frame Shifting

A photograph shows an attractive woman sitting on the top of a hill overlooking a lagoon. She's alone, taking in the breathtaking scenery, apparently deep in thought, but the photo provides no clear clues about what's going on in her mind. She could be lonely and in search of love. Or perhaps she is an independent-minded woman—a writer or an artist on an adventure—and she has found this lagoon in the course of her travels. Or maybe she is rich and lives nearby, but is unhappy with her life. The photograph is both striking and ambiguous—an image that provokes us to supply the missing information to complete the story that this scene represents.

Just such an ambiguous photograph was used in an experiment to test the relationship between culture and perception. Researchers wanted to find out if people who had grown up biculturally would use multiple cultural perspectives when interpreting the image. As they explain, "[B]iculturals may have distinct cognitive frameworks associated with each of the cultures and languages and . . . those mental frames may consist of different repertoires of values and behaviors as well as separate worldviews and identities."[9] The organizing concept in this research is *frame switching*, meaning that "individuals with extensive experience in two cultures seem to access different culture-specific cognitive structures, or mental frames, depending on the sociocultural context." The challenge was to see if researchers could catch the brain in the act of engaging these different cognitive structures.

The researchers tested Hispanic Americans who spoke Spanish at home and English in the outside community. They asked the same person to describe the same photo of the woman at the lagoon on two different occasions, once in each different language. They hoped to trigger different cultural frameworks in the participants as they interpreted the woman's story. The researchers also gathered a second group of test participants—people who were bilingual in Spanish and English but who had learned Spanish in the classroom. They were bilingual but not bicultural. The researchers wanted to find out if the choice of language would affect the interpretations of bilinguals who did *not* grow up biculturally.

They found some interesting contrasts. One participant, Sara, was shown the photograph of the woman and asked to imagine what the woman was doing and how she was feeling. This first time Sara did this, she saw the woman in this way:

> The woman looks very tranquil. She takes time for herself. She went for a walk after a long day at work. It is very beautiful landscaping, and she sits down to think. She is alone with her thoughts. I think she is a positive person who takes risks—she can express herself; she is independent. The fact that she is alone indicates that she knows how to take time for herself.

Six months later, Sara was asked to look at the same photo and create another story. This time, the narrative was quite different:

> She's by herself on her own. But she feels, she looks, hopeless. It looks like she's going through something, that she needs to get away from everything and go here and think and just let it all out. If it was just a yell—scream, nobody could hear her. But there is just, just that feeling of being alone, nobody to bother you. . . . She looks lonely too, and she looks very disturbed, confused, like she's got something on her mind. She's trying to figure out the answer for it.

The first story is of a strong, independent woman. The second is of someone weak and lonely. Why the change? Sara is both bilingual and bicultural. The first time she answered this question she used Spanish, while the second time she used English. This result was evident among other participants as well, who also told contrasting stories. The female protagonist in the Spanish story was strong and independent—more of an emotional pillar of strength—while the protagonist in the English story was, it seems, the *weaker sex*—more vulnerable and dependent.

This result matched researchers' predictions. They point out that in European American cultural traditions, women are historically and culturally associated with needing protection. In Latin American cultures, women are often associated with emotional fortitude. As for the monocultural group, they told similar stories in both languages, hinting that learning a foreign language in the classroom did not change their perceptions. Naturally, Sara and other participants weren't consciously thinking about cultural associations when looking at these photographs—they were caught up in creating a story. But the story they created takes place in mental frames shaped by cultural associations. Our cultural frames contain the canvas upon which we paint our narratives.

It's not necessary for us to consciously agree with these frames and associations for us to be influenced by them. Implicit association testing was also used to measure unconscious attitudes of biculturals like Sara. They were asked to categorize male and female names with words related either to self-sufficiency (e.g., "leadership," "assertive," "dominant") or other-dependency (e.g., "gentle," "tender," "compassionate"). This test was performed in both English and Spanish to see if there are differences in the unconscious associations related to gender. Researchers found, for example, that the concept *self-sufficient* was more strongly linked to *feminine* when the testing was done in Spanish. In English, on the other hand, self-sufficient was more strongly linked with the word *masculine*. And, as predicted, they found that when testing monocultural bilinguals—those who had learned Spanish without extensive intercultural experience—the results were the same in both languages.

Research like this hints that people are capable of maintaining distinct cultural-cognitive structures that, while integrated into a single individual, are activated situationally and affect perception and interpretation at a deep level of self. Not only were their stories different depending on the language, the unconscious associations differed as well. It's as though bicultural people can have *two sets of cultural intuitions* that are activated depending on the context.

I find it remarkable that researchers are learning to measure such unconscious phenomena. I have long heard sojourners talk about this, saying things like, "When I go back home, I put on a different pair of cultural glasses," or "Living in a foreign country gives you a new way of looking at the world." It's impressive that we have started to be able to understand and measure those shifts. It's not clear, however, how conscious the study participants were of this frame shifting. Were these frames something they could consciously choose from? Or do situational factors simply provoke different interpretive frameworks, with little conscious awareness of that process? The ability to shift frames is not the same as a meta-awareness of doing so.

Becoming a Bridge Person

Can people who were not raised biculturally, but who have had extensive intercultural experiences, also learn to shift frames at this very deep level of self?

Anecdotal evidence suggests that they can. I sometimes hear sojourners talk about this frame-shifting experience. Ye-jun, a student from Korea says:

> It's similar to a camera—especially an SLR, which is constructed with changeable lenses and a camera body. [In this case,] camera body means a person. He or she is born in a culture and gets their lens. Lens means culture. Without the lens, he or she cannot see anything. It is just black or white if they don't have any lens. Through the lens, he or she now can see and make a sense of some things around him or her. I think to understand different cultures means adding some other lenses to their own lens. Through two lenses at the same time, he or she can see some things around them in different ways.

It's possible, of course, that Ye-jun experienced a shift in perceptions, but that it was not as deep as for people who were raised biculturally. It's also possible, however, that those who gain cross-cultural insights through foreign experiences after childhood learn something that even biculturals don't. Milton Bennett makes a distinction between people who have grown up with multiple frameworks versus those who gain them through later intercultural experiences. He comments, "Not all biculturalism is culturally sensitive. In the case of 'accidental biculturalism,' people have simply received primary socialization into two cultures. Such people may be able to act appropriately in two different cultural contexts, but they cannot necessarily generalize that ability to a third culture."[10]

What use is an ability to shift cultural frames and have multiple sets of cultural intuitions? To find out, let's meet Khaled Abu Toameh, someone who is used to being caught in the middle. Toameh is an Arab journalist and filmmaker who is also a citizen of Israel and a fluent Hebrew speaker. He has reported for the Palestinian press under the PLO, for international news outlets such as the *Wall Street Journal* and the *Sunday Times*, and is currently a reporter on Palestinian affairs for the *Jerusalem Post*. He is known as a strong defender of freedom of the press, and has not been afraid to criticize the Palestinian Authority when he felt they were harassing journalists.

Toameh's work has put him at the nexus of conflict in the Middle East and made him something of a bridge person—someone who operates on two sides of a cultural line, in this case one that is etched deeply into a complicated and conflicted cultural landscape.[11] He speaks out in favor of Arabs in Israel, but also expresses respect for freedoms available there that can't be found in many Arab countries. This opens him to accusations that he is pro-Israeli. To statements like this, he responds, "I am not pro-Israel, I'm not pro-Palestinian, and I'm not pro-American. But as a journalist, I'm pro the facts and pro the truth."

I believe that frame shifting at this deep level of self is an important part of functioning as such a bridge person. Evidence of this is found in research that examines language use and prejudice. Consider, for starters, that the Arab-Israeli war of 1948 is referred to in Israel as the *War of Independence*, while in Arabic it is referred to as *nakba*—the catastrophe. This linguistic difference is representative of a perceptual split—what is heroic on one side of this divide is a disaster on the other. Each narrative negates the other. Can anyone fully bridge such a divide?

Implicit association testing has found that bilingual Israeli Arabs from Hebrew-speaking universities exhibited weaker anti-Jewish attitudes when measured in Hebrew than in Arabic.[12] This is significant because such tests measure *unconscious* associations—elements of cognition that may influence our attitudes or behavior without us knowing it. Likewise, French-Arabic bilingual Moroccans, as well as bilingual Hispanic Americans, displayed a stronger preference for each nationality or ethnicity when tested in a matching language. I interpret this research to mean that cultural frame shifting, which may be triggered by switching languages, involves very deep parts of the self. The ability to shift frames does not automatically solve conflict, but it provides hope for successful engagement across even such a wide perceptual gap.

Developmental Intercultural Learning

While those raised biculturally develop multiple cultural frames and thus contrasting sets of cultural intuitions, can the same ability be learned through intercultural experiences later in life? To answer this question, we need to know whether the ability to shift cultural frames can be learned developmentally. Saying that learning is *developmental* refers to the view that learning progresses through stages or levels of increased ability. One example of a developmental learning model is that of Jean Piaget's, which delineates stages of cognitive development in children.[13] Another is Kurt Fischer's *dynamic skill theory*, which proposes that cognitive abilities progress in predictable levels, from more concrete to more abstract thinking.[14]

How then, can we understand the developmental process for intercultural learning? Milton Bennett has tried to answer this question. His Developmental Model of Intercultural Sensitivity (DMIS) proposes that integrating cultural difference into our cognitive architecture engenders *"the construction of reality as increasingly capable of accommodating cultural difference."*[15] He posits six stages of development—*denial, defense, minimization, acceptance, adaptation,* and *integration*—each of which represents a more complex cognitive orientation towards cultural difference. Just as children start life as egocentric and gradually learn to consider the wellbeing and point of view of others as they grow up, we begin our intercultural experiences largely ethnocentric, and through a process of growth and increased understanding, learn to expand our intercultural horizons as well.

Bennett's model has been used to develop a related psychometric instrument called the Intercultural Development Inventory (IDI).[16] As a phenomenological model, the DMIS may provide a bridge from the realm of intercultural communication theory to that of cognitive neuroscience. I would like to see experienced interculturalists—those who measure high on the IDI scale—tested using the methodology of cognitive neuroscience. This may shed light on the cognitive architecture associated with effective bridge people. In particular, I wonder if highly experienced interculturalists do the kind of frame shifting found in biculturals.

I believe there are many possibilities for neurocognitive research in this area. Does switching languages activate different networks of unconscious cultural associations in experienced interculturalists? Do they have different unconscious reactions to novelty? Do they feel less threatened by out group members in general? What cognitive strategies or capacities help them resist jumping to ethnocentric conclusions? Do highly experienced interculturalists tend to be more empathetic in general? We're still at the early stages of finding the intercultural questions that can be asked and answered using the new science of mind, but I am hopeful that these areas will be explored.

Although I'm excited about the possibility of identifying key cognitive capacities that are important for an intercultural mindset, I don't expect that there is a single "magic ingredient" for intercultural competence. I don't look at the development of an intercultural mind as the pursuit of a singular cognitive ability. Rather, the idea of developing a more intercultural mind points us in the direction of greater cognitive flexibility across a wide range of capacities.

Tips for an Intercultural Mind

The starting point of developing a more intercultural mind, I believe, is *an awareness of the limits of our own cultural perspective, and an increasing ability to look at a situation through the cultural eyes of others.* I've argued that we can encourage this ability in two ways: (1) learning about the structure and cultural configurations of our own mind, and (2) through a trial-and-error process of developing new cultural intuitions through foreign experiences. The former is intercultural learning from the inside out—we learn about our own mind to gain more insight into our cultural learning processes. The latter is outside in—our intercultural experiences shed light on previously unnoticed elements of the self. Just as cultural patterns exist out in the world, and within the cognitive architecture of our minds, cultural learning should be oriented both inwards and outwards.

Intercultural learning must rest on a solid foundation of resilience and general psychological well-being—we can't develop an insightful, flexible intercultural mind upon a foundation of insecurity, defensiveness, or selfishness. This jibes with research showing that the abilities to have successful relationships, manage stress, regulate emotions, think critically, and remain open and flexible are all associated with intercultural success.[17, 18, 19] Qualities that make for psychological health generally also contribute to success when interacting cross-culturally.

With all this in mind, I'd like to review the main ideas we've talked about. What follows is a sort of laundry list of the points that I have been making through this book.

Oz moments are important.

Oz moments are a sign that your intuitive mind's pattern detection systems are finding anomalies, that your cognitive systems are being taxed, and that you should be aware of the *sense-making* aspect of your experiences. Some sojourners find it useful to keep a journal or talk to friends about what they experience. Actively reflecting on your cross-cultural experiences engages critical thinking skills and keeps you from being carried away by negative feelings and judgments.

Mind the intuitive mind.

Be mindful of your *gut reactions* to your experiences: the things you notice, the impressions you have, the thoughts that float into your mind, your tendency to judge, and your overall state of psychological well-being. The most common feedback I get from sojourners after learning about culture and cognition is: *Wow, there's so much more to foreign experiences than I realized.* That's a sign that they have become more sensitized to their intuitive mind.

Mind the attentive mind.
By paying active attention to the feelings and intuitions of your intuitive mind, you provide the attentive mind with more opportunity for critical thinking and analysis. Cultivate the ability to look at a situation from multiple perspectives. Pay attention to the big picture. Consciously cultivate cultural empathy—the ability to look at a situation from the perspective of someone with different perceptions than your own.

Foreign experiences are powerful.
Novelty taxes our cognitive systems. Cognitive overload can lead to stress and culture shock, sometimes without the attentive mind recognizing what's going on. You can't always be positive and tolerant. Don't be too hard on yourself.

Choose to go deeper.
You will face many choices about whether to retreat to a comfort zone or expose yourself to the unknown. While you need to be aware of your limits, in general the more challenging the experience, the more potential there is for growth and insight. Every foreign experience is a precious opportunity to explore.

Explore your cultural configuration.
Ethnocentrism is natural; resistance is natural; feeling frustrated by cultural difference is natural. Be tolerant of yourself. Over time, your intercultural boundaries will become more supple. You'll start to feel more comfortable with the uncertainty that comes from intercultural experiences. You may even learn to enjoy it!

Sharpen your cultural intuitions.
A deep understanding of a foreign community takes longer than you might expect. If you are living abroad, rather than just visiting, be ready for a long-term process of trial and error. You need plenty of interaction and experience to gain an intuitive understanding of the local perspective.

Learn a foreign language.
Nothing is harder. Nothing is more powerful. Language is much more than a tool for information exchange. Even if you think you'll never return, or don't have long enough to become fluent, the conscious decision to work on foreign language skills will change the flavor of your experience. Don't excuse yourself from language learning because locals speak English.

Focus on growth.
There are opportunities for intercultural learning everywhere. How far away you go is less important than how deep you go. Find ways to turn your journeys into an opportunity for personal growth.

Get in Touch
Have a story to share? Think I missed something important? Want to learn more? I'd love to hear from you. Contact me at info@japanintercultural.org, or through the website of the Japan Intercultural Institute at www.japanintercultural.org.

KEY CONCEPTS

Cultural frames: *These are the perceptual filters that we use to make sense of our experiences. Learning to look at things from multiple cultural perspectives is a long-term goal of intercultural learning.*

Developmental intercultural learning: *Our intercultural experiences change the way we perceive things, and this effect is cumulative. Over time, we can develop more complex ways of making sense of cultural difference.*

The intercultural mind: *We develop an intercultural mind by gaining an awareness of our own cognitive processes and cultural configuration, as well as interacting with people whose configurations are different from our own, thus developing new cultural intuitions.*

Discussion Quote: *Meeting these Americans reminded me of myself—and how wide-eyed we all are on our first trip abroad, and how much wiser we feel when we come home.*

Further Reading

I f you are interested in learning more about the ideas in this book, you'll need to decide where you want to start. The book that first hooked me—and many others—on the subject of intercultural communication, is *The Silent Language*, by Edward Hall. More than 50 years after it was first published, I still find it to be insightful. If you want to start with something more current, yet still focused on the unconscious impact of culture on our cognitive processes, I recommend *The Geography of Thought*, by Richard Nisbett.

There are lots of books that talk about the connection between brain and mind. Very few, however, focus much on the impact of culture. To get a general sense of how the intuitive mind works, I recommend books such as *Thinking Fast and Slow*, by Daniel Kahneman, *Strangers to Ourselves*, by Timothy Wilson, *Thinking Twice*, by Jonathan Evans, and *Subliminal*, by Leonard Mlodinow. It's a hot topic and new works are coming out all the time, but any of these will get you going.

If you are interested in embodiment, the idea that mental experiences engage us at many levels of self, you can start with *Descartes' Error*, by Antonio Damasio. A lot has happened since it was published in 1994, but his work has had a big impact. For more on language and embodied simulation, pick up a copy of *Louder Than Words*, by Benjamin Bergen. It provides lots of examples of research in this area.

If you are interested primarily in the process of adapting deeply to another cultural environment, I have written about that in my book *Deep Culture: The Hidden Challenges of Global Living*. While that's a fairly academic title, *Beneath the Surface: A Beginner's Guide to the Deep Intercultural Experience* is an easier read focused on how to get the most out of our intercultural experiences.

And finally, if you have an interest in cognitive neuroscience and want an overview of the research being done related to culture, you'll find a lot in *Culture Neuroscience: Cultural Influences on Brain Function*, edited by Joan Chiao, as well as *Handbook of Cultural Psychology*, edited by Kitayama and Cohen. An overview of work in unconscious cognition can be found in *The New Unconscious*, edited by Hassin, Uleman, and Bargh.

Acknowledgments

Thanks to my students at Keio University for their openness, enthusiasm, and patience as I experimented with much of the material found in this book. Thanks also to everyone at the Japan Intercultural Institute, and particularly the participants in the Deep Culture Seminars, for their strong interest and support. They are my intercultural family. Thanks to Matthieu Kollig for all these years of love, creativity, and collaboration—your illustrations add so much to this book. Thanks to Dan, Knik, Arik, Yoga, and Ketut for sharing your lives with me. See you again soon in Pemuteran! Thanks to the FAB team: Marc Helgesen, Curtis Kelley, Robert Murphy, and Tim Murphey for their enthusiasm and love of all things educational and neuro! Many people gave critical feedback and support at different stages in the writing of this book, including Sujata Banerjee, Jonathan Bolick, Mitch Goodman, Gordon Jolley, Val Hansford, Tsutomu Hashida, Karen Hill-Anton, Peter Hourdequin, Vincent Jeffries, Tim Keely, Matthieu Kollig, Yuko Koyama-Bolick, Anne-Claude Lambelet, Stefan Meister, Michael Mersiades, Anne Niesen, Harumi Ogawa, Elena Pruvil, Liisa Salo-Lee, James Shaules, Gabriela Schmidt, Stephen Shrader, Eliza Skowron, Maurice Splichal, Yvonne van der Pol, Bob Whiting, Patchareerat Yanaprasart, Tomoko Yoshida, and Steve Ziolkoski. Thanks for your time, intelligence, and interest. An additional special thanks to Kumiko Torikai for her mentoring and deep friendship, and Bob Whiting for ongoing guidance, support, and inspiration. Thanks to my family for their love and support, in particular my brother James, my brother David, my sister Ceja and husband Vince, my son David and his wife Liz, and of course my mother. Finally, my wife, friend, and partner Ayako supports me in so many ways. She is the anchor of my ship and my lighthouse in any storm. She bathes me in warm sunshine every single day. I can't imagine my life without her.

Endnotes

CHAPTER ONE

[1] J. M. Harlow, "Passage of an Iron Rod Through the Head," *The Boston Medical and Surgical Journal* 39(20) (1848): 389–393.

[2] W. M. Baum, *Understanding Behaviorism: Science, Behavior, and Culture* (New York: HarperCollins College Publishers, 1994).

[3] O. Sacks, *The Man Who Mistook His Wife for a Hat* (London: Picador, 1985).

[4] J. F. Kihlstrom, "The Cognitive Unconscious." *Science* 237 (1987): 1445–1452.

[5] O. Sporns. *Discovering the Human Connectome* (Cambridge, MA: MIT Press, 2013).

[6] R. Hassin, J. Uleman, et al., eds., *The New Unconscious* (Oxford: Oxford University Press, 2007).

[7] M. L. Brandao, ed., *Neurobiology of Mental Disorders* (New York: Nova Science Publishers, 2006).

[8] T. D. Wilson, *Strangers to Ourselves: Discovering the Adaptive Unconscious* (Cambridge, MA: Belknap Press, 2002); J. Evans, and K. Frankish, eds., *In Two Minds: Dual Processes and Beyond* (New York: Oxford University Press, 2009); J. Evans, *Thinking Twice: Two Minds in One Brain* (New York: Oxford University Press, 2010); D. Kahneman, *Thinking Fast and Slow* (New York: Farrar, Straus and Giroux 2011); L. Mlodinow, *Subliminal: How Your Unconscious Mind Rules Your Behavior* (New York: Pantheon Books, 2012).

[9] J. Medina, *Brain Rules* (Seattle: Pear Press, 2008).

[10] D. Sousa, ed., *Mind, Brain and Education: Neuroscience Implications for the Classroom* (Bloomington, IL: Solution Tree Press, 2010).

[11] M. Seligman, *Flourish: A Visionary New Understanding of Happiness and Well-being* (New York, Free Press: 2012).

[12] S. Iyengar, *The Art of Choosing* (New York: Twelve, 2010); S. Vedantam, *The Hidden Brain: How Our Unconscious Minds Elect Presidents, Control Markets, Wage Wars, and Save Our Lives* (New York: Spiegel & Grau, 2010).

[13] M. R. Banaji, and A. G. Greenwald, *Blind Spot: Hidden Biases of Good People* (New York: Delacorte Press, 2013); R. Dobelli, *The Art of Thinking Clearly* (London: Hodder & Stoughton, 2013); M. Gladwell, *Blink: The Power of Thinking Without Thinking* (New York: Back Bay Books 2005); G. Gigerenzer, *Gut Feelings: The Intelligence of the Uncon-*

scious (London: Penguin, 2007).

[14] T. Wilson, *Redirect: The Surprising New Science of Psychological Change* (New York: Little, Brown and Company, 2011).

[15] P. Boyer, *Religion Explained: The Evolutionary Origins of Religious Thought* (New York: Basic Books, 2001).

[16] C. Boehm, *Moral Origins: The Evolution of Virtue, Altruism, and Shame* (New York: Basic Books, 2012).

[17] K. Stanovich, *Rationality & The Reflective Mind* (New York: Oxford University Press, 2011).

[18] B. K. Bergen, *Louder Than Words: The New Science of How the Mind Makes Meaning* (New York: Basic Books, 2012).

[19] C. Keysers, *The Empathic Brain: How the Discovery of Mirror Neurons Changes Our Understanding of Human Nature* (Lexington, KY: Social Brain Press, 2011).

[20] A. Damasio, *The Feeling of What Happens* (New York: Harcourt, Inc., 1999); A. Damasio, *Self Comes to Mind: Constructing the Conscious Brain* (New York: Pantheon Books, 2010).

[21] R. E. Nisbett, *The Geography of Thought* (New York: Free Press, 2003).

[22] H. Markus and S. Kitayama, "Culture and the Self: Implications for Cognition, Emotion, and Motivation," *Psychological Review* 98 (1991): 224–253.

[23] S. Kitayama and D. Cohen, eds., *The Handbook of Cultural Psychology* (New York: The Guilford Press, 2007).

[24] J. Y. Chiao, ed., *Cultural Neuroscience: Cultural Influences on Brain Function* (New York: Elsevier 2009).

[25] H. S. Kim and J. Y. Sasaki, "Cultural Neuroscience: Biology of the Mind in Cultural Contexts," *Annual Review of Psychology* 65 (2014): 1–24.

[26] Nisbett, *The Geography of Thought*, 82.

[27] J. Evans, *Thinking Twice: Two Minds in One Brain* (New York: Oxford University Press 2010).

[28] Vedantam, *The Hidden Brain*; Kahneman, *Thinking Fast and Slow*; Banaji and Greenwald, *Blind Spot*.

[29] G. A. Klein, *Sources of Power: How People Make Decisions* (Cambridge, MA: MIT Press, 1998).

[30] Wilson, *Strangers to Ourselves*.

[31] N. Lund, *Attention and Pattern Recognition* (Hove, East Sussex: Routledge, 2001).

[32] S. Pinker, *How the Mind Works* (New York: W. W. Norton & Company, 1997); D. Marr and T. A. Poggio, *Vision: A Computational Investigation into the Human Representation and Processing of Visual Information* (Cambridge, MA: MIT Press, 2010).

[33] Kahneman, *Thinking Fast and Slow*; Banaji and Greenwald, *Blind Spot*; Dobelli, *The Art of Thinking Clearly*.

[34] Bergen, *Louder than Words*; Damasio, *The Feeling of What Happens*; Damasio, *Self Comes to Mind*; D. M. Amodio and S. A. Mendoza, "Implicit Intergroup Bias: Cognitive, Affective, and Motivational Underpinnings" in *Handbook of Implicit Social Cognition: Measurement, Theory, and Applications* by G. Payne (New York: The Guilford Press, 2010); C. K. W. D. Dreu, L. L. Greer, et al., "Oxytocin Promotes Human Ethnocentrism," *Proceedings of the National Academy of Sciences* (2011).

[35] Banaji and Greenwald, *Blind Spot*; Kahneman, *Thinking Fast and Slow*; A. Greenwald, "IAT Studies Showing Validity with 'Real-World' Subject Populations," list created 2008; A. G. Greenwald, C. T. Smith, et al., "Race Attitude Measures Predicted Vote in the 2008 U.S. Presidential Election," *Analyses of Social Issues and Public Policy* 9 (2009): 241–253.

[36] Cohen and Kitayama, *The Handbook of Cultural Psychology*.

[37] S. Herculano-Houzel, "The Human Brain in Numbers: a Linearly Scaled-Up Primate Brain," *Frontiers in Human Neuroscience* 3 (2009).

[38] Sporns, *Discovering the Human Connectome*.

[39] Neisser, U., *Cognitive Psychology* (New York: Appleton-Century-Crofts, 1967).

[40] Cohen and Kitayama, *The Handbook of Cultural Psychology*.

[41] Ibid.

CHAPTER TWO

[1] R. Slimbach, *Becoming World Wise: A Guide to Global Living* (Sterling, VA: Stylus, 2010), 7.

[2] Whereami. "How Are You Different?" *http://ak.typepad.com/whereami/2005/07/* (last accessed April 1, 2014).

[3] J. Trowbridge, *Samuel Finley Breese Morse* (London: Forgotten Books, 2012).

[4] C. Chen, G. Xue, et al., "Cultural Neurolinguistics" in *Progress in Brain Research* by J. Y. Chiao (New York: Elsevier, 2009).

[5] J. O. Goh and D. C. Park, "Culture Sculpts the Perceptual Brain" in *Progress in Brain Research* by J. Y. Chiao (New York: Elsevier, 2009).

[6] I. Johnson, "In China, Once the Villages are Gone, The Culture is Gone," *International New York Times*, February 1, 2014.

[7] A. Barnard and J. Spencer, eds., *Encyclopedia of Social and Cultural Anthropology* (London: Routledge, 1996).

[8] Wikimedia Foundation. "Culture" *http://en.wikipedia.org/wiki/Culture* (accessed April 1, 2014).

[9] E. Tylor, *Primitive Culture* (London: John Murray, 1871).

[10] A. Lincoln, "Fourth Lincoln Douglas Debate." Debate held in Charleston, IL, 1858.

[11] M. Gilbert, "Churchill and Eugenics." *www.winstonchurchill.org/support/the-churchill-centre/publications/finest-hour-online/594-churchill-and-eugenics* (posted 2009, last

accessed April 1, 2014); T. Roosevelt, *Theodore Roosevelt on Race, Riots, Reds, Crime* (West Sayville, NY: Probe Books, 1968); P. Schrag, *Not Fit for our Society: Immigration and Nativism in America* (Berkley, CA: University of California Press, 2010).

[12] E. Sapir, *Language: An Introduction to the Study of Speech* (San Diego, CA: Harcourt Brace & Company, 1921).

[13] M. Mead, *Coming of Age in Samoa* (New York: Perennial Classics, 1961).

[14] S. Pinker, *The Blank Slate: The Modern Denial of Human Nature* (New York: Penguin Books, 2002).

[15] S. Kitayama, "Mapping Mindsets: The World of Cultural Neuroscience," *Observer* 26 (2013).

[16] G. Downey, "Balancing Between Cultures: Equilibrium in Capoeira" in *The Encultured Brain: An Introduction to Neuroanthropology* by D. H. Lende and G. Downey (Cambridge, MA: MIT Press, 2012).

[17] B. Wexler, *Brain and Culture: Neurobiology, Ideology and Social Change* (Cambridge, MA: MIT Press, 2006), 5.

[18] S. Han, G. Northoff, et al., "Cultural Neuroscience Approach to the Biosocial Nature of the Human Brain," *Annual Review of Psychology* 64(1) (2011).

[19] S. Lash, *Intensive Culture: Social Theory, Religion and Contemporary Capitalism* (Los Angeles: SAGE, 2010).

CHAPTER THREE

[1] Lund, *Attention and Pattern Recognition*.

[2] Ibid., 62–63

[3] Wilson, *Strangers to Ourselves*, 50.

[4] Hassin, Uleman, et al., *The New Unconscious*, 227.

[5] Wilson, *Strangers to Ourselves*.

[6] Wilson, *Strangers to Ourselves*; Kahneman, *Thinking Fast and Slow*.

[7] Whereami. "How Are You Different?" *http://ak.typepad.com/whereami/2005/07/* (last accessed April 1, 2014).

CHAPTER FOUR

[1] E. T. Hall, *An Anthropology of Everyday Life* (New York: Doubleday, 1992).

[2] E. T. Hall, *The Silent Language* (New York: Anchor Books, 1959); E. T. Hall, *Beyond Culture* (New York: Anchor Books Doubleday, 1976); E. T. Hall, *The Dance of Life: The Other Dimension of Time* (New York: Anchor Books, 1984); C. M. Archer, *Living With Strangers in the U.S.A.: Communicating Beyond Culture* (Englewood Cliffs, NJ: Prentice Hall Regents, 1991).

[3] Hall, *Beyond Culture*, 12.

[4] Ibid., 239.

[5] Ibid., 166.

[6] Evans and Frankish, *In Two Minds*; Evans, *Thinking Twice*.

[7] Wilson, *Strangers to Ourselves*.

[8] Hassin, Uleman, et al., *The New Unconscious*.

[9] Wilson, *Strangers to Ourselves*.

[10] Ibid., 6–7.

[11] Kahneman, *Thinking Fast and Slow*.

[12] Wikimedia Foundation. "Dual Process Theory," *http://en.wikipedia.org/wiki/dual_process_theory* (accessed April 1, 2014).

[13] M. D. Lieberman, "The X- and C-Systems: The Neural Basis of Automatic and Controlled Social Cognition" in *Fundamentals of Social Neuroscience* by E. Harmon-Jones and P. Winkelman (New York: Guilford Press, 2007), 290–315.

[14] Ibid., 6.

[15] Evans, *Thinking Twice*, 7.

[16] Kahneman, *Thinking Fast and Slow*, 105.

[17] Wilson, *Strangers to Ourselves*, 73.

[18] Ibid., 77.

[19] G. Moskowitz, *Social Cognition: Understanding Self and Others* (New York: Guilford, 2005).

[20] Hall, *The Dance of Life*.

CHAPTER FIVE

[1] G. Jack and A. Phipps, *Tourism and Intercultural Exchange: Why Tourism Matters* (Clevedon, UK: Channel View Publications, 2005).

[2] E. Gilbert, *Eat, Pray, Love: One Woman's Search for Everything Across Italy, India and Indonesia* (London: Penguin Books, 2006).

[3] P. Ayer, *The Global Soul: Jet Lag, Shopping Malls, and the Search for Home* (New York: Vintage, 2000).

[4] S. Ross, "Transformative Travel: An Enjoyable Way to Foster Radical Change," *ReVision* 32(1) (2010): 54–61.

[5] J. A. Kottler and M. Montgomery, "Prescriptive Travel and Adventure-based Activities as an Adjunct to Counseling," *Guidance and Counseling* 15(2) (2000): 8–11.

[6] M. Ashdijian. "What NOT to Write your College Application Essay About," *www.examiner.com/article/what-not-to-write-your-college-application-essay-about* (last accessed April 1, 2014).

[7] Slimbach, *Becoming World Wise*.

[8] K. Oberg, "Culture Shock: Adjustment to New Cultural Environments," *Practical An-*

thropology 7(177) (1960).

⁹ Ibid., 142.

¹⁰ Archer, *Living With Strangers in the U.S.A.*; J. Bennett, *Transition Shock: Putting Culture Shock in Perspective* (Yarmouth, ME: Intercultural Press, 1998).

¹¹ Bennett, *Transition Shock*.

¹² R. F. Baumeister, E. Bratslavasky, et al., "Ego Depletion: Is the Active Self a Limited Resource?" *Journal of Personality and Social Psychology* 74(5) (1998): 1252–1265.

¹³ Kahneman, *Thinking Fast and Slow*.

¹⁴ G. Weaver, "Understanding and Coping with Cross-Cultural Adjustment Stress" in *Education for the Intercultural Experience* by R. M. Page (Yarmouth, ME: Intercultural Press, 1993).

¹⁵ M. Gallardo, C. Yeh, et al., eds., *Culturally Adaptive Counseling Skills: Demonstrations of Evidence-Based Practices* (Thousand Oaks, CA: SAGE, 2011).

¹⁶ Wilson, *Strangers to Ourselves*; Kahneman, *Thinking Fast and Slow*.

¹⁷ Iyengar, *The Art of Choosing*.

¹⁸ Ibid., 46.

¹⁹ B. D. Ruben, "General Systems Theory: An Approach to Human Communication" in *Approaches to Human Communication* by R. Budd and B. D. Ruben (New York: Spartan, 1972), 120–144.

²⁰ Y. Y. Kim, *Becoming Intercultural: An Integrative Theory of Communication and Cross-Cultural Adaptation* (London: SAGE, 2001).

²¹ Damasio, *The Feeling of What Happens*, 136.

²² J. Shaules, *Deep Culture: The Hidden Challenges of Global Living* (Clevedon, UK: Multilingual Matters, 2007).

²³ Kim, *Becoming Intercultural*.

²⁴ Shaules, *Deep Culture*.

²⁵ J. Bennett, "Cultural Marginality: Identity Issues in Intercultural Training" in *Education for the Intercultural Experience* by M. R. Paige (Yarmouth, ME: Intercultural Press, 1993), 109–135.

²⁶ J. Bennett, "A Developmental Approach to Training for Intercultural Sensitivity," *International Journal of Intercultural Relations* 10 (1986): 179–200.

CHAPTER SIX

¹ D. Nasaw, "US Election: 10 Oddities Explained," *BBC News Magazine*, 2012.

² E. L. Fox, "No Drama, King Obama," *Aeon*, February 4, 2013.

³ T. Drummond, "The Barack Obama Story: Harvard Law Review Gets Its First Black President," *The San Francisco Chronicle*, 1990.

[4] J. Scott, "Obama's Young Mother Abroad," *The New York Times*, April 20, 2011.

[5] A. Pascual-Leone, C. Freitas, et al., "Characterizing Brain Cortical Plasticity and Network Dynamics Across the Age-span in Health and Disease with TMS-EEG and TMS-fMRI," *Brain Topography* 24 (2011): 302–315.

[6] G. S. Berns, K. Blaine, et al., "Short- and Long-Term Effects of a Novel on Connectivity in the Brain," *Brain Connectivity* 3(6) (2013): 590–600.

[7] Wexler, *Brain and Culture*.

[8] Associated Press, "Soaring Putin Leads a Flock of Cranes," *The Moscow Times*, September 7, 2012.

[9] T. L. Brink, "Unit 12: Developmental Psychology," *Psychology: A Student Friendly Approach* (2008).

[10] F. M. Benes, "Konrad Lorenz, 1903–1989," *The American Journal of Psychiatry* 161 (2004): 1,767.

[11] J. F. Dominguez, E. D. Lewis, et al., "The Brain in Culture and Culture in the Brain: A Review of Core Issues in Neuroanthropology" in *Cultural Neuroscience: Cultural Influences on Brain Function* by J. Y. Chiao (New York: Elsevier, 2009).

[12] S. Gelman and J. Opfer, "Development of the Animate-Inanimate Distinction" in *Blackwell Handbook of Childhood Cognitive Development* by U. Goswami (Oxford: Blackwell, 2002).

[13] Han, Northoff, et al., "Cultural Neuroscience Approach to the Biosocial Nature of the Human Brain," *Annual Review of Psychology*.

[14] Y. Y. Tang and Y. Liu, "Numbers in the Cultural Brain" in *Cultural Neuroscience: Cultural Influences on Brain Function* by J. Y. Chiao (New York: Elsevier, 2009), 178.

[15] Chen, Xue, et al., "Cultural Neurolinguistics."

[16] C. A. Perfetti, Y. Liu, et al., "Reading in Two Writing Systems: Accommodation and Assimilation of the Brain's Reading Network," *Bilingualism: Language and Cognition* 101 (2007): 131–146.

[17] A. Damasio, *Descartes' Error: Emotion, Reason, and the Human Brain* (New York: Penguin, 1994).

[18] Ibid., xiii.

[19] Bergen, *Louder Than Words*.

[20] Ibid.

[21] L. K. Miles, L. K. Nind, et al., "Moving Through Time," *Psychological Science* 21 (2010): 222–223.

[22] N. Angier, "Abstract Thoughts? The Body Takes Them Literally," *The New York Times*, February 1, 2010.

[23] J. B. Freeman, N. O. Rule, et al., "Culture Shapes a Mesolimbic Response to Signals of Dominance and Subordination that Associates with Behavior," *NeuroImage* 47(1) (2009): 353–359.

[24] A. Kurata, J. S. Moser, et al., "Culture Shapes Electrocortical Responses During Emotion Suppression," *Social Cognitive and Affective Neuroscience* 8(5) (2013): 595–601.

[25] J. Y. Chiao and K. D. Blizinsky, "Culture-Gene Coevolution of Individualism-Collectivism and the Serotonin Transporter Gene," *Proceedings of the Royal Society* 277(1681) (2010): 529–537.

[26] D. Biello, "Culture Speeds Up Human Evolution," *Scientific American*, December 11, 2007.

[27] The term "software of the mind" comes from G. Hofstede in *Cultures and Organizations: Software of the Mind* (New York: McGraw-Hill, 2010); R. B. Zajonc and H. Markus, "Affect and Cognition: The Hard Interface" in *Emotions, Cognition, and Behavior* by C. E. Izard and R. B. Zajonc (Cambridge: Cambridge University Press, 1984), 63–103; Markus and Kitayama, "Culture and the Self: Implications for Cognition, Emotion, and Motivation."

[28] Hofstede, *Cultures and Organizations*.

[29] I. Castiglioni, "The Memetic Construction of Culture: Implications for Training and Research." Paper presented at SIETAR Europa Tallinn, 2013.

[30] S. Kitayama and A. Uskul, "Culture, Mind, and the Brain: Current Evidence and Future Directions," *Annual Review of Psychology* 62 (2011): 419–449.

[31] Ibid.

[32] S. Harkness, C. M. Super, et al., "Parental Ethnotheories of Children's Learning" in *Parents' Cultural Belief Systems: Their Origins, Expressions, and Consequences* by S. Harkness and C. M. Super (New York: The Guilford Press, 1996).

[33] Harkness and Super, "Parental Ethnotheories of Children's Learning" in *Parents' Cultural Belief Systems*; S. Harkness and C. M. Super, "Themes and Variations: Parental Ethnotheories in Western Cultures" in *Parenting Beliefs, Behaviors, and Parent-Child Relations: A Cross-cultural Perspective* by K. H. Rubin and O. B. Chung (New York: Psychology Press, 2006).

[34] Harkness and Super, "Parental Ethnotheories of Children's Learning" in *Parents' Cultural Belief Systems*, 69.

[35] Ibid., 71.

[36] Ibid., 10.

[37] F. Trompenaars and C. Hampden-Turner, *Riding the Waves of Culture* (New York: McGraw-Hill, 1998).

[38] Iyengar, *The Art of Choosing*.

[39] Markus and Kitayama, "Culture and the Self," *Psychological Review*.

[40] *World Values Survey 2014* (Stockholm, Sweden: World Values Survey Association, 2014).

[41] Kim and Sasaki, "Cultural Neuroscience," *Annual Review of Psychology*.

[42] Kitayama, "Mapping Mindsets," *Observer*.

[43] S. Kitayama, A. King, et al., "The Dopamine Receptor Gene (DRD4) Moderates Cul-

tural Difference in Independent versus Interdependent Social Orientation." University of Michigan, 2013.

[44] Kitayama, "Mapping Mindsets," *Observer*.

CHAPTER SEVEN

[1] Banaji and Greenwald, *Blind Spot*.

[2] Kahneman, *Thinking Fast and Slow*; Banaji and Greenwald, *Blind Spot*.

[3] Wilson, *Strangers to Ourselves*; Kahneman, *Thinking Fast and Slow*; Banaji and Greenwald, *Blind Spot*.

[4] Kahneman, *Thinking Fast and Slow*; Mlodinow, *Subliminal*.

[5] Kahneman, *Thinking Fast and Slow*, 105.

[6] M. H. Ashcraft, *Cognition* (Upper Saddle River, NJ: Pearson Education, 2006).

[7] V. Goel, M. Makale, et al., "The Hippocampal System Mediates Logical Reasoning about Familiar Spatial Environments," *Journal of Cognitive Neuroscience* 16(4) (2004): 654–664.

[8] R. B. Zajonc, "Mere Exposure: A Gateway to the Subliminal," *Current Directions in Psychological Science* 10(6) (2001): 224–228.

[9] Kahneman, *Thinking Fast and Slow*.

[10] Ibid., 43.

[11] M. Sherif, O. J. Harvey, et al., *Intergroup Conflict and Cooperation: The Robbers Cave Experiment* (Norman, OK: University Book Exchange, 1961).

[12] Wexler, *Brain and Culture*, 4.

[13] M. Sherif, "A Study of Some Social factors in Perception: Chapter 3," *Archives of Psychology* 27(187) (1935): 23–46.

[14] R. Cialdini, and N. Goldstein, "Social Influence: Compliance and Conformity," *Annual Review of Psychology* 55 (2004): 591–621.

[15] S. Lev-Ari, and B. Keysar, "Why Don't We Believe Non-Native Speakers? The Influence of Accent on Credibility," *Journal of Experimental Social Psychology* 46 (2010): 1093–1096.

[16] A. Baddeley, *Your Memory: A User's Guide* (London: Prion, 1993).

[17] Amodio and Mendoza, "Implicit Intergroup Bias" in *Handbook of Implicit Social Cognition*.

[18] H. Nishida, "Cultural Schema Theory" in *Theorizing About Intercultural Communication* by W. B. Gudykunst (Thousand Oaks, CA: SAGE, 1999), 401–418.

[19] B. Derks, M. Inzlicht, et al., "The Neuroscience of Stigma and Stereotype Threat," *Group Processes & Intergroup Relations* 11(2) (2008): 163–181.

[20] B. A. Nosek, M. R. Banaji, et al., "Harvesting Implicit Group Attitudes and Beliefs

from a Demonstration Website," *Group Dynamics* 6(1) (2002): 101–115.

[21] Greenwald, Smith, et al., "Race Attitude Measures Predicted Vote in the 2008 U.S. Presidential Election," *Analyses of Social Issues and Public Policy*.

[22] M. K. Nock and M. R. Banaji, "Assessment of Self-Injurious Thoughts Using a Behavioral Test," *American Journal of Psychiatry* 164 (2007): 820–823; M. K. Nock et al., "Measuring the 'Suicidal Mind': Implicit Cognition Predicts Suicidal Behavior," *Psychological Science* 21(4) (2010): 511–517.

[23] A. G. Greenwald, and M. R. Banaji, "Implicit Social Cognition: Attitudes, Self-Esteem, and Stereotypes," *Psychological Review* 102(1) (1995): 4–27.

[24] Amodio and Mendoza, "Implicit Intergroup Bias" in *Handbook of Implicit Social Cognition*.

[25] D. M. Amodio, "The Neuroscience of Stereotyping and Prejudice," Lecture, Inclusive Leadership, Stereotyping, and the Brain Conference, Columbia University, September 2009.

[26] Wanderlust, "20 Astonishing Holiday Complaints," *Wanderlust Travel Magazine* (2011).

[27] Wilson, *Strangers to Ourselves*, 37.

[28] Moskowitz, *Social Cognition*, 356.

[29] Wilson, *Strangers to Ourselves*, 15.

[30] Trompenaars and Hampden-Turner, *Riding the Waves of Culture*.

[31] M. J. Bennett, "Towards Ethnorelativism: a Developmental Model of Intercultural Sensitivity" in *Education for the Intercultural Experience* by M. R. Paige (Yarmouth, ME: Intercultural Press, 1993), 21-71.

[32] Ibid., 22.

[33] Hall, *Beyond Culture*.

[34] V. A. Harris, and E. E. Jones, "The Attribution of Attitudes," *Journal of Experimental Social Psychology* 3 (1967): 1–24.

[35] J. G. Miller, "Culture and the Development of Everyday Social Explanation," *Journal of Personality and Social Psychology* 46(5) (1984): 961–978.

[36] I. Choi and R. E. Nisbett, "Situational Salience and Cultural Differences in the Correspondence Bias and Actor-Observer Bias," *Personal Social Psychology* 24 (1998): 949–960.

[37] M. J. Bennett, "Towards Ethnorelativism: a Developmental Model of Intercultural Sensitivity" in *Education for the Intercultural Experience* by M. R. Paige (Yarmouth, ME: Intercultural Press, 1993), 21-71.

CHAPTER EIGHT

[1] Moskowitz, *Social Cognition*.

[2] Ibid., 155.

[3] Nishida, "Cultural Schema Theory" in *Theorizing About Intercultural Communication*.

[4] P. Ekman, and W. V. Friesen, "Constants Across Cultures in the Face and Emotion,"

Journal of Personality and Social Psychology 11 (1971): 124–129; P. Ekman, W. V. Friesen, et al., "Universals and Cultural Differences in the Judgments of Facial Expressions of Emotion," *Journal of Personality and Social Psychology* 53(4) (1987): 712–717.

[5] R. E. Jack, O. G. B. Garrod, et al., "Facial Expressions of Emotion Are Not Culturally Universal," *Proceedings of the National Academy of Sciences*, 2012.

[6] D. Matsumoto and B. Willingham, "Spontaneous Facial Expressions of Emotion of Congenitally and Noncongenitally Blind Individuals," *Journal of Personality and Social Psychology* 96(1) (2009): 1–10.

[7] Metaphysics Research Lab, "Empathy" in *The Stanford Encyclopedia of Philosophy*, Stanford University, 2008.

[8] G. di Pellegrino, L. Fadiga, et al., "Understanding Motor Events: A Neurophysiological Study." *Experimental Brain Research* 91 (1992): 176–180.

[9] Keysers, *The Empathic Brain*.

[10] J. Rifkin, *The Empathic Civilization: The Race to Global Consciousness in a World in Crisis* (New York: Penguin, 2009).

[11] Bennett, *Transition Shock*.

[12] Kahneman, *Thinking Fast and Slow*.

[13] Mlodinow, Subliminal; R. Dobelli, *The Art of Thinking Clearly* (London: Hodder & Stoughton, 2013).

[14] Kahneman, *Thinking Fast and Slow*, 11.

[15] Ibid., 244.

[16] M. J. Bennett, "Overcoming the Golden Rule: Sympathy and Empathy" in *Basic Concepts of Intercultural Communication* by M. J. Bennett (Yarmouth, ME: Intercultural Press, 1998), 272.

[17] Ibid., 31.

[18] Ibid., 33.

[19] A. Bechara, H. Damasio, et al., "Deciding Advantageously Before Knowing the Advantageous Strategy," *Science* 275(28) (1997): 1293–1294.

[20] Kahneman, *Thinking Fast and Slow*, 12.

[21] Gladwell, *Blink*.

[22] Gigerenzer, *Gut Feelings*.

[23] H. Poincare, *The Foundations of Science: Science and Hypothesis, The Value of Science, Science and Method* (New York: The Science Press, 1913).

[24] Klein, *Sources of Power*, 147.

[25] Ibid., 148–149.

[26] J. Gaston, *Cultural Awareness Teaching Techniques* (Brattleboro, VT: Pro Lingua Associates, 1984); R. M. Paige, "On the Nature of Intercultural Experiences and Intercultural Education" in *Education for the Intercultural Experience* by R. M. Paige (Yarmouth, ME:

Intercultural Press, 1993), 1–20; B. Tomlinson, "Materials for Cultural Awareness." *The Language Teacher* 24(2) (2000).

[27] Klein, *Sources of Power.*

[28] Ibid., 33.

CHAPTER NINE

[1] D. Matsumoto, R. J. Grissom, et al., "Do Between-Culture Differences Really Mean That People Are Different? A Look at Some Measures of Cultural Effect Size," *Journal of Cross-Cultural Psychology* 32(4) (2001): 478–490.

[2] Tylor, *Primitive Culture.*

[3] Hall, *The Silent Language*, 20.

[4] Ibid., 27.

[5] J. H. Barkow, L. Cosmides, et al., *The Adapted Mind: Evolutionary Psychology and the Generation of Culture* (New York: Oxford University Press, 1992).

[6] Chiao, *Cultural Neuroscience.*

[7] Hofstede, *Culture and Organizations.*

[8] G. Hofstede, *Culture's Consequences: International Differences in Work-Related Values* (Beverly Hills, CA: SAGE, 1980); G. Hofstede, "Dimensions of National Culture in Fifty Countries and Three Regions" in *Expications in Cross-Cultural Psychology* by J. B. Deregowski, S. Dziurawiec, and R. C. Annis (Lisse, Netherlands: Swetz and Zeitlinger, 1983); Hofstede, *Culture and Organizations.*

[9] M. H. Bond, "Reclaiming the Individual From Hofstede's Ecological Analysis: A 20-Year Odyssey," *Psychological Bulletin* 128(1) (2002): 73–77; D. Oyserman, H. M. Coon, et al., "Rethinking Individualism and Collectivism: Evaluation of Theoretical Assumptions and Meta-Analyses," *Psychological Bulletin* 128(1) (2002): 3–72.

[10] *World Values Survey 2014.*

[11] D. Matsumoto and L. Juang, *Culture and Psychology* (Belmont, CA: Thomson Wadsworth, 2004).

[12] D. Matsumoto, *Cultural Influences on Research Methods and Statistics* (Prospect Heights, IL: Waveland Press, 2000), 4–5.

[13] Amodio and Mendoza, "Implicit Intergroup Bias" in *Handbook of Social Cognition*, 28.

[14] Markus and Kitayama, "Culture and the Self," *Psychological Review.*

[15] Ibid., 229.

[16] Chiao, Cultural Neuroscience; Goh and Park, "Culture Sculpts the Perceptual Brain" in *Progress in Brain Research.*

[17] Y. Zhu, L. Zhang, et al., "Neural Basis of Cultural Influence on Self-Representation," *NeuroImage* 34 (2007): 1310–1316.

[18] S. Han and G. Northoff, "Culture-Sensitive Neural Substrates of Human Cognition: A Transcultural Neuroimaging Approach," *Nature Reviews Neuroscience* 9 (2008): 646–654.

[19] Ibid., 248.

[20] R. E. Nisbett and D. Cohen, Culture of Honor: *The Psychology of Violence in the South* (Boulder, CO: Westview, 1996).

[21] Ibid.

[22] Ibid.

[23] Ibid.

CHAPTER TEN

[1] Pinker, The Language Instinct, 81.

[2] Ibid., 57.

[3] Pinker, *The Language Instinct*; Damasio, *The Feeling of What Happens.*

[4] Damasio, *The Feeling of What Happens*, 108.

[5] D. Bickerton, *Adam's Tongue: How Humans Made Language, How Language Made Humans* (New York: Hill and Wang, 2009).

[6] Ibid., 108.

[7] D. Everett, *Language: The Cultural Tool* (London: Profile Books, 2012).

[8] E. Sapir, "The Status of Linguistics as a Science" in *Culture, Language and Personality* by D. G. Mandelbaum (Berkeley, CA: University of California Press, 1958), 69.

[9] P. Kay and W. Kempton, "What Is the Sapir-Whorf Hypothesis?" *American Anthropologist* 86 (1984): 65–89.

[10] J. B. Carrol and J. B. Casagrande, "The Function of Language Classifications in Behavior" in *Readings in Social Psychology* by E. L. Hartley (New York: Holt, 1958), 18–31.

[11] A. H. Bloom, *The Linguistic Shaping of Thought: A Study in the Impact of Language on Thinking in China and the West* (Hillsdale, NJ: Erlbaum, 1981).

[12] T. K. Au, "Chinese and English Counterfactuals: The Sapir-Whorf Hypothesis Revisited," *Cognition* 15 (1983): 155–187; I. R. L. Davies, P. T. Sowden, et al., "A Cross-Cultural Study of English and Setswana Speakers on a Colour Triads Task: A Test of the Sapir-Whorf Hypothesis," *British Journal of Psychology* 89(1) (1998): 1–15.

[13] G. Deutscher, *Through the Looking Glass: Why the World Looks Different in Other Languages* (London: Random House, 2010).

[14] A. Motluk, "You Are What You Speak," *New Scientist* (2002): 34–38.

[15] M. Fields, "15 Fantastic Untranslatable Words," *http://travel.allwomenstalk.com/fantastic-untranslatable-words* (last accessed February 18, 2014).

[16] J. Scott, "Obama's Young Mother Abroad," *The New York Times*, April 20, 2011.

[17] T. Doi, *Anatomy of Dependence* (New York: Kodansha, 1995).

[18] "ALC," *www.alc.co.jp/* (last accessed April 1, 2014).

[19] C. Y. Chiu, A. Leung, et al., "Language, Cognition, and Culture: Beyond the Whorfian Hypothesis" in *Handbook of Cultural Psychology* by S. Kitayama and D. Cohen (New York: The Guilford Press, 2010).

[20] Bergen, *Louder Than Words.*

[21] M. E. Wheeler, S. E. Peterson, et al., "Memory's Echo: Vivid Remembering Reactivates Sensory-Specific Cortex," *Proceedings of the National Academy of Sciences* 97(20) (2000): 11125–11129.

[22] Bergen, *Louder Than Words*, 44.

[23] J. Driskell, C. Copper, et al., "Does Mental Practice Enhance Performance?" *Journal of Applied Psychology* 79 (1994): 481–492.

[24] C. W. Perky, "An Experimental Study of Imagination," *American Journal of Psychology* 21 (1910): 422–452.

[25] Bergen, *Louder Than Words.*

[26] Kahneman, *Thinking Fast and Slow*, 50.

[27] Ibid., 51.

[28] G. Lakoff and M. Johnson, *Metaphors We Live By* (Chicago: University of Chicago Press, 1980), 3.

[29] M. K. Hiraga, *Metaphor and Iconicity: A Cognitive Approach to Analysing Texts* (New York: Palgrave Macmillan, 2005).

[30] Bergen, *Louder Than Words*, 202.

[31] Ibid., 177.

CHAPTER ELEVEN

[1] J. M. Bennett, "Cultivating Intercultural Competence" in *The SAGE Handbook of Intercultural Competence* by D. K. Deardorff (Thousand Oaks, CA: SAGE, 2009).

[2] B. H. Spitzberg and G. Changon, "Conceptualizing Intercultural Competence" in *The SAGE Handbook of Intercultural Competence* by D. K. Deardorff (Thousand Oaks, CA: SAGE, 2009).

[3] P. C. Earley and S. Ang, *Cultural Intelligence* (Stanford, CA: Stanford Business Press, 2003); S. Ang and L. V. Dyne, eds., *Handbook of Cultural Intelligence: Theory, Measurement, and Applications* (Armonk, NY: M. E. Sharpe, 2008).

[4] S. J. Gould, *The Mismeasure of Man* (New York: Norton, 1996).

[5] W. R. Sieck, J. L. Smith, et al., "Metacognitive Strategies for Making Sense of Cross-Cultural Encounters," *Journal of Cross-Cultural Psychology* 44(6) (2013): 1007–1023.

[6] D. E. Brown, *Human Universals* (New York: McGraw-Hill, 1991), 1.

[7] Ibid.

[8] S. Pinker, *The Language Instinct* (London: Penguin, 1995); Pinker, *The Blank Slate*.

[9] D. Luna, T. Ringberg, et al., "One Individual, Two Identities: Frame Switching among Biculturals," *Journal of Consumer Research* 35 (August 2008).

[10] M. J. Bennett, "Intercultural Competence for Global Leadership." Lecture at The Intercultural Development Research Institute, 2001, 12.

[11] A. Ostrovsky, "Abu Toameh: What the Western Media Misses," *FrumForum* (2010).

[12] S. Danziger and R. Ward, "Language Changes Implicit Associations Between Ethnic Groups and Evaluation in Bilinguals," *Psychological Science* 21 (2010): 799–800.

[13] J. Piaget, *The Child's Conception of the World* (London: Routledge & Kegan Paul, 1929).

[14] K. Fischer and Z. Yan, "The Development of Dynamic Skill Theory" in *Conceptions of Development: Lessons From the Laboratory* by R. Lickliter and D. Lewkowicz (Hove, UK: Psychology Press, 2002).

[15] Bennett, "Cultural Marginality" in *Education for the Intercultural Experience*, 21.

[16] R. M. Paige et al., "Assessing Intercultural Sensitivity: A Validation Study of the Hammer and Bennett Intercultural Development Inventory." Paper presented at the International Academy of Intercultural Research Conference, Kent State University, April 1999; M. R. Paige, "The Intercultural Development Inventory: A Critical Review of the Research Literature," *Journal of Intercultural Communication* 6 (2003): 53–61.

[17] K. Cushner and R. Brislin, *International Interactions* (Thousand Oaks, CA: SAGE, 1996).

[18] M. Hammer, W. B. Gudykunst, et al., "Dimensions of Intercultural Effectiveness: An Exploratory Study," *International Journal of Intercultural Relations* 2 (1978): 382–393.

[19] D. Matsumoto, J. LeRoux, et al., "Development and Validation of a Measure of Intercultural Adjustment Potential in Japanese Sojourners: The Intercultural Adjustment Potential Scale (ICAPS)," *International Journal of Intercultural Relations* 25(5) (2001): 488–510.

Index

deep. *See* Deep culture
definition of, 13–14, 18,
    27–28, 155–156
embodied, 95–99, 111
everyday usage of, 27–28
extensive, 31, 33
fractal view of, 103, 109,
    111
globalization and, 21–22,
    32–33
honor, 166–168
ignorance of influences
    of, 10
intensive, 32–33
interactions across, 31
intuitive nature of, 168
intuitive understanding
    across, 195
language and, 173–175,
    184
learning about, x–xi
metaphors of, 10
mind and, connection
    between, 18
nineteenth-century origins
    of, 28
parenting attitudes affected
    by, 104–106
past and, 168
quantification of, 158
reading the air across,
    137–139
reification fallacy of, 30
searching for, 27–30
shared meanings and, 15
surface, 85–88
thinking affected by, 6–7
unconscious mind and,
    10–12
Culture and the Self:
    Implications for
    Cognition, Emotion,
    and Motivation, 160
Culture bumps, 72
Culture shock
as occupational disease,
    71, 77
causes of, 71–72
description of, 7, 38, 75
history of, 71
intuitive overload of,
    71–72

mental exhaustion
    secondary to, 75
unconscious learning and,
    77
Culture stress, 72–75
Culture surprise, 72, 75
Cultures and Organization:
    Software of the Mind,
    99

D

Damasio, Antonio, 81, 96,
    174
Decision-making, 182
Declarative knowledge, 142
Deep acceptance, 87
Deep adaptation, 87
Deep culture
as social autopilot, 61–63
conditioned responses
    in, 62
configuration of, 62
definition of, 88
description of, 30–33,
    85–87
intercultural experiences
    and, 63
Deep culture difference,
    159–160
Deep culture knowledge, 62
Deep culture patterns, 85
Deep resistance, 87
Dependent self-construals,
    161
Descartes' Error: Emotion,
    Reason, and the
    Human Brain, 96
Development, critical periods
    in, 93–95
Developmental intercultural
    learning, 205
Developmental learning
    model, 201
Developmental model
    of intercultural
    sensitivity, 201–202
Differentiation, 129
DMIS. *See* Developmental
    model of intercultural
    sensitivity
Doi, Takeo, 178
Dominance, 97–98

Dual inheritance theory, 110
Dual processing model, 54
Dynamic skill theory, 201

E

East Asians, 6
Egalitarianism, 12
Ego depletion, 73–77, 119
Ekman, Paul, 137
Embodied cultural knowledge,
    183–184, 189
Embodied culture, 95–99,
    111
Embodied simulation, 179–
    183, 189
Embodiment, 181
Emotion, 96–98
Empathy, cultural, 139–141,
    194
Emphatic civilization, 140
Enculturation, 95
Ethnocentricity, 8
Ethnocentrism, 125–130,
    133, 204
Ethnotheories, parental,
    103–106, 111
Etiquette, 196
Eugenics, 28
Evans, Jonathan, 54–55,
    58–59
Expert intuitions, 141–144,
    150
Explicit culture, 85
Explicit representations, 54
Extensive culture, 31, 33

F

Facial expressions, 137–138
FAE. *See* Fundamental
    attribution error
Familiarity bias, 117–119, 133
Familiarity heuristics, 117
Fast thinking, 56
Feature analysis, 38
Fischer, Kurt, 201
Folk psychology, 54
Foreign experiences
changes learned through,
    68–71
culture stress effects on, 74
making sense of, 115–116
power of, 204